Sustainable Development in Water-stressed Developing Countries

A Quantitative Policy Analysis

Satoshi Kojima

Institute for Global Environmental Strategies, Japan

Edward Elgar

Cheltenham, UK • Northampton, MA, USA

Published by
Edward Elgar Publishing Limited
Glensanda House
Montpellier Parade
Cheltenham
Glos GL50 1UA
UK

Edward Elgar Publishing, Inc.
William Pratt House
9 Dewey Court
Northampton
Massachusetts 01060
USA

A catalogue record for this book
is available from the British Library

Library of Congress Control Number: 2006940749

ISBN 978 1 84720 062 4

Printed and bound in Great Britain by MPG Books Ltd, Bodmin, Cornwall

Contents

Preface

This book is a research monograph presenting a novel approach to studying sustainable development policies in developing countries. The main building blocks of this research are not new, but I have attempted to analyse critically and put them together in an original manner. The reader will see that the innovation of this book includes a critical examination of somewhat controversial concepts such as the perfect foresight assumption and also the meaning of the utility function in dynamic optimisation which is usually not challenged.

When I started my PhD at the University of York, upon which this book is based, my intention was to conduct an empirical study of sustainable development policies focusing on developing countries using some existing tools. But I soon realised the difficulty in finding suitable ready-made analytical tools. Moreover, I realised that the existing literature on sustainable development focused more on sustainability than on development. In other words, sustainable development is primarily about 'development' which means changing the current situation, I believe, while most existing sustainable development studies are about 'sustainability' which means maintaining the current situation. It is of course not wrong to discuss how to maintain the current situation or theorise about the necessary conditions of non-declining welfare for an infinite time horizon, but these seem to be less relevant to real global concerns and consequently to my research interest. Moreover, it seems to me wrong if the dominant majority of the existing literature interprets sustainable development in this way. Therefore I decided to develop an original analytical framework based on my own definition of sustainable development based on a critical review of the existing literature. This made the nature of the research less empirical, but I hope that my intention to address practical policy problems is intelligible to the reader.

This book is written as a coherent description of my research and it follows the standard structure of this type of research monograph, but I also provided a detailed account of how I customised a published social accounting matrix and calibrated the applied model in Chapter 5. In addition, an application of the Maximum Principle of optimal control theory to dynamic optimisation models in both continuous and discrete time settings is explained in detail in the Appendices to Chapter 3 and Chapter 4. I hope that they will not only improve the reproducibility of my research but also serve as a reference for postgraduate students who are interested in quantitative policy analysis. Even though there are excellent textbooks regarding these topics, in the course of my research I often wished for a detailed explanation about how these techniques were actually applied to specific empirical problems.

In writing this book I have acquired a deep debt of gratitude to many individuals. First of all, I would like to express my sincere gratitude to my academic supervisor Charles Perrings. I never could have finished my research successfully without his ingenious and effective guidance. My sincere gratitude also extends to Ric Scarpa who continuously encouraged me in various ways and also introduced me to Edward Elgar Publishing. I also would like to thank Giovanni Baiocchi, Mick Common and Malcolm Cresser for their helpful comments and suggestions. My University of York colleagues Jim Smart and Mark Bulling, and my IGES (Institute for Global Environmental Strategies) colleagues Henry Scheyvens, Mark Elder and Andrew Wong read the manuscript and improved my English. I am very grateful to them. I was definitely very lucky to have wonderful friends throughout my PhD experience. In particular I received invaluable support from Jan Minx. Whenever I came up with some ideas (often in the form of criticism against some 'common sense' in economics) I first bounced my ideas off him. In addition to constructive discussion and helpful references, he always provided me with encouragement to explore an unfamiliar path in order to develop an original analytical framework. I cannot thank him enough. I should not forget to acknowledge spiritual and financial support received from my parents Reishi and Hiroko Kojima. My parents-in-law Ryuichi and Miyuki Suzuki also supported me in various ways in the course of writing this book.

Lastly I would like to express my deepest gratitude to my wife Michiyo Suzuki for providing me with crucial moral support as well as for her patience; and to our children Amane and Aruma for cheering me up by their very existence. They may have wondered why their father sometimes could not play with them and spent entire weekends writing this book, and my sense of guilt is deepened by my inability to give a clear answer to their questions of what this book is about.

Satoshi Kojima
Hayama, Kanagawa
December 2006

1. Introduction

1.1 BACKGROUND

1.1.1 Call for Policy-Relevant Sustainable Development Research

Sustainable development entered the international political stage nearly two decades ago when the Brundtland Report defined this term as 'development that meets the needs of the present without compromising the ability of future generations to meet their own needs' (WCED 1987, p. 43). Subsequently, sustainable development has been stated as a universal policy goal in numerous official documents of international organisations and governments.

The progress towards this policy goal is, however, painfully slow. The Millennium Development Goals Report (United Nations 2005) observed that the situation for the very poor is getting worse. In sub-Saharan Africa, the number of people with insufficient food increased by 34 million between 1990 and 2002, and the number of underweight children increased from 29 million to 37 million between 1990 and 2003. The average under-five mortality rate per thousand live births marginally improved for developing countries from 105 to 88 between 1990 and 2003, but this is a tragically high rate compared with the OECD average of 7.3 in 2003 (WHO 2005). Obviously, the ongoing development process of global society fails to meet the needs of the present generation.

At the same time, serious anthropogenic ecological destruction continues to compromise the basis for prosperous living of future generations. The rich countries have given very high political priority to global warming which would cause huge economic and human losses in these countries, but there are even more urgent environmental issues requiring immediate action from global society. For example, rapid deforestation of tropical forests and mangrove forests severely undermines the sustainable livelihood of local communities in many developing countries. Furthermore, such unprecedented massive ecological destruction may cause irreversible damage to ecosystems as life support systems.

This is the reality we face. In spite of the official commitment of the world leaders to pursue sustainable development, the current development pattern neither satisfies the basic needs of the present world's poor nor secures the very basis of the survival of future generations. On the surface, the problem appears to be a lack of political will. Devarajan et al. (2002) estimated the annual costs to achieve the health-related Millennium Development Goals at US$20 to 25 billion, while the United States spent on average US$60 billion a year on the Iraq War between 2003 and 2005 (Bennis et al. 2005). But simply grieving over the lack of real political will to achieve sustainable development cannot change the situation, as political will reflects popular will. Indeed, the problem is associated with the value judgements of ordinary people, and scientific researchers have a crucial role to play in informing public opinion so as to lobby for sustainable development.

The mainstream sustainable development research in environmental and ecological economics has not fulfilled this duty, unfortunately. Most research in this field interprets the objective of sustainable development as eternally non-declining social welfare, as exemplified by the following definition of sustainable development from a standard textbook in this literature: 'The general definition of SD [sustainable development] adopted here is that every future generation must have the option of being as well off as its predecessor' (Hanley et al. 1997, pp. 433–4). Imagine how this definition sounds for the current world poor who cannot satisfy their basic needs either for their survival or for their dignity. Apparently, only the richer portion of the world's population would find this definition appealing. In the worst case, such a definition could be abused to justify suppression of the economic development of the developing countries for the sake of preventing some environmental problems affecting rich countries. This fear is not imaginary. The current political debate on greenhouse gas emissions reduction, in which developed countries often prioritise environmental protection over poverty reduction, may reflect such a mainstream interpretation of sustainable development.

This study aims to fill this gap and to respond to the urgent call for policy-relevant sustainable development research.

1.1.2 Water Scarcity and Sustainable Development

Water plays a vital role in sustainable development. The hydrological cycle forms the backbone of ecosystems. Its disruption often triggers irreversible collapse of life support systems, such as desertification as one of the most conspicuous cases.

At the same time, water is a vital resource for meeting human needs. International conflicts have long occurred over water resources (Gleick 1994, 1998; Postel 1999). In 1995 Ismail Serageldin (then vice-president of the World Bank) warned: 'if the wars of this century were fought over oil, the wars of the next century will be fought over water' (Shiva 2002). The same concern prompted the United Nations to declare 2005 to 2015 as the 'International Decade for Action – Water for Life'.

Everybody needs clean water for drinking, cooking and hygiene purposes. But the reality is that 1.1 billion people all over the world do not have access to clean and safe water (WHO and UNICEF 2000). The lack of safe water access causes various waterborne diseases, which account for around 80 per cent of infections in developing countries. It is estimated that nearly 4 billion cases of diarrhoea cause 2 million deaths each year in developing countries, and most of the victims are young children under the age of five (WHO and UNICEF 2000). 200 million people are infected with schistosomiasis, and 10 per cent of the people living in developing countries are infected with intestinal worms. Moreover, it is estimated that trachoma blinds 6 million people and risks inflicting sight impairment on 500 million people each year (Hoffman 2004).

Food production requires an adequate amount of water at the necessary points in time, which can be achieved only by introducing irrigation in the arid and semi-arid regions of the world. Global food demand could not have been satisfied without a drastic increase in irrigated areas, nearly a fivefold increase during the last century (Rosegrant et al. 2002a). On the other hand, this rapid irrigation expansion results in massive water consumption that often accounts for around 80 to 90 per cent of total water use (Rosegrant et al. 2002a, 2002b). Its direct effect is unsustainable exploitation of groundwater. The situation is alarming as groundwater tables in many major irrigation areas such as northern China and the southern Indian state of Tamil Nadu have been rapidly sinking at the rate of more than 1 metre per year (Postel 1992). Moreover, salinisation and waterlogging induced by inappropriate irrigation has severely degraded soil productivity particularly in the arid and semi-arid regions. According to the latest worldwide assessment by the United Nations Environment Programme (Morris et al. 2003), salinisation has severely affected productivity on about 22 million hectares of the irrigated land, and this figure will keep growing by an additional 1.5 to 2 million hectares each year.

Water is essential for industrial production as well. Various industries, in particular energy, textiles and paper industries, require a vast amount of water, and their products constitute a part of subsistence goods. Industrialisation is expected to play a key role in materialising economic growth indispensable for meeting basic human needs in poor countries, while an increase in industrial water demand aggravates already strong competition over scarce water.

Against the increasing water demands for meeting basic human needs, the available amount of water per person is decreasing. During the period between 1970 and 1990 the average water supply worldwide per person dropped by a third, and this tendency is expected to continue due to world population growth (United Nations 2003). This means that water-stressed developing countries will face further difficulty in promoting sustainable development.

This study is fully aware of the importance of these linkages between water scarcity and sustainable development. It thus focuses on sustainable development in the water-stressed developing countries.

1.2 OPERATIONAL PRINCIPLES OF SUSTAINABLE DEVELOPMENT

The definition of sustainable development in the Brundtland Report is deliberately phrased and in a sense vague. It was successful in achieving the primary task of the Brundtland Commission; that is, to establish a worldwide consensus on basic principles to deal with poverty and environmental issues, which can be summarised by stating that the global community is neither sustainable nor worth sustaining unless intragenerational equity is achieved. As Jacobs (1991) indicated, sustainable development in the Brundtland Report is coined as a contestable concept, such as those of liberty, social justice and democracy, which 'have basic meanings and almost everyone is in favour of them, but deep conflicts remain about how they should be understood and what they imply for policy' (p. 60). A more rigorous and narrow definition of sustainable development could not have gained such a worldwide consensus (Lélé 1991).

On the other hand, Lélé (1991) correctly pointed out that 'clarification and articulation is necessary if SD [sustainable development] is to avoid either being dismissed as another development fad or being coopted by forces opposed to changes in the status quo' (p. 618). Such clarification and articulation must be a subject of political consensus of stakeholders and it has a case-specific nature. For instance, the operational definition of needs for a whole nation may differ from that for one local community. Thus, the task to establish the operational definition must be, by nature, undertaken by individual projects and researches.

This task requires clarification of both the meaning of 'needs' and the necessary conditions not to 'compromise the ability of future generations to meet their own needs', for which one cannot avoid making one's value judgement explicit. As Common (1995) emphasised, manifesting one's value judgement explicitly is essential to make the sustainability debate constructive.

1.2.1 The Meaning of Needs

Two different approaches to human needs may be useful to understand and operationalise sustainable development; one is the basic human needs approach and the other is the fundamental human needs approach.

The basic human needs approach is widely adopted by international development agencies. Basic human needs are defined as food, clothing, shelter, access to safe water, primary education and so on. Poverty is defined as a lack of opportunity to meet these basic human needs. This approach is conceptually simple and easy to operationalise when these needs are not satisfied, because both the ends and the means of development are visible.

The fundamental human needs approach views human needs from broader perspectives. Among others, Max-Neef (1992) proposed an interesting and powerful theory of fundamental human needs. He classified ten fundamental human needs, such as subsistence and creation, by distinguishing needs from satisfiers that are the means to satisfy the needs.[1] He argued that fundamental human needs do not have a hierarchical structure except for in situations where subsistence needs are insecure, and that they are common to all cultures and to all historical periods, with the exception of the evolutionary change of human species. Consequently, 'any fundamental human need that is not adequately satisfied reveals a human poverty' (p. 200). On the other hand, selection of satisfiers varies across cultures and historical periods. Max-Neef classified satisfiers into five types of which three types (violator, pseudo-satisfier and inhibiting satisfier) do not actually satisfy needs.

Max-Neef's theory helps us to distinguish the satisfaction of needs from material consumption. Jackson and Marks (1999) argued that a large part of the current prodigal consumption in the rich nations is likely to be associated with the satisfaction of non-material needs, and 'material consumption may offer at best a pseudo-satisfaction of non-material needs and at worst may actually inhibit or violate the satisfaction of those needs' (p. 439). They refer to mismatch theory proposed by evolutionary psychologists, that the mismatch between material consumption and the nature of human needs satisfaction may account for the symptoms of poverty in rich countries such as high incidence rates of suicide and depression.

The fundamental needs approach helps to recognise that poverty exists in both rich and poor countries whenever any fundamental human needs, either material or non-material, are not satisfied. This recognition is crucial for sustainable development in rich countries where overconsumption is one of the principal threats to sustainable development and a shift in social values is urgently called for in order to fill the gap between current prodigal consumption patterns and the nature of fundamental needs satisfaction. Sustainable development policy in rich countries must primarily address this challenge to make consumption patterns consistent with fundamental needs satisfaction (Ekins 1992; Dodds 1997; Jackson and Marks 1999). In addition, the established consumption patterns must be such that all members of the global community can pursue them without compromising the ability of future generations to meet their own needs.

On the other hand, in underdeveloped countries where subsistence needs are not adequately satisfied, the basic human needs approach seems effective and operational. Moreover, it is recognised that in developing countries the connection between material consumption and satisfaction of needs is more direct than in rich countries (Ekins 1992; Jackson and Marks 1999). The conventional idea of economic growth-oriented social welfare improvement seems still relevant to developing countries to a certain extent.

1.2.2 Constraints not to Compromise the Ability of Future Generations to Meet Their Own Needs

Many sustainable development studies interpret sustainability constraints imposed by sustainable development as non-declination of either proxies of welfare or determinants of welfare such as per capita consumption, production capacity or capital stock. For example, increase of genuine savings is interpreted as sustainability of the current development path (Pearce and Atkinson 1993; Hamilton and Clemens 1999). It is obvious, however, that this cannot be true if the needs of the present generation are not currently satisfied. To operationalise sustainable development in the spirit of the Brundtland Commission, another way must be sought.

Recall that Brundtlandian sustainable development employs a negative form of constraint: 'without compromising the ability of future generations to meet their own needs'. It is apparently more natural to define sustainability as a negative form, in which sustainable means 'not unsustainable' (Becker et al. 1999). This negative definition form of sustainability is easily associated with the resilience of a dynamic system.

Holling (1973) defined resilience as the propensity of a system to retain its organisational structures after perturbations. Based on this concept, Perrings and Dalmazzone (1997) defined the resilience of a system as the maximum perturbation of the system that does not cause the system to leave the original stability domain. According to this definition, resilience at time t is determined not only by system parameters but also by distance between the system's location at time t and the boundary of the stability domain. Once dynamic behaviour of a system is modelled, sustainability constraints can be represented by the condition that the perturbations caused by development should be less than the system's resilience at any t.

Rigorously, loss of resilience is not equal to unsustainability of the system, since leaving the original stability domain does not necessarily mean collapse of the system. Nevertheless, the fact that the system outside the original stability domain is associated with a high degree of uncertainty makes sense of employing resilience conditions as sustainability constraints.

It is apparently nonsense to impose sustainability constraints on all the systems surrounding us. It seems reasonable to confine the scope of sustainability constraints to the ecosystems functioning as life support systems, such as hydrological and nutrient cycles, soil regeneration or food chains. There may be no objection against the fact that the loss of resilience of these life-supporting ecosystems will compromise the future generations' ability to meet their needs. This definition of sustainable development is close to that of Choucri (1999): 'Sustainable development means meeting the needs and demands of human populations without undermining the resilience of life-supporting properties' (pp. 143–4). Also see Common (1995) for this definition.

Implementation of sustainability constraints based on the resilience concept is not an easy task due to non-linearity, path-dependence, discontinuity, and uncertainty associated with ecosystems (Perrings et al. 1995). The extreme difficulty in predicting outcomes of irreversible environmental changes requires a precautionary approach. It might be realistic to establish safe minimum standards for each target ecosystem based on precautionary principles with the currently available scientific knowledge and information. Any costs accrued by adopting safe minimum standards should not be regarded as unacceptable in this case, because maintaining the resilience of ecosystems underpinning life support systems is a precondition of human well-being and must be prioritised above all else. This assertion constitutes an important assumption of this book.

1.2.3 Study-specific Operational Principles of Sustainable Development

Based on the above discussion, this book articulates the study-specific operational principles of sustainable development as follows:

- The primary objective of sustainable development is to meet basic human needs throughout the world, particularly in developing countries.
- Economic growth is required to meet basic human needs through higher material consumption and higher employment rates in developing countries, while appropriate policy interventions are also required to address distributional issues including infrastructure development such as provision of access to safe water.
- The resilience of ecosystems underpinning life support systems must be maintained as the very basis for future generations to meet their needs. For this purpose, sustainability constraints, mainly in terms of safe minimum standards, must be set and observed. The determination of sustainability constraints must follow the precautionary principle and scientific uncertainty cannot be an excuse not to implement them.

Sustainability constraints may be imposed on, for instance, water withdrawal, pollutant emissions, forest clearance and so on.

This study sets aside the sustainable development issues in the rich countries that are no less important and challenging than those in the poor countries. For example, the developed countries must be responsible for establishing consumption patterns that all members of the global community can adopt without losing the resilience of ecosystems underpinning life support systems. These issues have been discussed in the rapidly growing literature of sustainable consumption and production and/or industrial ecology, and they are excluded from the scope of this study.

1.3 RESEARCH OUTLINE

1.3.1 Study Objectives

This study aims to propose an innovative quantitative policy analysis framework that is consistent with the operational principles of sustainable development explained in the previous section. This study rejects the mainstream definition of sustainable development in environmental and ecological economics literature, that is, non-declining social welfare based on either the weak or the strong sustainability principle. Such a definition does not adequately reflect the real concerns of global society, in particular those of its members trapped in poverty, while the Brundtland Report declares that overriding priority must be given to the essential needs of the poor (WCED 1987, p. 43).

This study responds to a challenge to develop an alternative model for studying poverty alleviation without compromising the basis of living of future generations in terms of the resilience of ecosystems functioning as life support systems. The basic requirements for the proposed framework are:

- Performance of sustainable development policies can be evaluated in terms of both social welfare and poverty alleviation.
- Sustainability constraints can be anchored in resilience of ecosystems functioning as life support systems.

In order to produce tangible outcomes from such a challenging research enterprise, it is obviously necessary to confine the study's scope to a part of the whole problem. The study's scope is explained below.

1.3.2 Study Scope

Focusing on the water crisis

Among the various forms of ecological destruction that must be addressed to realise sustainable development, this study focuses exclusively on the water crisis in water-stressed developing countries. The rationale is the importance of the linkages between the water crisis and sustainable development explained in Section 1.1.2, and the necessity to narrow down the scope for the sake of analytical tractability.

The costs of focusing exclusively on the water crisis must be mentioned. Recently, the interrelationships between water and energy have drawn particular attention in sustainable development debates. In his opening speech to the International Conference on Freshwater held in Bonn in 2001, Klaus Töpfer, then executive director of the United Nations Environmental Programme, asserted that 'there are only two issues that are so intensively interrelated and important for development and they are water and energy'.

Hoffman (2004) described various direct and indirect linkages between water and energy. As direct linkages, extraction, treatment and transportation of water require large quantities of energy inputs, while energy production requires large quantities of water such as cooling water for thermal power plants, water injection to oil wells and so on. As indirect linkages, he counts water pollution caused by energy production and use. In addition, Rosenfeld (2000) warned that emissions from fossil fuel combustion may suppress precipitation. All of these linkages reveal the importance of addressing water and energy issues in an integrated manner.

Nevertheless, it is likely that the inclusion of energy into the scope of this study would make the problem intractable. The integrated treatment of water and energy issues must be an important future research topic of sustainable development studies.

Focusing on economic aspects

This study assumes that sustainability constraints necessary for keeping the resilience of ecosystems underpinning life support systems are given. This is not because this study underestimates the importance of or difficulty in formulating them. On the contrary, this study claims that such an important and difficult task must be rendered by proper interdisciplinary collaboration across ecology, environmental science, engineering and economics, at the very least. Moreover, a high degree of uncertainty and severe knowledge limitation concerning this issue may rule out clear-cut solutions. Instead, it might be necessary to prepare several alternative versions of sustainability constraints and to build political consensus on the choice among them.

This study sets aside this genuinely interdisciplinary task and focuses on economic aspects of sustainable development. Instead of asking what sustainability constraints are or how they are formulated, this study asks how they can be incorporated and utilised in sustainable development policies. It is also expected that answers to the latter question will be helpful to address the former questions. Nevertheless, it must be re-emphasised here that best efforts to establish appropriate sustainability constraints through both inter-disciplinary collaboration and adequate political process are essential to operationalise sustainable development.

Focusing on quantitative policy analysis

This study adopts the method of quantitative policy analysis, which consists of model construction and policy simulations (Sadoulet and de Janvry 1995). The notion of policies in this study is narrowly referred to as the government's quantitative policies which are defined as 'the changing, within the qualitative framework of the given structure, of certain political parameters or political instruments' (Tinbergen 1952, p. 2).

Focusing on quantitative policies does not imply that qualitative policies are less important than quantitative policies. Ciriacy-Wantrup (1967) argued that water policy is better defined as 'a set of decision rules in a multistage decision process' which comprises three different levels (p. 179). At the lowest level, the decision maker chooses proper values of control variables such as the amount of water withdrawal. At the second level, the decision maker controls the institutional framework within which the lowest-level decisions are made. Selection of a property right regime or a particular type of water management organisation might be the subjects of decision making at this level. At the highest level, the second-level decision-making process is itself the subject of decision making.

The rationale of Ciriacy-Wantrup's argument is that the institutional conditions are themselves the outcomes of decision making rather than merely a given constraint within social decision making. He claimed that 'the second level is the most significant one for the study of water policy' and that it is necessary to seek 'criteria that could serve as conceptually and operationally meaningful proxies for the functional construct of optimizing welfare' (p. 183). From this standpoint the most relevant analysis is not quantitative optimisation itself but comparative analysis of the institutional setting in which such optimisation is pursued.

Nevertheless, the benefits obtained from applying quantitative policy analysis seem to be large enough to compensate for the costs incurred. Government policies which are studied in this book, such as setting rates for water charges and levels of public investment, will have complex and often interdependent direct and indirect effects on various sectors of the economy.

Quantitative policy analysis provides the most effective way, indeed often the only way, to reveal overall consequences with reasonable accountability (Sadoulet and de Janvry 1995). Furthermore, when the policy target consists of multiple objectives, quantitative policy analysis enables policy makers to understand the trade-offs between each objective.

Single-country framework

This study adopts a single-country framework due to its advantages in both modelling and data collection. Although policy analysis in a multi-country framework has recently attracted research interest, the complex nature of the problems studied imposes severe restrictions on the selection of analytical methods (see Turnovsky 1995, 1997). It seems wiser to establish a policy analysis framework relevant to the established operational principles of sustainable development in a single-country framework focusing on developing countries, and to extend the scope in the future.

On the other hand, a severe drawback of the single developing country framework is that actions of developed countries cannot be properly incorporated. In this regard, this study simply assumes that developed countries can afford significant amounts of capital transfer if this is required to implement sustainable development in developing countries. Although the volume of international aid flows is currently reducing, the demonstration of positive impacts of such capital transfer on sustainable development could help to convince developed countries to increase international aid flows.

1.4 STRUCTURE OF THIS BOOK

This book is structured as follows. Chapter 2 establishes the basic methodological framework of this study. This chapter reviews the existing analytical frameworks from the viewpoint of compatibility with the established operational principles of sustainable development. Further, relevance of several innovative ideas is examined by locating them in the existing literature.

The policy simulation models are constructed in two steps described respectively in Chapter 3 and Chapter 4. In Chapter 3 an analytic model for investigating interactions between water and economy is developed. Policy implications obtained by theoretical analysis using the analytic model are summarised in propositions. These policy implications are further investigated through numerical simulations. The analytic model constructed in this chapter provides the model platform of an applied model constructed in Chapter 4. Moreover, some insights obtained in this chapter are indispensable to solve the applied model numerically. Chapter 4 presents the applied model for conducting policy simulations. The applied model is developed by incorporating stylised facts commonly observed in water-stressed developing countries, such as vulnerability of rain-fed agriculture, high incidence of lack of access to safe water and so on, into the analytic model. The applied model departs from the deterministic world of the analytic model by introducing several uncertainties such as production risks. Furthermore, tax and trade issues are incorporated in order to accommodate empirical data such as an existing social accounting matrix described in Chapter 5.

Chapter 5 reports calibration and validation of the applied model along with data description. In addition to detailed descriptions of datasets, general features of Morocco, the case-study country, are also described in this chapter. A detailed explanation of calibration procedure, which seems useful but is rarely found in the existing literature, is also provided.

Chapter 6 reports policy simulations. Since the model involves uncertainty, policy planning and policy implementation must be clearly distinguished. This chapter addresses this issue in detail, and establishes simulation procedures and policy evaluation criteria. Policy scenarios cover not only policy alternatives but also alternative environments (or exogenous drivers) such as tax regimes, climate change and so on. This wide coverage of policy scenarios demonstrates the applicability of the applied model developed in this study.

Chapter 7 summarises the major achievements of this study and concludes this book by suggesting future tasks.

NOTE

1. The ten fundamental human needs are: subsistence, protection, affection, understanding, participation, creation, idleness, identity, freedom and transcendence. Max-Neef (1992) also classified five types of satisfiers, that is, destroyers, inhibiting satisfiers, pseudo-satisfiers, singular satisfiers and synergistic satisfiers.

2. Basic Framework for Quantitative Policy Analysis

2.1 INTRODUCTION

This chapter develops an analytical framework which is consistent with the operational principles of sustainable development which were established in the previous chapter. It was found, through the literature review, that such a framework has not yet been developed, although Ramsey-Cass-Koopmans models (RCK models), which are dynamic utility optimisation models pioneered by Ramsey (1928) and elaborated by Cass (1965) and Koopmans (1965), seem to serve as a foundation for developing an appropriate analytical framework.

This chapter is organised as follows. Section 2.2 justifies the selection of RCK models as a basis for establishing the analytical framework, while the limitations of RCK models are also mentioned. In Section 2.3, innovative features such as a decentralised setting are introduced. Section 2.4 proposes a model development procedure in a stepwise manner considering the innovative features of the proposed framework. Lastly, the basic analytical framework established in this chapter is summarised in Section 2.5.

2.2 FOUNDATION FOR THE PROPOSED QUANTITATIVE MODELS

2.2.1 Relevance of Ramsey-Cass-Koopmans Models

The methodological framework of this study is constructed on the basis of dynamic computable general equilibrium models. More specifically, this study employs multi-sector RCK models as a foundation for establishing its analytical framework.[1] The rationale behind this choice is as follows.

Relevance of computable general equilibrium models

Along with the rapid expansion of computational capacities as well as development of accessible and easy-to-use modelling packages over the last few decades, computable general equilibrium (CGE) models have become the most popular tool for applied work on a wide range of policy issues, such as tax and subsidy policies, public investment policies, changes in economic and social structures, terms of trade and exchange policies and so on. In particular, when the economic policies subject to analysis affect socio-economic structure such as sectoral composition and income distribution along with price changes, CGE models are often regarded as the most powerful analytical framework (Sadoulet and de Janvry 1995). Furthermore, CGE models are able to investigate a wide range of issues across not only economic but also social and environmental problems in a coherent way.

Because of these properties, CGE models are very suitable for quantitative analysis of sustainable development policies in accordance with established operational principles.

The requirement for dynamic models

The choice between a static and a dynamic model is an important step in the design of an analytical framework. Mäler (1974) provided a good treatment of this issue. He illustrated the comparative advantages of both static and dynamic models in sustainable development studies by locating each model in a very general analytical framework for investigating interactions between the economic system and its environment. He sketched a general equilibrium model incorporating flows of both materials and energy, which play a central role in the materials balance approach (Ayres and Kneese 1969; Kneese et al. 1972), and in intertemporal aspects such as capital and waste accumulation, population growth, exhaustion of non-renewable resources and so on. Because such a model is too complex to obtain useful implications, Mäler constructed: (1) a static general equilibrium model which adopted a materials balances approach reflecting environmental effects of waste discharges; and (2) a highly aggregated RCK model for a finite time horizon.

In the former static model, several assumptions, for example convexity of the production possibility set and consumer preferences, were introduced as the model became a special case of Arrow-Debreu general equilibrium models, for which the existence of a unique equilibrium can be proved by appealing to the proof of Debreu (Debreu 1959, p. 19). For the latter dynamic model, four variations of aggregate RCK models were constructed by incorporating environmental quality as an argument of the instantaneous utility function and including exhaustible natural resources as a material balance constraint. The four variations differ from each other in their ability to control population, the number of environmental qualities (single or multiple) depicted, and the possibility of recycling. Mäler proved that all four variants are associated with the turnpike property, with which the optimal trajectories tend to approach the optimal steady state and spend most of the planning period at the optimal steady state if the time horizon is enough long (Samuelson 1965). This turnpike property enables the optimal trajectories to be approximated by the optimal steady state. Hence, under these conditions, Mäler claimed that the former static general equilibrium model could be regarded as a good approximation to the dynamic general equilibrium model along the optimal growth path.

This might not be the case, however, for economies which lie some way from the optimal growth path, as is often assumed to be the case for many developing countries. In addition, an absolute speed of convergence towards the optimal steady state matters from the practical viewpoint. If it were to take decades for an economy to realise the optimal steady state, such an approximation would provide misleading information.

Because the main concern of this study is sustainable development of water-stressed developing countries where optimality can scarcely be assumed, full dynamic models are required for this study.

The requirement for dynamic optimisation models

The current treatment of dynamic aspects in CGE models is quite problematic as most of the current fully dynamic CGE models, which are based on dynamic optimisation, employ a strong assumption of households' perfect foresight. The model of Jorgenson and Wilcoxen (1993) exemplifies this line of research.[2]

Although this assumption seems justifiable in first-best optimal policy analysis, it appears unrealistic for applied purposes (Robinson 1989). It is thus common for applied CGE models to accommodate economic dynamics as a succession of temporary equilibria (obtained as solutions of static optimisation) linked by dynamic adjustment mechanisms such as exogenous growth of capital and labour supply. CGE models of this type are called recursive dynamic models, or sometimes 'quasi-dynamic models' because they lack dynamic optimisation mechanisms. For analysing development policies which are inherently associated with transitional dynamics rather than steady states, dynamic optimisation CGE models are highly desirable. Sustainable development policy certainly falls within this category.

Thus, currently available options for dealing with dynamics in CGE models are either recursive dynamic models that are criticised for their lack of dynamic optimisation, or forward-looking dynamic optimisation models that are criticised for their inclusion of the unrealistic assumption of perfect foresight. If we could liberate RCK models from the perfect foresight assumption, they would become a powerful tool for studying sustainable development policies. This is the strategy which is adopted by this study.

2.2.2 Limitations of Multisector RCK Models

The selection of multisector RCK models as the basis of the framework for this study does not mean that these models satisfy perfectly the basic requirements for the proposed framework mentioned in Chapter 1. Mainly due to the limitation of the computational capacity, multisector RCK models are highly aggregated and they therefore have difficulty in explicitly incorporating income distribution across social classes. This difficulty is an impediment to assessing proposed policies for poverty alleviation. In this regard, Löfgren et al. (1997) provided a good example of recursive dynamic CGE studies addressing income distributional issues. RCK models also have difficulty in reflecting aspects of spatial distribution such as hydrological systems or crop patterns which are important for studying sustainable water policies in detail. In this regard, Bouhia (1998) provided an integrated framework consisting of a hydrology-based water management model developed by McKinney and Cai (1997) and an economic model based on an input-output framework.

2.3 INNOVATIVE FEATURES OF THE PROPOSED FRAMEWORK

The standard RCK models have served almost exclusively as analytic models for investigating important assumptions and causal mechanisms of the interesting issues, except for a few dynamic CGE models such as the one developed by Jorgenson and Wilcoxen (1993). There appear to be two major reasons for this lack of applied dynamic CGE models: one is technical and the other is conceptual. The former is a limitation in computational capacity, as the introduction of dynamics exponentially increases the complexity of the model. The latter is the restrictions inherent in the strong assumptions employed by the standard RCK models, such as the perfect foresight assumption. The following three innovations are introduced in order to make the RCK models more relevant for conducting applied policy simulations. They collectively contribute to the development of an adequate policy simulation tool to deal with sustainable development in water-stressed developing countries.

2.3.1 Alternative Interpretation of Dynamic Utility Optimisation

The objective function of the standard RCK model is defined as follows:

$$U = \int_0^{\infty} e^{-\rho t} u(c(t))dt \qquad (2.1)$$

where U: lifetime utility, ρ: rate of pure time preference, $c(t)$: per capita consumption at time t, and $u(\ )$: the instantaneous utility function.

The basic assumption behind this definition is that the current utility level (instantaneous utility) is solely determined by the current activities represented by the current consumption level. This is indeed a strong assumption, as we know that our current utility level (happiness) is certainly influenced by past experience and future expectations. Strotz (1956) clearly recognised the possibility of utility experienced at a point of a time 'depending on the consumption of a later date', and criticised the term 'instantaneous utility function' as a 'misnomer' (Strotz 1956, footnote 2, p. 167). Other authors also avoided the term 'instantaneous utility' and adopted alternatives. For example, Tinbergen (1952) labelled it 'ophelimity', which may have been borrowed from the works of Vilfredo Pareto who defined 'ophelimity' as satisfaction derived from current economic activities and 'utility' as satisfaction derived from all causes including both economic and non-economic causes (Tarascio 1969). Similarly, Arrow and Kurz (1970), following Gorman (1957), used the term 'felicity' instead of instantaneous utility.

This study observes the tradition of these authors and employs the term 'felicity' to refer to enjoyment derived only from the current conditions, which corresponds to $u(c(t))$ in (2.1). Further, it is assumed that the utility level experienced at this moment, $U(0)$, is determined as a discounted sum of a stream of expected felicities. For further discussion on the implications of this alternative interpretation, see Kojima (2006).

2.3.2 Decentralised Setting

In the standard RCK model literature, it is commonly assumed that a benevolent social planner, who can dictate everything including consumption levels of individuals, maximises social welfare by controlling both public and private decision variables. This is obviously an unrealistic assumption, but Barro and Sala-i-Martin (1995) explained that the benevolent social planner setting is 'useful in many circumstances for finding the economy's first-best outcomes' (p. 71). From the policy perspective, however, the first-best outcomes are important only if they are achievable by particular policies, for instance a Pigouvian tax. Finding such a policy requires an analysis in the second-best world where the social planner (the government) cannot directly control private decision variables such as consumption levels.[3] Therefore, policy-relevant quantitative policy analysis requires a decentralised setting in which private and public decision making are distinguished.

The importance of a decentralised setting in studying public policy was clearly recognised by Arrow and Kurz (1970). They argued that the government in a decentralised society does not have discretion to make all allocative decisions but 'has the choice of values of a limited range of instruments' (p. 115). This understanding, which they regarded as a dynamic version of the theory of economic policy proposed by Tinbergen (1952), led them to set out a theory on the controllability of public policy in which a central issue is the necessary conditions for the government to achieve the publicly optimal path, and a dynamic theory of the second-best policy which is defined as the best policy in non-controllable situations with the given set of instruments.

In order to study these issues, Arrow and Kurz (1970) formulated dynamic optimisation models in which private sector optimisation and public sector optimisation are dealt with separately. In private sector optimisation, the representative individual maximises the total net present value of all individuals' welfare in an economy, taking the government policy such as the tax rate and the stock of public capital as exogenously given. In public sector optimisation, the government selects only the rates of public investment, taxes and government borrowing subject to a budget limitation.

The decentralised setting investigated by Arrow and Kurz, in more general form, can be formalised as follows.

Let $\boldsymbol{V}^P$ and $\boldsymbol{V}^G$ denote the objective functions and $\boldsymbol{f}^P$ and $\boldsymbol{f}^G$ denote the constraint sets of the private and the public sectors, respectively. Each sector maximises (or minimises, depending on model specification) its objective function by choosing the values of its instruments (control variables) subject to the given constraint sets. Let vectors $\boldsymbol{x}^P$ and $\boldsymbol{x}^G$ denote the control variables and $\boldsymbol{y}^P$ and $\boldsymbol{y}^G$ denote the state variables of the private and the public sectors, respectively.

The private sector problem is

$$\underset{\boldsymbol{x}^P}{Max}\, V^P\left(\boldsymbol{x}^P,\boldsymbol{y}^P;\boldsymbol{x}^G,\boldsymbol{y}^G\right) \text{ subject to } \boldsymbol{f}^P(\boldsymbol{x}^P,\boldsymbol{y}^P;\boldsymbol{x}^G,\boldsymbol{y}^G)=\boldsymbol{0} \qquad (2.2)$$

The semicolon in the argument of functions separates the endogenous (left) and the exogenous (right) variables. The private optimal solution can be described as functions of the exogenous variables, which are denoted as $\hat{\boldsymbol{x}}^P\left(\boldsymbol{x}^G,\boldsymbol{y}^G\right)$ and $\hat{\boldsymbol{y}}^P\left(\boldsymbol{x}^G,\boldsymbol{y}^G\right)$.

Now the public sector problem can be expressed as

$$\underset{\boldsymbol{x}^G}{Max}\, V^G\left(\hat{\boldsymbol{x}}^P\left(\boldsymbol{x}^G,\boldsymbol{y}^G\right),\hat{\boldsymbol{y}}^P\left(\boldsymbol{x}^G,\boldsymbol{y}^G\right),\boldsymbol{x}^G,\boldsymbol{y}^G\right)$$
$$\text{subject to } \boldsymbol{f}^G\left(\hat{\boldsymbol{x}}^P\left(\boldsymbol{x}^G,\boldsymbol{y}^G\right),\hat{\boldsymbol{y}}^P\left(\boldsymbol{x}^G,\boldsymbol{y}^G\right),\boldsymbol{x}^G,\boldsymbol{y}^G\right)=\boldsymbol{0} \qquad (2.3)$$

While the optimal solution of this public sector problem is in general the second-best policy, it is the optimal policy from practical viewpoint. If we insist on the first-best policy, we must first set up the following benevolent social planner problem in order to find the first-best outcome:

$$\underset{x^P, x^G}{Max}\ V^G\left(\boldsymbol{x}^P, \boldsymbol{y}^P, \boldsymbol{x}^G, \boldsymbol{y}^G\right) \quad \text{subject to}$$
$$\boldsymbol{f}^P(\boldsymbol{x}^P, \boldsymbol{y}^P, \boldsymbol{x}^G, \boldsymbol{y}^G) = \boldsymbol{0} \ \text{ and } \ \boldsymbol{f}^G(\boldsymbol{x}^P, \boldsymbol{y}^P, \boldsymbol{x}^G, \boldsymbol{y}^G) = \boldsymbol{0} \qquad (2.4)$$

Then, we have to find the solution of (2.3) resulting in the first-best outcome. Whether such a solution exists or not depends on the controllability. In any case we need to employ a decentralised setting if we want to find the feasible optimal policy. This study adopts a decentralised setting of the Arrow-Kurz type, which is referred to as a 'two-stage optimisation' setting.

Objective function of the private sector

Arrow and Kurz (1970) advocated that the private objective function has to include population size even if the decision-making unit is the single representative individual, and proposed the following objective function for the representative private agent:

$$V^P \equiv \int_0^\infty e^{-\rho t} L(t) u(c(t)) dt \qquad (2.5)$$

where ρ: rate of pure time preference, $L(t)$: population at time t, $c(t)$: per capita consumption at time t, and $u(\ )$: the felicity function.

They showed that if population is not included in (2.5) the optimal solution requires that less per capita consumption is allocated to the more populous generations. It is, however, not clear why the representative (average) individual, who is assumed to be 'selfish', has to care about a social equity issue of this type. In this respect their treatment of the private setting is not fully convincing.

Specification (2.5) is widely adopted in the recent growth literature, but from a different perspective. In this regard Barro and Sala-i-Martin (1995) provided the following lucid explanation. It is assumed that the decision-making unit is not the representative individual but the representative household, and that the population growth takes the form of increase of the household size. Then the household felicity is assumed to be the sum of each household member's felicity.

This reasoning is simple and intuitive if we accept the underlying assumptions that a household is the basic decision unit and that the number of households in the economy is constant over the whole time horizon. Though it is standard in the neoclassical microeconomics literature to regard the household as a single decision-making unit, it has been pointed out that this approach violates the basic rule underpinning neoclassical microeconomic theory. Bourguignon and Chiappori (1992) argued that aggregating individual preference 'within the ad-hoc fiction of a collective decision unit' cannot meet the principle of individualism (p. 356). Moreover, it is claimed that incorporating the intra-household decision-making process in policy analysis produces significantly different implications concerning individuals' welfare from those provided by the standard approach.[4]

Nevertheless, this study follows the standard approach, mainly because it provides a suitable framework to address the chronically high urban unemployment rate induced by rural-urban migration, which is explained in Chapter 4. The latter assumption of constant household number is clearly a fiction for analytical purposes but it appears quite harmless, and is useful to clarify the main issue. This study thus employs the specification (2.5) as a basis for constructing the private objective function which will be explained in the next chapter.

Objective function of the public sector

One of the advantages of a two-stage optimisation setting would be its capacity to accommodate both positive and normative approaches in a harmonised way. In this setting the modelling of private optimisation is a positive task in the sense that its success depends on how well the private sector's response to government policy can be predicted. Modelling public optimisation, however, is essentially a normative task in the sense that its success depends on how well collective general interests can be represented in the objective function V^G as well as in the constraint sets.

In his famous paper on the social welfare function, Bergson stated that:

> The number of sets [of value propositions which is sufficient for the evaluation of all alternatives] is infinite, and in any particular case the selection of one of them must be determined by its compatibility with the values prevailing in the community the welfare of which is being studied. For only if the welfare principles are based upon prevailing values, can they be relevant to the activity of the community in question. (Bergson 1938, p. 323)

To capture 'the values prevailing in the community' in economic models is obviously far from easy. Nevertheless, the adoption of utilitarian social welfare functions for this purpose, in which social welfare is defined as an aggregate of individual utilities, is widely accepted in the RCK literature.

It seems particularly relevant that it has been proved that the Bergson-Samuelson social welfare function must have, with some additional assumptions,[5] the form of a weighted mean of all members' individual utilities (Harsanyi 1955) or of an unweighted sum of them (Ng 1975), though Bergson explicitly disfavoured the use of an unweighted sum of individual utilities as the social welfare function, claiming that it 'is not a useful tool for welfare economics' (Bergson 1938, p. 327). As there is no a priori reason to deny the claims of Harsanyi and Ng, this study follows the tradition of the literature in adopting a social welfare function defined as the arithmetic mean (or unweighted sum) of all members' individual utilities as the maximand of the public sector. Consequently, the social welfare function is defined as follows:

$$V^G \equiv \sum_i U^i(0) = \sum_i \int_0^{\infty} e^{-\rho t} L^i(t) u\left(\hat{c}^i(t)\right) dt \tag{2.6}$$

where the same notation as in (2.5) holds with the superscript i denoting the ith household.

This portrayal represents the social welfare of the present generation at the present moment, which can be referred to as the 'intra-generational' social welfare function of the present generation. Mäler (1974) correctly pointed out that this social welfare specification 'reflects the choices of the present government and does not involve those of future generations (whose preferences we obviously do not know)' (p. 61). This is a strength, not a weakness, in a social welfare function, because it avoids the unsolvable problem of representing the welfare of unborn future generations. This study adopts this intra-generational social welfare function as the public sector objective function since it is perfectly consistent with the established operational principles of sustainable development, the main goal of which is improving intra-generational social welfare in terms of poverty alleviation, without violating given sustainability constraints. Intergenerational aspects of sustainable development are represented by the sustainability constraints within this framework, rather than by the social welfare function itself.

In this regard, Toman et al. (1995) argued that it would be desirable to incorporate a 'sustainability function' into the social welfare function on the ground that a sustainability constraint approach does not allow 'tradeoffs between intergenerational concern and other social goods' (Toman et al. 1995, p. 142). However, if we construct the intergenerational social welfare function in consistence with the discussion above, it takes the following form:

$$V^G \equiv \int_0^T e^{-\gamma s} \left\{\sum_i \hat{U}^i(s)\right\} ds = \int_0^T e^{-\gamma s} \left\{\sum_i \int_s^{\infty} e^{-\rho t} L^i(t) u\left(\hat{c}^i(t)\right) dt\right\} ds \tag{2.7}$$

where T is the time horizon of the public sector, s are generations, and γ is the discount rate of future social welfare.

This social welfare function is obviously not applicable to practical policy analysis because of its cumbersome double integral together with the difficulty in representing the social welfare of unborn future generations. On the other hand, this specification might resolve the controversy over the choice of discount rates in the social objective function, since both the 'normative' and the 'positive' discount rates of Arrow et al. (1996) coexist as γ and ρ, respectively, in (2.7). Ramsey's famous aphorism that any non-zero discount rate is 'ethically indefensible' sounds persuasive in the case of γ (Ramsey 1928, p. 543).

2.3.3 Expectation Formation without Perfect Foresight

The standard RCK models employ a very strong assumption that the individuals (or households) have perfect foresight when they form their expectations of time paths of price variables such as rental rates of capital, wage rates and exogenous prices. Although this apparently unrealistic assumption is helpful in seeking for first-best outcomes, as is the benevolent social planner setting, it is inappropriate for conducting policy-relevant quantitative policy analysis.

A systematic investigation of alternative rationality concepts in economic theory was initiated by Simon (1955). He defined his task as replacing omniscient rationality, as often assumed in economics, with 'a kind of rational behavior that is consistent with the access to information and the computational capacities that are actually possessed by organisms, including man' (Simon 1955, p. 99). He suggested the concept of 'bounded rationality', a kind of conditional rationality given the limited ability of decision makers to gather and process information. It seems an adequate concept consistent with the approach of this study, taking into account the fact that any level of information is inadequate to enable households to predict perfectly entire time paths of exogenous prices, unless the households themselves make public decisions as in the benevolent social planner setting.

It is important to notice that the implications of bounded rationality are not confined purely to information processing, such as the selection of input information. Rather, an awareness of bounded rationality would urge decision makers to tailor their decision-making procedure in accordance with their cognitive ability.[6] For instance, the standard RCK model literature assumes that households make a decision only once, since unbounded (omniscient) rationality enables them to find, with full confidence, the first-best optimal consumption path for the entire period at the beginning of the planning period. Intuitively, replacing unbounded rationality with bounded rationality in this framework would be likely to introduce frequent monitoring–feedback processes into the decision procedure. In fact, if we assume that the monitoring–feedback process is costless, as assumed in this study, continuous monitoring–feedback for the entire planning period will emerge as a logical consequence of bounded rationality.

Now we turn to investigate decision input with bounded rationality. In the two-stage optimisation setting the central issue is whether the government can approximate the households' expectations sufficiently well to allow it to predict the response of the households to government policies with adequate accuracy. The task is not to model the actual expectation formation mechanisms of the households in detail, but rather to assume some simple but 'reasonable' approximation of the households' expectations from which the government can predict the household response to the government policy reasonably accurately within its cognitive limitation.

Stiglitz (1974) identified basic properties for expectation formation models to be 'reasonable'. He expressed, in discrete time, the expectation formation process as

$$p_{t+1}^{e} = \phi\left(p_t, p_{t-1,} \cdots, p_{t-n,} \cdots; t\right) \tag{2.8}$$

where p_{t+1}^{e} is expected price at period $t + 1$.

Stiglitz claimed that this function must satisfy: (1) linear homogeneity with respect to all arguments; (2) stationarity (or time independency); and (3) convergence of the expectation into the real price at the steady state. Even after screening candidates based on these three conditions, there still exist numerous valid alternatives for the reasonable expectation formation process.

The final selection of a decision input from these alternatives has to rely on one's intuition, and its correctness can be judged only by empirical tests. In his pioneering work of the rational expectation hypothesis, Muth (1961) compared his rational expectation model with other alternatives such as cobweb-type models ($p_{t+1}^{e} = p_t$), and adaptive expectation models, by testing how closely model prediction of the pig price cycle between 1911 and 1931 corresponded with actual observations. His conclusion was, with a caveat of potential bias due to serial correlation, that the rational expectation model, which is equivalent to perfect foresight in the deterministic world, would have relative advantages over its rivals. Although his empirical test is too sketchy to be a basis for choice among various expectation formation processes, its implication that a highly unrealistic hypothesis could generate better proxies of real behaviour is important.

The expectation formation process assumed in this study is a combination of a decision procedure embedding continuous monitoring and feedback with the simplest decision input based on the current values only. The households expect that exogenous variables will remain constant at the current values, but at the next moment they are free to update this expectation based on the realised values of exogenous variables at that moment. It can easily be seen that this expectation process satisfies three necessary conditions of Stiglitz

(1974). Furthermore, this specification can be regarded as an example of the 'consistent planning' strategy of Strotz (1956) which he defines as the strategy 'to find the best plan among those that he will actually follow' (p. 173). Notice that the estimated optimal consumption path at each moment in this specification is not a plan, as the household will almost certainly not follow this course due to expectation errors, but it serves as decision input through which households optimise their instantaneous consumption level at that moment. It is this instantaneous consumption level which corresponds to what Strotz referred to as 'the best plan' that households actually follow.

2.4 STEPWISE MODEL DEVELOPMENT PROCEDURE

Since the analytical framework of this study is unique in respect of the above-mentioned innovations, there is no readily available prototype for this study in the existing literature. It is in general difficult to construct a quantitative model for applied purposes without directly relevant prototypes that can provide a clue as to the main causal mechanisms behind the problems, considering the inevitable trade-off between analytical tractability and empirical realism in modelling analysis.

In this regard, Robinson (1989) classified quantitative policy analysis models into analytic models, stylised numerical models and applied models, as described in Table 2.1. He suggested that it is generally desirable to employ more than one kind of model for improving analysis of any particular model, because the different kinds of models provide different insights.

Table 2.1 Classification of models for quantitative policy analysis

Type	Description
Analytic models	Highly stylised models associated with closed-form solutions which help to extract important assumptions and causal mechanisms that can rarely be revealed by more realistic and complicated models.
Stylised numerical models	Generalised version of an analytic model which contributes, through numerical simulations, to both quantifying various effects and investigating causal mechanisms of which implications depend on functional forms or parameter values.
Applied models	More realistic and complicated model incorporating structural and institutional details of the economy being studied in order to secure policy relevance of the policy simulations.

Robinson's suggestion is particularly useful for this study, because the applied model of this study will be quite complicated for conducting dynamic quantitative policy analysis taking into account various stylised facts of water-stressed developing economies. Starting from the construction of an analytic model as a prototype significantly facilitates the model construction process. This study adopts a stepwise model development procedure in which an analytic model is developed first and then an applied model is developed based on the analytic model.

2.5 ESTABLISHED QUANTITATIVE POLICY ANALYSIS FRAMEWORK

This study adopts RCK models as a foundation for building the quantitative policy analysis framework, because of their capability to reveal the overall consequences of the complex and often interdependent effects of sustainable development policies whilst also capturing dynamic aspects in sustainable development.

The standard RCK models tend to focus on the first-best optimal outcomes without considering their controllability or achievability in the second-best world. Although the first-best optimal studies have played an important role not only in establishing a theoretical framework but also in providing useful benchmarks, it might be misleading to apply these outcomes directly to policy analysis. In order to customise the RCK models for conducting quantitative policy analysis which is consistent with the operational principles of sustainable development, where full consideration should be given to 'second-best', the following three innovative features are introduced. Firstly, an alternative interpretation of utility is introduced, in which intertemporal aspects of dynamic utility optimisation are distinguished from their inter-generational aspects. Secondly, the established analytical framework employs a two-stage optimisation setting consisting of the private and public optimisation processes. Thirdly, it liberates RCK models from the perfect foresight assumption, which is criticised by proponents of static or recursive dynamic CGE models as being unacceptably unrealistic.

The established analytical framework employs a stepwise model development procedure in which an analytic model and an applied model are developed sequentially. The analytic model is a stylised RCK growth model which assumes imperfect foresight of household expectations with two-stage optimisation. Based on the analytic model, the applied model is developed by incorporating key stylised facts of water-stressed developing countries.

NOTES

1. The pioneering work in applying RCK models to the water crisis issue is due to Barbier (2004). He developed an RCK model for investigating the interaction between water scarcity and economic growth based on congestible public good models of Barro and Sala-i-Martin (1992, 1995). As main conclusions, Barbier claimed that his model predicts an inverted U-shaped relationship between economic growth and water utilisation which is consistent with cross-country data. Barbier's paper is an important contribution to the sustainable water literature which introduces the appealing idea of applying RCK models to this issue. It contains interesting information and discussion relevant to sustainable water policy, but his main conclusions are not well founded for the following reasons. Firstly, Barbier regards utilised water itself as a public good subject to congestion, but the congestible public good at issue here must be 'water systems' in terms of water supply facilities, rather than water itself, if the models of Barro and Sala-i-Martin are applied correctly. Sorting out this confusion without changing the model specification requires a constant marginal product of water with respect to water supply facilities, but this assumption is not only rejected by empirical evidence, which suggests a diminishing marginal product for water production (Rosegrant et al. 2002a), but is also inconsistent with Barbier's own statement: 'as water becomes increasingly scarce in the economy, the government must exploit less accessible sources of fresh water through appropriating and purchasing a greater share of aggregate economic output' (Barbier 2004, p. 2). Secondly, even if the constant marginal product assumption were accepted, Barbier's model actually predicts, as an interior solution of the optimisation problem, a unique combination of economic growth and water utilisation rates, which is depicted as a point on a graph, rather than an inverted U-shaped curve.
2. Devarajan and Go (1998) provide a simplified version of a dynamic optimisation CGE model.
3. The word 'second-best' was first coined by Meade (1955) in which the problems of second-best optimality were discussed against an empirical background. Lipsey and Lancaster (1956) investigate the theoretical implications of this issue.
4. Haddad and Kanbur (1992) list the empirical evidence for this claim.
5. In Harsanyi (1955) the expected utility property is the key assumption, while finite sensibility of individual and the Weak Majority Preference Criterion are the key assumptions in Ng (1975).
6. The tailored decision procedure is not necessarily 'optimal'. Lipman (1991) points out the logical inconsistency in assuming an optimal decision procedure when modelling bounded rationality.

3. Analytic Model of Water–Economy Interaction

3.1 INTRODUCTION

In this chapter a stylised Ramsey-Cass-Koopmans (RCK) model is developed as an analytic model. The analytic model provides a model platform based on which an applied model for policy simulations is constructed. In addition, it helps to clarify impacts of water supply constraints on sustainable development by abstracting from other stylised facts commonly observed in water-stressed developing countries, such as vulnerability of rain-fed agriculture and high incidence of lack of access to safe water, particularly in the rural areas. These stylised facts will be incorporated into the applied model in Chapter 4.

The structure of this chapter is as follows. Section 3.2 explains general features of the analytic model, in particular the specification of a two-stage optimisation without an assumption of perfect foresight. Section 3.3 shows the results of the first-stage optimisation in which households and private firms optimise their objective functions. Section 3.4 explains the second-stage optimisation by the government and shows that there are two candidates for the second-stage solution, and that only numerical simulations can determine the second-stage solution. Section 3.5 shows the numerical simulations of the analytic model, which not only provide further insight into the results of qualitative analysis but also clarify the properties of the optimal trajectories. Section 3.6 presents the conclusions of this chapter.

3.2 OUTLINE OF THE ANALYTIC MODEL

The analytic RCK model is designed so as to be compatible with the applied model described in Chapter 4. Like the applied model, the analytic model solves for the optimal consumption levels of the market good and domestic water for the household, factor inputs including water for the private firms, public investment and the water price for the public water producer.

The analytic model assumes a closed economy consisting of numerous identical households and identical competitive firms, output from which is the numeraire of the economy. The population grows at a constant rate ν and capital depreciates at a constant rate δ. Further, it is assumed that a budget-neutral government provides water to households and private firms and collects a volumetric water charge.

The social optimisation process consists of two stages. In the first stage, households maximise utility by choosing consumption levels and private firms maximise profits by choosing the levels of factor inputs taking the rate of water charge as given. In the second stage, the government maximises social welfare by choosing a rate of volumetric water charge and by investing the collected water charge in public capital which is the sole factor input to the water supply service. More precisely, the first-stage optimisation represents the government's forecast of the policy responses of households and firms. This reflects the fact that the optimiser in this situation is different from the subject of optimisation: this is the essence of social optimisation.

Households form expectations without perfect foresight. Conventional RCK models assume that households determine their optimal consumption trajectory by deriving optimal conditions for instantaneous rates of change of consumption. RCK models also determine an optimal initial level of consumption based on a consumption function derived from the intertemporal budget constraint. This assumes that households can precisely predict trajectories for the wage rate, the water price and the interest rate. In the model developed here, households decide upon their consumption levels based on their expectations of the future trajectories of those exogenous variables, but they are then free to modify their expectations continuously based on the realised levels of the exogenous variables. The realised consumption trajectories satisfy the second-best optimality conditions discussed in Chapter 2. At the optimal steady state the second-best outcomes coincide with the first-best outcomes derived from the perfect foresight assumption.

3.3 FIRST-STAGE OPTIMISATION

The first-stage optimisation consists of households' utility maximisation and firms' profit maximisation, taking water price as exogenously given.

3.3.1 The Household's Problem

Problem formulation

It is assumed that households hold assets as equity shares of private capital stock. Population is defined as the labour force population and each person supplies one unit of labour services per unit of time. This means, in the real world, that we assume a constant ratio between the consumption level of a person of labour force age and the consumption level of his or her dependents, such as young children and elderly people, throughout the time horizon. In other words, 'a person' in this model comprises one person of labour force age and his or her dependents. This assumption is important in empirical analysis. Households earn wage and capital income, and use that income to purchase publicly supplied water and manufactured goods for consumption, and to invest in private capital stock. As a result the per capita budget constraint of the representative household is

$$w + rm = c_M + pq_H + I \tag{3.1}$$

where w is the wage rate, r is the real rate of return to equity shares, m is the household assets, c_M is per capita consumption of the manufactured good, q_H is per capita domestic water consumption, p is the rate of water charge (water price), and I is the household investment in private capital. Note that all variables are time varying, such as $w(t)$ and $r(t)$, but time is omitted for notational simplicity.

The equation of motion for per capita household assets is $\dot{m} = I - vm$. Note that the dot superscript indicates the time derivative throughout this book. The far right term depicts 'dilution' due to the increase in household size as the total population grows (Aghion and Howitt 1998, p. 14). It is assumed that the equity shares do not depreciate, unlike the corresponding private capital, as the firm pays the dividends based on the amount of household investment. With (3.1) this equation of motion can be rewritten as

$$\dot{m} = w + (r - v)m - c_M - pq_H \tag{3.2}$$

Suppose that households produce a flow of satisfaction by consuming the manufactured good and water:

$$c(c_M, q_H) = c_M{}^{\varphi} q_H{}^{1-\varphi}, \; 0 < \varphi < 1 \tag{3.3}$$

where φ is a weighting accorded to the manufactured good in the household's production process.

It is assumed that households' utility at time t is determined by the discounted sum of felicities for some finite time period T. The felicity function is assumed to be of CIES (constant intertemporal elasticity of substitution) form.

$$U(t) = \int_t^{t+T} e^{-(\rho-v)s} u(c(s))ds + V(t+T), \; u(c(t)) \equiv \frac{\{c(t)\}^{1-\sigma}}{1-\sigma} \tag{3.4}$$

where $c(t)$: the consumption of flow of satisfaction produced by the household itself at time t, T: the length of the planning period, ρ: the rate of pure time preference, σ: the elasticity of marginal felicity with respect to consumption, and $V(t+T)$: a function that represents the value of the household assets at the terminal time.

In this book $\rho > v$ and $\sigma > 1$ are assumed. The former assumption is plausible according to Ostry and Reinhart (1992) who estimated ρ for African countries at 6.4 per cent based on the data of Morocco, Egypt, Ghana and Côte d'Ivoire between 1968 and the mid-1980s. For the latter assumption, Arrow et al. (1996) reported that the majority of studies use values in the range of 1–2 for σ.

We have little idea about the length of planning period T that might be influenced by economic and social circumstances and education levels in the real world. For example, Perrings (1989) argued that poverty may drive poor farmers to an extremely myopic outlook such that 'all that matters is consumption today' (p. 20). When we employ a finite period for T, say 20 years, we must also specify the value function V at the terminal time $t+T$. Both the choice of T and that of the terminal value function are arbitrary. Aronsson et al. (2004) argued that for the optimal solution the value function must be a discounted sum of a stream of felicities along the optimal trajectories after the terminal time. This study does not employ the perfect foresight assumption and consequently households cannot precisely specify a terminal value function in this way, but it seems reasonable to assume that households' guesses of terminal value are adequate for this specification. This specification gives the utility function the following form:

$$U(t) = \int_t^{\infty} e^{-(\rho-v)s} u(c(s))ds \tag{3.5}$$

Each household maximises its utility subject to its budget constraint, taking the water price as given. The representative household's optimisation problem at time t is therefore:

$$\max_{c_M, q_H} U(t) = \int_t^{\infty} e^{-(\rho-v)s} \frac{c(c_M(s), q_H(s))^{(1-\sigma)}}{1-\sigma} ds \tag{3.6}$$

subject to the equation of motion for household assets (3.2), and the initial assets $m(t)$ historically determined at time t.

Optimal consumption level

The optimisation problem (3.6) is solved analytically using the Maximum Principle of optimal control theory (see Barro and Sala-i-Martin 1995 for the application of the Maximum Principle to RCK models). Instead of the perfect foresight assumption of the standard RCK models, the analytic model of this study assumes that households optimise their current consumption levels, not the entire consumption trajectory, based on dynamic utility optimisation at the moment of decision making, and they are then free to repeat this optimisation based on their updated expectations. Therefore we must derive the optimal consumption level at the moment of decision making. The essence of this derivation of the optimal consumption level is explained below. For mathematical details of the derivation, see Appendix 3.1.

The current value Hamiltonian for this problem is

$$H = \frac{c(c_M, q_H)^{(1-\sigma)}}{1-\sigma} + \lambda\{w + (r - v)m - c_M - pq_H\} \tag{3.7}$$

where λ is the Lagrange multiplier associated with household assets m. λ represents the marginal felicity of those assets.

Assuming an interior solution, the necessary and sufficient conditions for optimality are $\partial H/\partial c_M = 0$, $\partial H/\partial q_H = 0$ and $\dot{\lambda} - (\rho - v)\lambda = -\partial H/\partial m$ and the transversality condition is $\lim_{s\to\infty}\left[e^{-(\rho-v)(s-t)}\lambda(s)\cdot m(s)\right] = 0.$[1]

From these conditions, the optimal growth rate of per capita consumption is obtained as

$$\frac{\dot{c}}{c} = \frac{1}{\sigma}\left\{(r - \rho) - (1-\varphi)\frac{\dot{p}}{p}\right\} \tag{3.8}$$

Its counterpart of the standard RCK model is $\dot{c}/c = (r - \rho)/\sigma$. The far right term in (3.8) represents the negative effect of a water price rise on consumption growth. The larger the weight accorded to water consumption in household production, $(1-\varphi)$, the larger this effect is. It is plausible that developing economies would be more sensitive to this negative impact of water price rise on consumption growth, because of the higher share of water expenditure within total household expenditure.

Given the optimal growth rate of consumption, the trajectories of both consumption level and household assets will be uniquely determined by initial consumption level as the initial asset holdings are historically given. The optimal initial consumption level is determined such that the trajectory of asset holdings satisfies the transversality condition. Solving the differential equations (3.2) and (3.8) by applying the transversality condition, we can derive the following consumption function for 'clairvoyant' households who can predict the future trajectories of w, r and p perfectly:

$$c(t) = \eta(t)\left[m(t) + \int_t^{\infty} w(s) e^{-\int_t^s \{r(\tau)-\nu\} d\tau} ds \right] \tag{3.9}$$

where $\eta(t) \equiv \varphi^{\varphi}(1-\varphi)^{(1-\varphi)} \Big/ \left[\{p(t)\}^{\frac{\sigma-\varphi}{\sigma}} \int_t^{\infty} \{p(s)\}^{\frac{(\sigma-1)(1-\varphi)}{\sigma}} e^{\int_t^s \left\{ \nu - \frac{\rho}{\sigma} - \frac{\sigma-1}{\sigma} r(\tau) \right\} d\tau} ds \right]$.

The term $\eta(t)$ is the propensity for the household to consume out of wealth at t. It is noted that clairvoyant households refer to the consumption function only once when they choose their initial consumption. Subsequently, they just need to change their level of consumption based on the optimal consumption growth rate (3.8) in order to achieve the first-best outcome.

Now let us relax the perfect foresight assumption. Instead, it is assumed that the households' expectations about the trajectories of the exogenous variables is that they will remain constant at their current values, that is, $p(s) = p(t)$ for all $s \geq t$ and so on. Although it is possible to incorporate past information within the expectation formation process, this kind of sophistication is rather ad hoc and its rewards might not be sufficient to justify the extra complexity involved. With this particular form of imperfect foresight assumption, the optimal consumption level at the moment of planning is obtained as summarised by the following proposition.

Proposition 3.1 If $r(t) > \nu$, the optimal per capita consumption level of satisfaction at the moment of decision is given by

$$c^*(t) = \varphi^{\varphi} \left\{ \frac{1-\varphi}{p(t)} \right\}^{1-\varphi} \left\{ r(t) - \nu - \frac{r(t)-\rho}{\sigma} \right\} \left\{ m(t) + \frac{w(t)}{r(t)-\nu} \right\} \tag{3.10}$$

and consumption of the manufactured good and domestic water are given by $c_M^*(t) = \left(\frac{\varphi}{1-\varphi} \right)^{1-\varphi} \{p(t)\}^{1-\varphi} c^*(t)$ and $q_H^*(t) = \left(\frac{\varphi}{1-\varphi} \right)^{-\varphi} \{p(t)\}^{-\varphi} c^*(t)$.

If $r(t) \leq \nu$, these optimal consumption levels diverge towards infinity.

Proof: See Appendix 3.1.

In the following analysis, the real rate of return is assumed to be strictly greater than the population growth rate ($r > \nu$). Now $c^*(t)$ is determined solely by the current values of the exogenous variables at t. This optimal consumption coincides with the first-best optimal consumption based on the perfect foresight assumption, provided that the economy is in a steady state. Otherwise, $c^*(t)$ is larger or smaller than the first-best optimal solution depending on the differences between the steady-state values and the realised values of p, r and w. For instance, if actual wage rates in future are higher than the steady-state value whilst other prices take their steady-state values, $c^*(t)$ is unambiguously greater than the first-best solution. Nevertheless, it is the second-best optimal consumption level given the assumed process for expectation formation.

3.3.2 The Firms' Problem

It is assumed that all competitive firms employ the same production technology described by the following Cobb-Douglas production function with constant returns to scale:

$$Y = F(K, Q_M, L) = K^{\beta_K} Q_M{}^{\beta_Q} L^{\beta_L} \tag{3.11}$$

where Y: aggregate output, K: aggregate private capital input, and Q_M: aggregate water input, L: aggregate labour input, and β_K, β_Q and β_L: factor shares of private capital, water and labour with $\beta_K, \beta_Q, \beta_L \in (0,1)$ and $\beta_K + \beta_Q + \beta_L = 1$.

The constant return to scale assumption enables the above production technology to be expressed as the following intensive form:

$$y = f(k, q_M) = k^{\beta_K} q_M{}^{\beta_Q} \tag{3.12}$$

where y: per worker output, k: per worker private capital input, and q_M: per worker water input.

The firms' per worker profit (π) is given as $\pi = y - (r+\delta)k - pq_M - w$. Note that the rental price of capital must be $r + \rho$ in order to compensate for the depreciation of capital (see Barro and Sala-i-Martin 1995, p. 69).

All the competitive firms maximise their per-worker profit by controlling factor inputs k and q_M such that the partial derivatives of π with respect to k and q_M become zero ($\partial\pi/\partial k = 0$ and $\partial\pi/\partial q_M = 0$), taking r and p as exogenously given.

From (3.12) and the optimality conditions, the optimal levels of per worker output (y^*)and water input (q_M^*) are determined as follows:

$$y^* = (\beta_Q/p)^{\beta_Q/(1-\beta_Q)} k^{\beta_K/(1-\beta_Q)} \tag{3.13}$$

$$q_M^* = (\beta_Q/p)^{1/(1-\beta_Q)} k^{\beta_K/(1-\beta_Q)} \tag{3.14}$$

From the optimality conditions and (3.13), the optimal per worker capital input (k^*) is determined by r and p as

$$k^* = \{\beta_K/(r+\delta)\}^{(1-\beta_Q)/\beta_L}(\beta_Q/p)^{\beta_Q/\beta_L} \tag{3.15}$$

By putting the optimality conditions into the per worker profit function with (3.13) and (3.14), we obtain the optimal per worker profit (π^*) as a function of the wage rate (w) and the optimal per worker capital input (k^*):

$$\pi^* = \beta_L(\beta_Q/p)^{\beta_Q/(1-\beta_Q)}(k^*)^{\beta_K/(1-\beta_Q)} - w \tag{3.16}$$

Thus w determines the sign of per worker profit as

$$\pi^* \begin{matrix} > \\ = \\ < \end{matrix} 0 \text{ if } w \begin{matrix} < \\ = \\ > \end{matrix} \beta_L\left(\frac{\beta_Q}{p}\right)^{\frac{\beta_Q}{1-\beta_Q}}(k^*)^{\frac{\beta_K}{1-\beta_Q}} \tag{3.17}$$

3.3.3 Market Equilibrium and First-stage Solution

Equilibrium in the labour, capital and goods markets is achieved by a set of prices r^* and w^* such that these markets clear. Since the market good is our numeraire, its equilibrium price is always unity.

The assumption of a market of competitive firms drives the optimal profit towards zero, which, together with (3.17), determines the equilibrium wage rate as

$$w^* = \beta_L(\beta_Q/p)^{\beta_Q/(1-\beta_Q)}(k^*)^{\beta_K/(1-\beta_Q)} \tag{3.18}$$

With this equilibrium wage rate the labour market clears such that total labour force population equals number of total workers, which means that per capita values and per worker values coincide. In these circumstances the capital market clearance condition is given by $k^* = m$.

The equilibrium rate of return to private capital is determined from (3.15) as

$$r^* = \beta_K(1/k^*)^{\beta_L/1-\beta_Q}(\beta_Q/p)^{\beta_Q/1-\beta_Q} - \delta \tag{3.19}$$

By putting w^* and r^* into the optimal consumption level (Proposition 3.1) with the capital market clearance condition, the optimal per capita consumption level of satisfaction can be expressed as follows:

$$\hat{c}\left(\hat{k}(t),p(t)\right)=\varphi^{\varphi}\left\{\frac{1-\varphi}{p(t)}\right\}^{1-\varphi}\left\{r^{*}\left(\hat{k}(t),p(t)\right)-\nu-\frac{r^{*}\left(\hat{k}(t),p(t)\right)-\rho}{\sigma}\right\}\times$$
$$\times\left\{\hat{k}(t)+\frac{w^{*}\left(\hat{k}(t),p(t)\right)}{r^{*}\left(\hat{k}(t),p(t)\right)-\nu}\right\} \tag{3.20}$$

The superscript hat here is used to denote the first-stage solution. With the equilibrium prices and (3.20), the equation of motion for per capita private capital can be expressed as the following first-order differential equation:

$$\dot{\hat{k}}(s)=(1-\beta_Q)/\varphi^{\varphi}\{(1-\varphi)p(s)/\beta_Q\}^{\varphi-1}\{\hat{k}(s)\}^{\beta_K/(1-\beta_Q)}$$
$$-(\delta+\nu)\hat{k}(s)-\{\beta_Q/p(s)\}^{\beta_Q/(1-\beta_Q)}\hat{c}\left(\hat{k}(s),p(s)\right)\ \text{ for } s\geq t \tag{3.21}$$

and $\hat{k}(t)=m(t)$ is historically determined.

These two equations (3.20) and (3.21) uniquely determine the first-stage solution. Once the government determines a water pricing schedule for $s \geq t$, the optimal consumption level at t, $\hat{c}(t)$, is uniquely determined by (3.20) since $\hat{k}(t) = m(t)$ is given. This household decision on consumption determines the optimal household asset holdings at the next moment $\hat{k}(t+1)$ based on (3.21), in which 't+1' denotes the next moment after t for notational convenience (in spite of continuous time setting). Then, the households determine $\hat{c}(t+1)$ based on (3.20) and this then determines $\hat{k}(t+2)$ and so on.

The other first-stage solutions required for the second-stage optimisation are as follows:

$$\hat{q}_H\left(\hat{k}(t),p(t)\right)=(1-\varphi)^{\varphi}\{\varphi\, p(t)\}^{-\varphi}\hat{c}\left(\hat{k}(t),p(t)\right) \tag{3.22}$$
$$\hat{q}_M\left(\hat{k}(t),p(t)\right)=\{\beta_Q/p(t)\}^{1/(1-\beta_Q)}\{\hat{k}(t)\}^{\beta_K/(1-\beta_Q)} \tag{3.23}$$

Recall that the first-stage optimisation is the government's forecast of households' response to water pricing policy. These first-stage solutions provide all the information necessary for the government to achieve its objective by means of the second-stage optimisation. Nevertheless, it is worth investigating the properties of the first-stage solution which can be interpreted as the optimal solution without water supply constraints. From this benchmark, the implications of water supply constraints can be clarified.

3.3.4 Properties of the First-Stage Solution

The following two propositions summarise the important properties of the first-stage solution.

Proposition 3.2 If there is no supply-side constraint, the following relationship between the optimal growth rate of private capital and water price holds for $s \geq t$:

$$g_k(s) \equiv \frac{\dot{\hat{k}}(s)}{\hat{k}(s)} \begin{array}{c} > \\ = \\ < \end{array} 0 \text{ if and only if } p(s) \begin{array}{c} < \\ = \\ > \end{array} \beta_Q \left(\frac{\beta_K}{\delta + \rho} \right)^{\frac{1-\beta_Q}{\beta_Q}} \left\{ \frac{1}{\hat{k}(s)} \right\}^{\frac{\beta_L}{\beta_Q}}$$

Moreover, $\lim_{p(s) \to 0+} g_k(s) = +\infty$ and $\lim_{p(s) \to p_{max}-} g_k(s) = -\infty$, in which $p_{max} \equiv \beta_Q \{ \beta_K / (\delta + \nu) \}^{(1-\beta_Q)/\beta_Q} \{ 1/\hat{k}(s) \}^{\beta_L/\beta_Q}$.

Consequently, the government can induce any level of private capital stock by controlling the water price, if the economy is free from supply-side constraints.

Proof: See Appendix 3.2.

Proposition 3.3 Once any constant water price is given, the first-stage solution always converges to the steady state. In other words, the optimal steady states given any constant water price are globally stable in the absence of supply-side constraints. The steady-state private capital stock is expressed as $\bar{k} = (\beta_Q / \bar{p})^{\beta_Q/\beta_L} \{ \beta_K / (\delta + \rho) \}^{(1-\beta_Q)/\beta_L}$.

Proof: See Appendix 3.3.

These two propositions are policy relevant. For instance, if the economy is free from supply-side constraints in water provision and the government has discretion in freely setting the water price, the government can induce any desirable household consumption level by setting the water price. Needless to say, these 'desirable' results are largely due to strong assumptions such as no supply-side constraint, full employment and full market equilibrium which are very unlikely to hold in the real world. Nevertheless, these propositions provide a useful benchmark from which we can investigate the implications of relaxing each assumption. Moreover, they facilitate analysis of supply-side problems that are particularly important in water-stressed developing economies.

3.4 SECOND-STAGE OPTIMISATION

3.4.1 Sustainable Water Production

As was the case of for private goods production, we drastically simplify the actual water production processes comprising the harnessing of raw water from the natural hydrological cycle, water purification, transmission and so forth into an aggregate water production function $Q = F^W(G)$, where Q is an aggregate water production and G is an aggregate public capital stock.

Weitzman (1970) argued that 'social overhead capital' including sanitation facilities, irrigation facilities and water supply facilities belong to the 'β sector' characterised by very high capital intensity. Indeed, the World Bank (2004) reported that 'the fixed costs of water supply are typically high relative to variable costs, more so than for other utilities such as electricity. For example, fixed costs account for more than 80 per cent of water supply costs in the United Kingdom' (p. 223). This could justify the above specification of the water production function. Note that here we use an aggregate production function because the water constraint is manifested in absolute terms rather than in per capita terms.

Another basic feature of the β sector discussed by Weitzman (1970) is the existence of substantial economies of scale due to indivisibility and cost lumpiness. This is highly relevant to the case of water production, which is often associated with large-scale facilities such as dams, treatment plants and pipelines (Young and Haveman 1985). Hence the shape of the water production function might not be smooth but kinked at several points as illustrated in Figure 3.1.

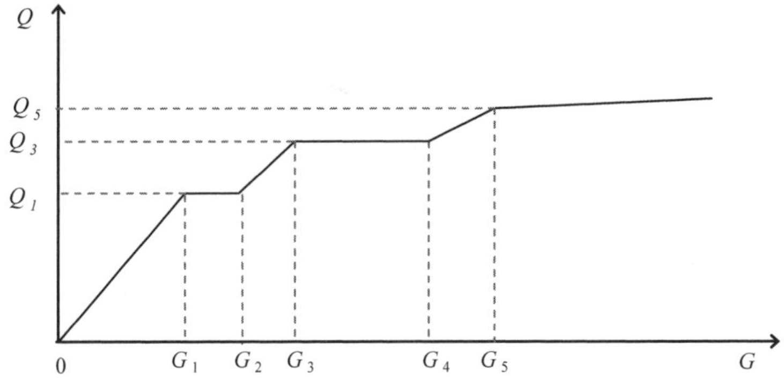

Figure 3.1 Conceptual illustration of water production function

In order to reflect a sustainability constraint in a tractable way, this function must be interpreted as the relationship between public capital stock and capacity to produce clean water, on condition that water production and consumption do not endanger the resilience of ecosystems underpinning life support systems. This sustainability constraint prohibits, for instance, exploiting surface water or groundwater beyond a sustainable yield, or discharging pollutants or wastewater to water bodies in excess of their assimilating capacities. Consequently, technological choice within a 'sustainable production function' is limited and the required amount of public capital covers not only narrowly defined water supply costs but also wastewater treatment costs. This 'sustainable production function' approach will be discussed further in Chapter 5.

When the amount of water to be supplied is smaller than Q_1, harnessing water from the hydrological cycle is technically easy and water-related capital might be divisible. To supply more than Q_1 some large-scale facility such as a large dam may need to be installed, which requires an amount of capital corresponding to G_2–G_1 for its construction. Only after installation of this facility does it become possible to increase water supply capacity up to Q_3 by further capital accumulation (from G_2 to G_3). In other words, the marginal product of water with respect to the public capital stock G is zero between G_1 and G_2 ($dF^W/dG = 0$). After repeating this process several times the water supply capacity will reach an upper limit for the conventional technologies (Q_5). Though it is possible to increase water supply capacity above this level by introducing unconventional technologies such as water importing, water recycling or desalinisation of seawater, it is highly likely that the marginal water product of these technologies would be very low, as is shown in Figure 3.1. Note that the sustainable water production function is assumed to be twice continuously differentiable, at least from the left side, at any point.

Based on this approach, the sustainability constraint can be expressed as

$$N_0 e^{vt}\left\{\hat{q}_H\left(\hat{k},p\right)+\hat{q}_M\left(\hat{k},p\right)\right\}\leq F^W(G) \tag{3.24}$$

where N_0 is the initial population.

The left-hand side is aggregate water demand, while the right-hand side is the water supply capacity which can be delivered without endangering sustainability, since F^W is the sustainable water production function.

3.4.2 The Government's Problem

It is assumed that the budget-neutral government collects volumetric water charges from both households and firms and spends all the collected charges on public capital investment (I^G):

$$p\left\{\hat{q}_H(\hat{k},p)+\hat{q}_M(\hat{k},p)\right\}N_0e^{\nu t}=I^G \tag{3.25}$$

The assumption that the government undertakes water service provision is not only justifiable considering the natural monopolistic features of water provision, but also realistic in most developing countries. In the context of a closed economy, the assumption of a budget-neutral government is sensible. With this assumption of budget neutrality, the equation of motion of public capital becomes

$$\dot{G}=p\left\{\hat{q}_H(\hat{k},p)+\hat{q}_M(\hat{k},p)\right\}N_0e^{\nu t}-\delta G \tag{3.26}$$

The objective of the government is to maximise the 'intra-generational' social welfare of the current generation by choosing a time trajectory for the water price whilst simultaneously observing the sustainability constraint. As discussed in Chapter 2, this study defines social welfare as the unweighted sum of all households' utilities. Since we assume identical households, the government's problem can be expressed as

$$\underset{p}{Max}\int_0^{\infty}e^{-(\rho-\nu)t}\frac{\hat{c}(\hat{k},p)^{(1-\sigma)}}{1-\sigma}dt \tag{3.27}$$

subject to the equation of motion for private capital (3.21) with an initial capital stock (k_0), the equation of motion for public capital (3.26) with an initial capital stock (G_0), and the sustainability constraint (3.24).

In the above problem, $\hat{c}$ and $\hat{k}$ are the first-stage solutions that represent the government's anticipation of households' response to water price. The government's problem is thus understood as an attempt to maximise social welfare by indirectly controlling households' consumption decisions through setting a water pricing schedule by anticipating households' response to it.

It must be noted that the infinite time horizon of the government's problem does not entail an infinite planning period for the government or for the consideration of intergenerational welfare. It simply reflects the infinite time horizon of the private utility function as discussed in Section 3.3.1. Although the solution of this optimisation problem is a trajectory of water price for infinite time, it is not necessary for the government actually to implement this trajectory for an infinite time in order to achieve its policy goal designed for a finite planning period. To allow for inevitable errors in expectation, the government may choose to set a relatively short planning period, say 5 to 20 years, and then to repeat the optimisation process periodically. This point does not affect the discussions which follow in this chapter but will be important for the policy simulations in Chapter 6.

3.4.3 The Second-Stage Solution: Two Candidates

The second-stage solution is a water pricing schedule for the planning period that can attain the highest possible level of social welfare whilst simultaneously satisfying the sustainability constraint.

If the sustainability constraint takes a form of an equality constraint, such a water pricing schedule is uniquely determined by this constraint as follows. At the outset ($t = 0$), the initial public capital stock (G_0) determines sustainable water supply capacity, and the sustainability constraint with this supply capacity uniquely determines the market-clearing water price such that water demand is equal to the water supply. This water price determines the levels of both public investment and anticipated private investment, which jointly dictate sustainable water production capacity in the next moment, and so on. Let us call such a water pricing schedule 'the market-clearing pricing schedule'. This pricing schedule is formally described in the following proposition.

Proposition 3.4 The market-clearing pricing schedule for water price is determined by the following system of equations with the initial capital stock levels k_0 and G_0:

$$\begin{cases} F^W(G) - N_0 e^{\nu t}\left\{\hat{q}_H(\hat{k}, p) + \hat{q}_M(\hat{k}, p)\right\} = 0 \\ \dot{G}/G = pF^W(G)/G - \delta \equiv g_G^{MC}(G, p) \\ \dot{\hat{k}}/\hat{k} = g_k(\hat{k}, p) \end{cases} \tag{3.28}$$

The rate of change of water price along the market-clearing pricing schedule is given by

$$g_p^{MC} \equiv \dot{p}/p = $$
$$= \frac{\varepsilon_G F^W g_G^{MC} - N_0 e^{\nu t}\{\nu(\hat{q}_H + \hat{q}M)\} + \hat{k}\left(\partial\hat{q}_H/\partial\hat{k} + \partial\hat{q}_M/\partial\hat{k}\right) g_k}{N_0 e^{\nu t} p\left(\partial\hat{q}_H/\partial\hat{k} + \partial\hat{q}_M/\partial\hat{k}\right)} \tag{3.29}$$

where $\varepsilon_G \equiv \left(dF^W/F^W\right)/(dG/G)$ is the elasticity of sustainable water production with respect to public capital.

The market-clearing pricing schedule always satisfies the sustainability constraint but cannot be an interior solution to the government problem, except for the very special case in which $\partial\hat{c}/\partial p = 0$ holds at the steady state.

Proof: See Appendix 3.4.

It must be noted that $\partial\hat{c}/\partial p = 0$ is possible since higher water price induces substitution of domestic water consumption with manufactured good consumption. Nevertheless, such a case requires very particular values of not only parameters but also state variables, and consequently $\partial\hat{c}/\partial p = 0$ holds only instantaneously unless it holds at the steady state. The probability of having a steady state associated with $\partial\hat{c}/\partial p = 0$ is negligible, and the market-clearing pricing schedule cannot be an interior solution of the government problem in a practical sense.

Still, this pricing schedule appears to be optimal as it is the lowest water price which satisfies the original inequality sustainability constraint on sustainability at the moment of decision making. If the government problem were static, this would be correct. For the dynamic problem, however, a water price which is higher than the market-clearing price could generate higher social welfare in the long run through faster capital accumulation. Indeed, the sign of the partial derivative of the accumulation speed of private capital stock with respect to water price ($\partial\dot{\hat{k}}/\partial p$) depends on parameter values.

Because of this possibility, there is another candidate for the optimal water pricing schedule when the sustainability constraint holds with strict inequality, or in other words, when sustainable water supply capacity exceeds the optimal water demand. This candidate is labelled as the 'excess-supply pricing schedule', and it is formally described in the following proposition.

Proposition 3.5 The excess-supply pricing schedule of water price is determined by the following system of equations with the initial capital stock levels k_0 and G_0:

$$\begin{cases} \hat{c}(\hat{k},p) - p\left\{\hat{q}_H(\hat{k},p) + \hat{q}_M(\hat{k},p)\right\} - \left\{g_k(\hat{k},p) + \delta + \nu\right\}\hat{k} = 0 \\ \dfrac{\dot{G}}{G} = \dfrac{p}{G}\left\{\hat{q}_H(\hat{k},p) + \hat{q}_M(\hat{k},p)\right\}N_0 e^{\nu t} - \delta \equiv g_G^{ES}(G,\hat{k},p) \\ \dot{\hat{k}}/\hat{k} = g_k(\hat{k},p) \end{cases} \tag{3.30}$$

This system gives the rate of change of water price as follows:

$$g_p^{ES}(p,\hat{k}) \equiv \dot{p}/p = -\left\{\delta + \rho + \sigma\varepsilon_k g_k(p,\hat{k})\right\}/\sigma\varepsilon_p \tag{3.31}$$

where $\varepsilon_p \equiv (d\hat{c}/\hat{c})/(dp/p)$ and $\varepsilon_k \equiv (d\hat{c}/\hat{c})/(d\hat{k}/\hat{k})$ are the elasticities of the optimal consumption with respect to water price and private capital stock, respectively.

The excess-supply pricing schedule is an interior solution to the government problem with the strict inequality form of sustainability constraint, but this solution does not necessarily satisfy the sustainability constraint. Only numerical simulations can tell us whether the excess-supply pricing schedule satisfies the sustainability constraint or not. Further, it can be shown that the excess-supply pricing schedule cannot satisfy the transversality condition with respect to the public capital stock.

Proof: See Appendix 3.5.

These propositions indicate that the second-stage solution cannot be determined without numerical simulations, although we can obtain two candidates analytically.

3.4.4 Local Stability Analysis of the Optimal Steady State

Before obtaining the second-stage solution by numerical simulation, it seems worthwhile to conduct a local stability analysis of the optimal steady state using the linearisation method, since many theoretical studies of RCK models have derived major conclusions from such an analysis. As we will see later, this study provides an interesting case where the policy implications obtained from local stability analysis are not consistent with the global stability properties observed in numerical simulations.

The steady state in this study is characterised by zero growth rates of private and public capital stock and a constant water price. Because of the zero growth condition on public capital, the steady state must be associated with zero population growth ($\nu = 0$), which is assumed throughout this subsection.

It is easily confirmed that the excess-supply pricing schedule cannot achieve a steady state. Under the steady-state conditions ($g_p^{ES} = 0$ and $g_k = 0$), we obtain $-(\delta+\rho)/(\sigma\varepsilon_p) = 0$ from (3.31), which can hold if and only if ε_p diverges to positive or negative infinite in the steady state. Let $\bar{\varepsilon}_p$ denote the steady-state value of ε_p. From Proposition 3.2, $\bar{\varepsilon}_p$ is evaluated as follows:

$$\bar{\varepsilon}_p = \varphi - 1 + \frac{\beta_Q\{\delta - (\delta+\rho)/\sigma\}\{(\delta-\rho)\beta_K - (\delta+\rho)\beta_L\}}{\rho(1-\beta_Q)\{\rho\beta_K + (\delta+\rho)\beta_L\}} + \frac{\beta_Q(\delta-\rho)}{\rho(1-\beta_Q)} \tag{3.32}$$

Since the denominators of the right-hand side are not infinitesimal, $\bar{\varepsilon}_p$ cannot diverge to positive or negative infinite. Consequently, the excess-supply pricing schedule cannot attain a steady state.

In contrast, the market-clearing pricing schedule can have a steady state if and only if the following set of conditions is satisfied:

$$\begin{cases} \hat{k} = \{\beta_K/(\delta+\rho)\}^{\frac{1-\beta_Q}{\beta_L}}(\beta_Q/p)^{\frac{\beta_Q}{\beta_L}} \equiv \bar{k}(p) \\ G = pN_0\{\hat{q}_H(p,\bar{k}(p)) + \hat{q}_M(p,\bar{k}(p))\}/\delta \equiv \bar{G}(p) \\ F^W(\bar{G}(p)) - N_0\{\hat{q}_H(p,\bar{k}(p)) + \hat{q}_M(p,\bar{k}(p))\} = 0 \end{cases} \tag{3.33}$$

where $\bar{k}$ and $\bar{G}$ are the steady-state private and public capital stocks.

The first condition is immediately obtained from Proposition 3.2, and the second condition is obtained from the second equation of (3.28) as the necessary and sufficient condition to have $g_G^{MC} = 0$ when $\hat{k} = \bar{k}$. Since setting $g_k = g_G^{MC} = 0$ in (3.29) automatically produces $g_p^{MC} = 0$, the market-clearing steady state exists if and only if the first equation of (3.28) is satisfied along with the first and the second conditions, as is summarised in the third condition.

That only the market-clearing pricing schedule can attain a steady state does not necessarily indicate that the excess-supply pricing schedule is suboptimal. If the latter can achieve higher social welfare than the former whilst observing the sustainability constraint, the latter is clearly the optimal pricing schedule even if there is no optimal steady state. Keeping this reservation in mind, steady states attained via the market-clearing pricing schedule are referred to as the optimal steady states.

The trajectories along the market-clearing pricing schedule are described by the following vector differential equation given the initial values, $G(0) = G_0$, $\hat{k}(0) = k_0$ and $p(0)$ that satisfies $F^W(G_0) = N_0[\hat{q}_H\{k_0, p(0)\} + \hat{q}_M\{k_0, p(0)\}]$:

$$\frac{d}{dt}\begin{bmatrix} G \\ \hat{k} \\ p \end{bmatrix} = \begin{bmatrix} Gg_G^{MC}(G,p) \\ \hat{k}g_p^{MC}(p,\hat{k}) \\ pg_p^{MC}(G,p,\hat{k}) \end{bmatrix} \tag{3.34}$$

Before applying the linearisation method, Liapunov's second method was used to confirm whether global stability analysis was possible.[2] An application of the second method with a Euclidean distance function as a candidate Liapunov function shows that the time derivative of this candidate is neither positive nor negative definitive, which is consistent with the partial stability frequently observed in the optimal growth models. Hence we focus on analysing the local stability of the steady state of the original system described as (3.34) with the linearisation method.

Because this system is autonomous, which means that time is not contained as an explicit argument, the linearised system near steady state is certainly a uniformly good approximation to the original system around the optimal steady state (Gandolfo 1997). The following proposition summarises the local stability of the optimal steady state.

Proposition 3.6 The optimal steady state along the market-clearing pricing schedule is saddle-path stable in the neighbourhood of the steady state, and the stability properties depend on the value of the elasticity of sustainable water production with respect to public capital at the steady state as follows.

If $\varepsilon_G(\overline{G}) < 1$, it is possible to position the economy on a stable manifold towards the optimal steady state if *either* G_0 *or* k_0 can be adjusted properly.

If $\varepsilon_G(\overline{G}) \geq 1$, it is possible to position the economy on a stable manifold towards the optimal steady state if *both* G_0 *and* k_0 can be adjusted properly.

Proof: See Appendix 3.6.

The local stability analysis carries two main implications. Firstly, the introduction of a supply-side constraint on water provision replaces the global stability of the optimal steady state in the world without supply-side constraints (Proposition 3.3) with a saddle-path stability of the optimal steady state. With a supply side-constraint, either one or both of G_0 and k_0 must be adjusted appropriately to achieve this optimal steady state, even if the economy has reached the neighbourhood of the steady state. Secondly, the elasticity of sustainable water production with respect to public capital defines the local stability properties of the optimal steady state.

It appears plausible that both of these factors should influence the convergent path towards the optimal steady state. In particular, the influence which the elasticity of sustainable water production with respect to public capital exerts over the local stability of the steady state seems to make sense because this elasticity represents the impact of a supply-side constraint on the economy.

What appears to be somewhat counterintuitive is that a higher elasticity of sustainable water production ($\varepsilon_G \geq 1$), which must make it easier to increase water production capacity, makes it more difficult to achieve the optimal steady state. It is, however, possible that a combination of the water market clearance condition and the assumption of budget-neutral government may make an elastic water production system excessively sensitive to changes in the level of capital stock.

It should be emphasised here that these implications would have been the main conclusion of this study, if numerical simulations had not been conducted. As noted previously, we shall see in the next section that the numerical simulations paint a quite different picture.

3.5 NUMERICAL SIMULATIONS

3.5.1 Model Specification

This section briefly describes the numerical simulation model, a discrete-time version of the analytic model.

First-stage optimisation in a discrete-time setting
The representative household's problem in discrete time becomes

$$\underset{c_s^M, q_s^H}{Max}\, U_t \equiv \sum_{s=t}^{\infty}\left(\frac{1+\nu}{1+\rho}\right)^s \frac{1}{1-\sigma}\{c(c_s^M, q_s^H)\}^{1-\sigma} \quad \text{subject to} \tag{3.35}$$

$$m_{s+1} - m_s = \frac{1}{1+\nu}\{w_s + (r_s - \nu)m_s - c_s^M - p_s q_s^H\} \tag{3.36}$$

with the initial asset holding m_t historically determined at time t.

The discrete-time version of the optimal consumption, which corresponds to Proposition 3.1 in continuous time, is as follows.

Proposition 3.7 If $r_t > \nu$ is satisfied, the optimal consumption is given by

$$c_t^* = \varphi^{\varphi}\left(\frac{1-\varphi}{p_t}\right)^{1-\varphi}\left\{1 + r_t - (1+\nu)\left(\frac{1+r_t}{1+\rho}\right)^{1/\sigma}\right\}\left(m_t + \frac{w_t}{r_t - \nu}\right) \tag{3.37}$$

Otherwise, c_t^* cannot have a positive finite value.

Proof: See Appendix 3.7.

Recall that $(1+x)^t$ in discrete time corresponds to e^{xt} in continuous time, or, equivalently, that $ln\,(1+x)$ in discrete time corresponds to x in continuous time, where x is any constant such as the population growth rate or the rate of pure time preference. Hence $\nu + \dfrac{r(t) - \rho}{\sigma}$ in continuous time corresponds to $ln(1+\nu) + \dfrac{ln(1+r_t) - ln(1+\rho)}{\sigma} = ln\left\{(1+\nu)\left(\dfrac{1+r_t}{1+\rho}\right)^{1/\sigma}\right\}$ in discrete time. This fact illustrates the correspondence between Propositions 3.1 and 3.7.

The firms' problem is identical with the continuous-time case because of its static nature. To provide more flexibility in the numerical simulations in order to facilitate calibration, however, a technological parameter τ is introduced.

This makes the firms' per labour term production function $y_t = \tau(k_t)^{\beta_K}(q_t^M)^{\beta_Q}$, and the equilibrium prices $r_t^* = \tau\beta_K(\beta_Q/p_t)^{\beta_Q/(1-\beta_Q)}(1/k_t)^{\beta_L/(1-\beta_Q)} - \delta$ and $w_t^* = \tau\beta_L(\beta_Q/p_t)^{\beta_Q/(1-\beta_Q)}k_t^{\beta_K/(1-\beta_Q)}$.

With these equilibrium prices the first-stage solution in discrete time is determined by the following system:

$$\hat{c}(\hat{k}_t, p_t) = \varphi^{\varphi}\left(\frac{1-\varphi}{p_t}\right)^{1-\varphi}\left[1 + r^*(\hat{k}_t, p_t) - (1+\nu)\left\{\frac{1+r^*(\hat{k}_t, p_t)}{1+\rho}\right\}^{1/\sigma}\right] \times$$
$$\times\left[\hat{k}_t + w^*(\hat{k}_t, p_t)/\{r^*(\hat{k}_t, p_t) - \nu\}\right] \tag{3.38}$$

$$\hat{k}_{t+1} - \hat{k}_t = \left[(r_t^* - \nu)\hat{k}_t + w_t^* - \varphi^{-\varphi}\{p_t/(1-\varphi)\}^{1-\varphi}\hat{c}_t\right]/(1+\nu) \tag{3.39}$$

The remaining first-stage solutions in the discrete time setting are as follows:

$$\hat{q}^H(\hat{k}_t, p_t) = (1-\varphi)^{\varphi}(\varphi p_t)^{-\varphi}\hat{c}(\hat{k}_t, p_t) \tag{3.40}$$

$$\hat{q}^M(\hat{k}_t, p_t) = (\beta_Q/p_t)^{1/(1-\beta_Q)}\hat{k}_t^{\beta_K/(1-\beta_Q)} \tag{3.41}$$

Second-stage optimisation in discrete time

The discrete-time versions of Propositions 3.4 and 3.5 are as follows.

Proposition 3.8 The market-clearing pricing schedule in discrete time is determined by the following system with G_0 and k_0 given:

$$\begin{cases} F^W(G_t) - N_0(1+\nu)^t\left\{\hat{q}^H(\hat{k}_t, p_t) + \hat{q}^M(\hat{k}_t, p_t)\right\} = 0 \\ G_{t+1} - G_t = p_t F^W(G_t) - \delta G_t \\ \hat{k}_{t+1} - \hat{k}_t = \left[(r_t^* - \nu)\hat{k}_t + w_t^* - \varphi^{-\varphi}\{p_t/(1-\varphi)\}^{1-\varphi}\hat{c}_t\right]/(1+\nu) \end{cases} \tag{3.42}$$

The excess-supply pricing schedule in discrete time is determined by the following system with G_0 and k_0 given:

$$\begin{cases} \hat{c}_t \left\{ 1 + \nu + \dfrac{1}{\varphi^{\varphi}} \left(\dfrac{p_t}{1-\varphi} \right)^{1-\varphi} \right\} - (1+\nu) p_t (\hat{q}_t^H + \hat{q}_t^M) - (r_t^* + \delta) \hat{k}_t - w_t^* = 0 \\ G_{t+1} - G_t = p_t N_0 (1+\nu)^t (\hat{q}_t^H + \hat{q}_t^M) - \delta G_t \\ \hat{k}_{t+1} - \hat{k}_t = \left[(r_t^* - \nu) \hat{k}_t + w_t^* - \varphi^{-\varphi} \{ p_t / (1-\varphi) \}^{1-\varphi} \hat{c}_t \right] / (1+\nu) \end{cases} \quad (3.43)$$

Proof: See Appendix 3.8.

Specification of water production function

Depending on the purpose of the numerical simulations, two sets of sustainable water production functions are constructed.

The first set of sustainable production functions is designed for analysing the stability of the optimal steady state. This set is constructed such that there exist three steady states, as shown in Figure 3.2, only the middle one of which is associated with the elasticity of sustainable water production being greater than unity ($\varepsilon_G(\overline{G}) \geq 1$).

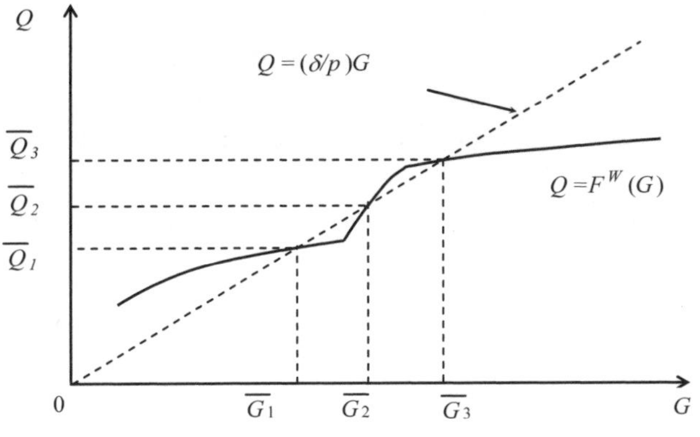

Figure 3.2 Water production function for numerical simulations

From the second condition of (3.33), the relationship $p\overline{Q} = pF^W(\overline{G}) = \delta\overline{G}$ holds at a steady state. It means that once the steady-state water price $\overline{p}$ is fixed, the line $Q = (\delta/\overline{p})G$ is fixed. From the second condition of (3.31), three steady-state points $(\overline{G}^i, \overline{Q}^i)$ are obtained by changing the population size N^i for i = 1, 2, 3 along this line, and the water production function $Q = F^W(G)$ is calibrated such that it goes through these steady-state points. The functional forms used are $F^W(G) = a_i lnG - b_i$ ($i = 1,3$) for the outer sections and $F^W(G) = a_2G^{b2} - c_2$ for the middle section, in which a_i, b_i and c_i are production parameters to be calibrated.

The second set of sustainable production functions is designed for comparing the two candidates for the optimal water pricing schedule: the market-clearing and the excess-supply pricing schedules. This set is constructed by scaling up the first set of sustainable production functions such that sustainable water production capacity along the excess-supply pricing schedule exceeds the optimal water demand for a reasonably long period. Scaling up means that if the first set of sustainable production functions is $Q = F^W(G)$, the second set is $Q = \alpha F^W(G)$ in which α is a scaling-up factor. This scaling up is necessary since it is found that the excess-supply pricing schedule results in a water deficit throughout the simulation period with the first set of sustainable production functions when initial capital stock levels are set at the steady-state capital stock levels. By contrast, the second set of sustainable production functions is not suitable for analysing the stability of the optimal steady state because it cannot contain a section where the elasticity of sustainable water production is larger than unity. This is why two sets of sustainable production functions are constructed. The scaling-up factor for the second set is empirically set at five.

Calibration

Most of model parameters are exogenously given but the technological parameter (τ), the steady-state private and public capital stocks ($\bar{k}$ and $\overline{G}^i$) and parameters in the water production functions are calibrated endogenously.

The technological parameter τ is calibrated as $\tau = (\bar{r} + \delta)/(\rho + \delta)$, where $\bar{r}$ is the steady-state value of r_t^*. The steady-state private capital stock and wage rate are calibrated as $\bar{k} = (\beta_Q/\bar{p})^{\beta_Q/\beta_L}\{\tau\beta_K/(\delta + \rho)\}^{(1-\beta_Q)/\beta_L}$ and $\bar{w} = \tau\beta_L\bar{k}^{\beta_K/(1-\beta_Q)}(\beta_Q/\bar{p})^{\beta_Q/(1-\beta_Q)}$. The steady-state public capital stock $\overline{G}^i$ is calibrated as follows. First, the steady-state aggregate water demand is obtained as $\overline{Q}^i = (\bar{q}^H + \bar{q}^M)N^i$, where

$$\bar{q}^H = (1-\varphi)/\bar{p}\left\{1 + \bar{r} - (1+\nu)(1+\bar{r})^{1/\sigma}(1+\rho)^{-1/\sigma}\right\}\{\bar{k} + \bar{w}/(\bar{r} - \nu)\}, \text{ and}$$
$$\bar{q}^M = \tau\bar{k}^{\beta_K/(1-\beta_Q)}(\beta_Q/\bar{p})^{1/(1-\beta_Q)}$$

Then the steady-state public capital stock is calibrated as $\overline{G}^i = \bar{p}\overline{Q}^i/\delta$. The parameters in the water production functions are calibrated such that all the steady-state points $(\overline{G}^i, \overline{Q}^i)$ are achieved and the elasticity of sustainable water production has the desired value at each steady state.

The following exogenous parameter values are chosen:

- Population growth rate: $\nu = 0.02$ (but $\nu = 0$ for the steady-state analysis)
- Elasticity of marginal felicity: $\sigma = 3$
- Weighting accorded to the consumption of the market good in household satisfaction production: $\varphi = 0.98$
- Depreciation rate: $\delta = 0.05$
- Rate of pure time preference: $\rho = 0.075$
- Factor share of private capital in market commodity production: $\beta_K = 0.5$
- Factor share of water in market commodity production: $\beta_Q = 0.2$
- Factor share of labour in market commodity production: $\beta_L = 0.3$

The population sizes are set at $N^1 = 1000$, $N^2 = 2000$ and $N^3 = 3000$. The water price and the real rate of return at the steady state are set at $\overline{p} = 1$ and $\overline{r} = 0.1$ in the calibration process. Calibrated water production parameters are as follows:

$a_1 = 5476.4$ $\quad b_1 = 61\,077.8$
$a_2 = 45\,526.4$ $\quad b_2 = 0.1$ $\quad c_2 = 121\,759.2$
$a_3 = 14\,400.4$ $\quad b_3 = 143\,107.1$

Solution algorithm

The economic situation to be studied is given as a set of (N^i, G_0, k_0) in which initial capital stock levels are specified as a proportion of their steady-state values, for example, $G_0 = 0.8\,\overline{G}^2$, $k_0 = 1.1\overline{k}$, and so on.

For notational convenience we will denote the left-hand sides of the implicit functions in (3.42) and (3.43) as

$$f^{MC}\left(G_t, \hat{k}_t, p_t\right) \equiv F^W(G_t) - N_0(1+\nu)^t\left\{\hat{q}^H\left(\hat{k}_t, p_t\right) + \hat{q}^M\left(\hat{k}_t, p_t\right)\right\}, \text{ and}$$

$$f^{ES}\left(\hat{k}_t, p_t\right) \equiv \hat{c}_t\left(\hat{k}_t, p_t\right)\left\{1 + \nu + p_t^{1-\varphi}/\varphi^{\varphi}(1-\varphi)^{\varphi-1}\right\} - w^*\left(\hat{k}_t, p_t\right)$$
$$- \left\{r^*\left(\hat{k}_t, p_t\right) + \delta\right\}\hat{k}_t - (1+\nu)p_t\left\{\hat{q}^H\left(\hat{k}_t, p_t\right) + \hat{q}^M\left(\hat{k}_t, p_t\right)\right\}$$

Given the initial values of the state variables, the water prices at $t = 0$ along the market-clearing and the excess-supply pricing schedules are obtained by solving the implicit functions $f^{MC}(p_0;\, G_0,\, k_0) = 0$ and $f^{ES}(p_0;\, k_0) = 0$, respectively. The water prices obtained, in turn, determine the capital stock levels in the next period $(G_1, \hat{k}_1)$ via the equations of motion. The water prices at $t = 1$ along the market-clearing and the excess-supply pricing schedules are then obtained by solving $f^{MC}(p_1;\, G_1, \hat{k}_1) = 0$ and $f^{ES}(p_1; \hat{k}_1) = 0$, and the water prices so obtained then determine $(G_2, \hat{k}_2)$, and so on.

This solution algorithm is specified as a mixed complementarity problem in the GAMS modelling software and solved by the MILES solver (see Brooke et al. 1988 for GAMS and Rutherford 1993 for MILES). All simulations are executed for 200 time periods.

3.5.2 Simulation Results

Convergence property of the first-stage solution

First, the first-stage optimisation is simulated for testing the validity of Proposition 3.3 that predicts the global stability of the optimal steady state given a constant water price. For this purpose, water price is fixed at unity. Figure 3.3 demonstrates the validity of Proposition 3.3.

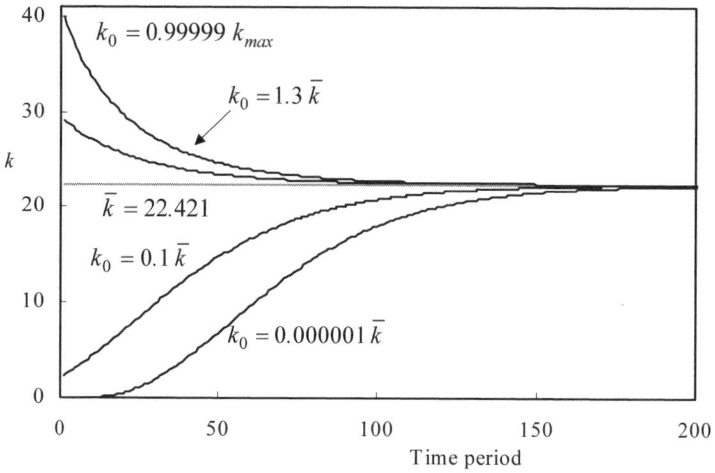

Figure 3.3 Global stability of the optimal steady state without a supply-side constraint

As Proposition 3.3 predicts, Figure 3.3 clearly shows that $\hat{k}$ always converges to its steady-state value $\bar{k} = (\beta_Q/\bar{p})^{\beta_Q/\beta_L}\{\tau\,\beta_K/(\delta+\rho)\}^{(1-\beta_Q)/\beta_L}$ from everywhere within its domain $\hat{k} \in (0, k_{max})$, in which the upper limit of the domain is $k_{max} \equiv (\beta_Q/\bar{p})^{\beta_Q/\beta_L}\{\tau\,\beta_K/(\delta+\nu)\}^{(1-\beta_Q)/\beta_L}$.

Comparison between two candidates for the second-stage solution

Before comparing the two candidate solutions, it is desirable to investigate the compatibility of the excess-supply pricing schedule with the sustainability constraint. The fact that significant scaling-up of the first set of sustainable production functions was necessary to prevent violation of the sustainability constraint along the excess-supply pricing schedule indicates that the proportion of Q_t to G_t is one of major factors which will determine whether the sustainability constraint can hold or not. In addition, it is observed through simulation that the initial stock of private capital also determines whether the sustainability constraint can be satisfied or not, and for how long this condition can hold, given the set of sustainable water production functions. Figure 3.4 illustrates this observation.

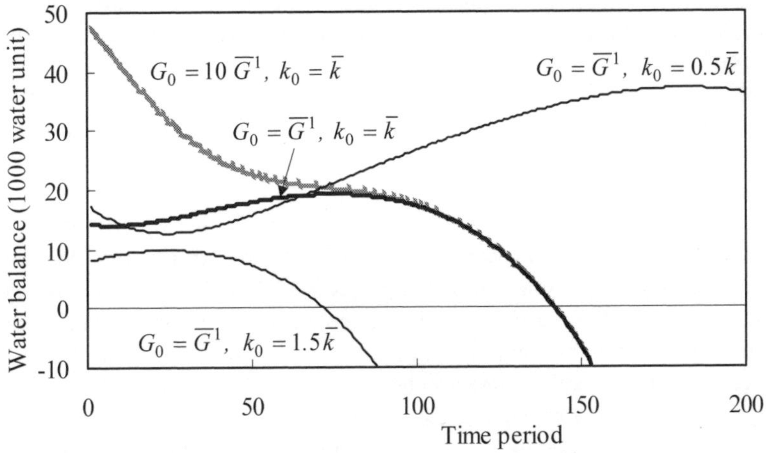

Figure 3.4 Sustainability constraint acting on the excess-supply trajectories

When the initial stock of public capital is set at $G_0 = \overline{G}^1$, a 50 per cent increase in the initial private capital stock (k_0) from $\overline{k}$ to $1.5\overline{k}$ drastically shortens the length of time for which the sustainability constraint can be satisfied from 141 to 71 time periods. A 50 per cent decrease in k_0 to $0.5\overline{k}$ prolongs this duration to considerably more than 200 time periods. In contrast, the initial level of public capital stock hardly affects the duration over which the sustainability constraint can be satisfied, as both $G_0 = \overline{G}^1$ and $G_0 = 10\overline{G}^1$ (accompanied by the same initial private capital stock $k_0 = \overline{k}$) produce a result which satisfies the sustainability constraint for exactly the same duration (141 time periods).

Based on the above observation, the two candidate solutions are compared under two contrasting initial conditions in terms of capital stock levels. The initial condition $(G_0, k_0) = (\overline{G}^1, 0.5\overline{k})$ represents a low development level in terms of capital accumulation but allows the excess-supply pricing schedule to satisfy the sustainability constraint for the entire simulation period, while the other initial condition $(G_0, k_0) = (10\,\overline{G}^1, \bar{k})$ represents a high development level. The results are shown in Figure 3.5 in which the trajectories along the market-clearing pricing schedule are labelled as 'MC' and those along the excess-supply pricing schedule are labelled as 'ES'.

Note that the trajectories are shown only when the sustainability constraint is satisfied. Figure 3.5 clearly demonstrates that the market-clearing pricing schedule always results in both a higher consumption level of satisfaction and higher stock levels of private and public capital than the excess-supply pricing schedule. When the excess-supply trajectories approach to (and appear to surpass) the corresponding market-clearing trajectories, the sustainability constraint is no longer satisfied. This observation leads us to the following corollary.

Corollary 3.1 The market-clearing pricing schedule is *the* second-stage solution which attains the highest level of social welfare without violating the sustainability constraint.

Since the social welfare function is specified for an infinite time horizon, higher satisfaction consumption with higher stock levels of private and public capital for a finite time horizon cannot automatically guarantee higher social welfare. This is why this central result of the analytic model is presented as a corollary, not a proposition. Nevertheless, the possibility of the excess-supply pricing schedule being the optimal second-stage solution is virtually ruled out by the observed tendency for the excess-supply pricing schedule to satisfy the sustainability constraint only when it produces a lower satisfaction consumption level than the market-clearing pricing schedule. In the next chapter, this crucial result greatly facilitates the second-stage optimisation in the applied model.

Convergence property of the second-stage solution

Figure 3.5 also shows that the market-clearing trajectories tend to converge on a unique path regardless of the initial conditions.

This property is investigated further. Figure 3.6 shows the optimal trajectories generated by the highly heterogeneous initial conditions $(G_0, k_0) = (0.1\,\overline{G}^1, 5\,\bar{k})$, $(0.1\,\overline{G}^1, 0.1\,\bar{k})$ and $(100\,\overline{G}^1, 0.1\,\bar{k})$.

Figure 3.6 clearly demonstrates the strong convergence tendency of the optimal trajectories on a unique set of paths that reflect the influence of a positive rate of population growth.

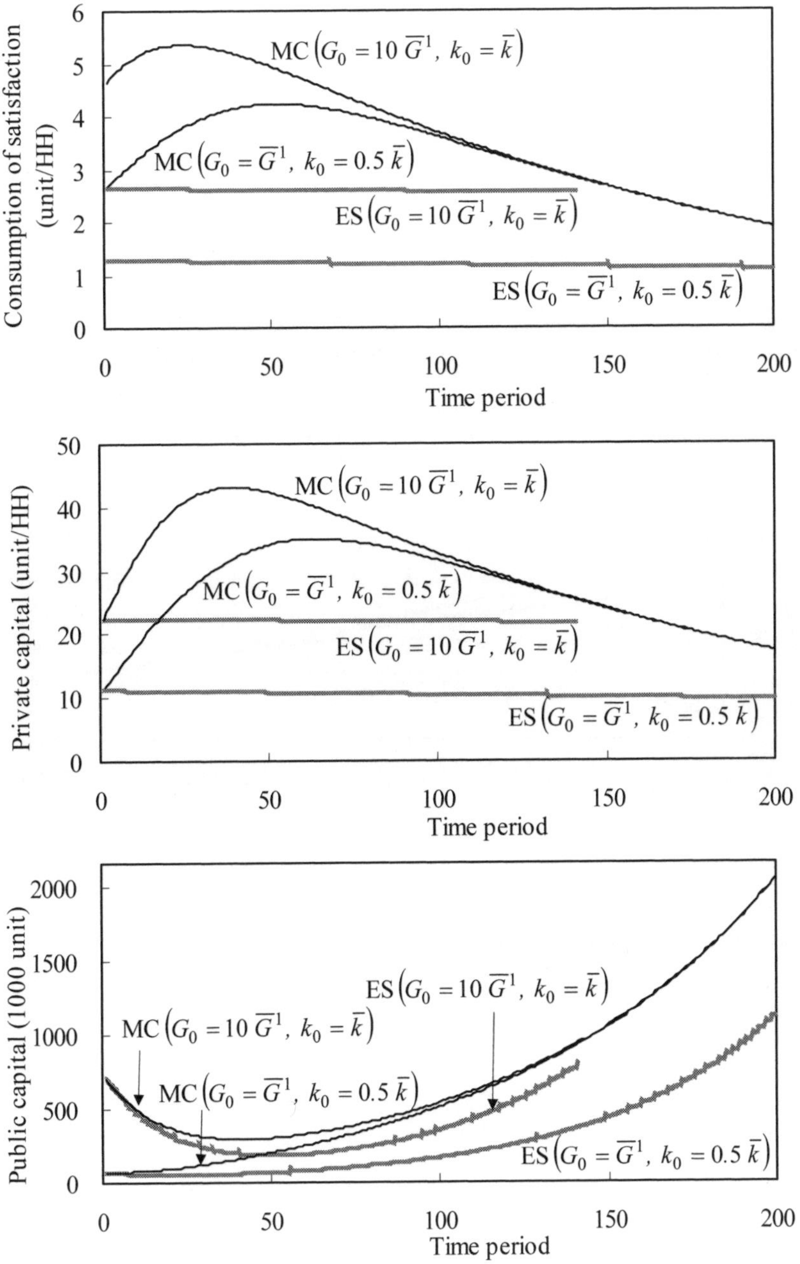

Figure 3.5 Comparison of the two candidates for the optimal trajectories

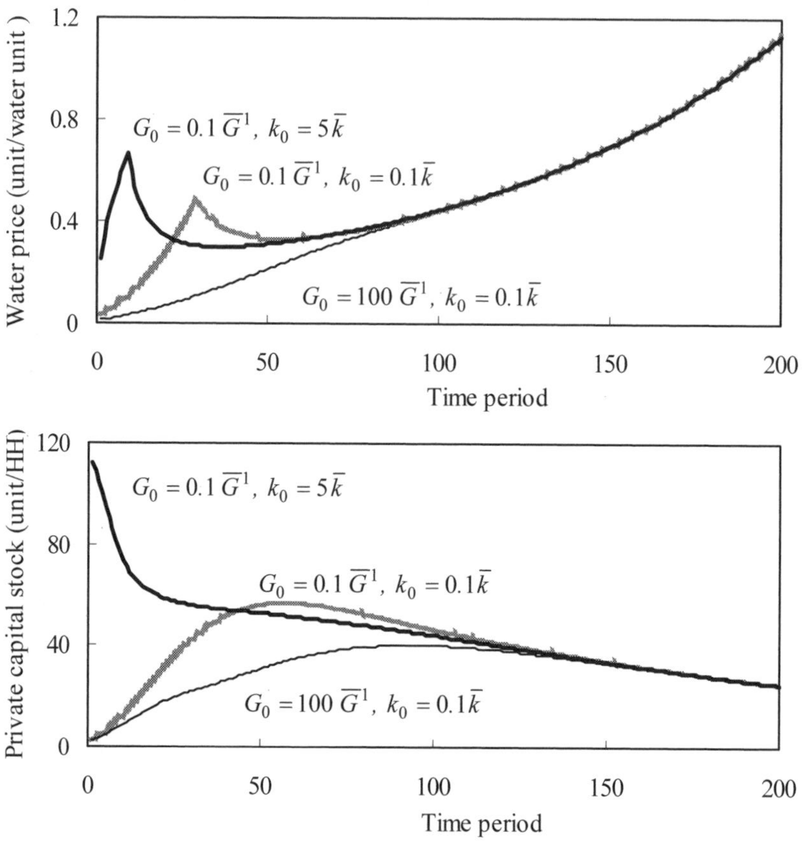

Figure 3.6 Convergence property of the optimal trajectories

Stability of the optimal steady state

Proposition 3.6 suggests that the optimal steady state is characterised by saddle-path local stability. This proposition also tells us that it is necessary to adjust the initial conditions of two state variables, G_0 and k_0, in order to position the economy on the stable manifold when the elasticity of sustainable water production at the steady state, $\varepsilon_G(\overline{G})$, is greater than unity. The steady state associated with N^2, which is designed to have $\varepsilon_G(\overline{G})>1$, is chosen to investigate this proposition, and highly heterogeneous combinations of public and private capital stock levels are set. Note that for the steady-state analysis population growth rate is set at zero. The outcome of this simulation is shown in Figure 3.7.

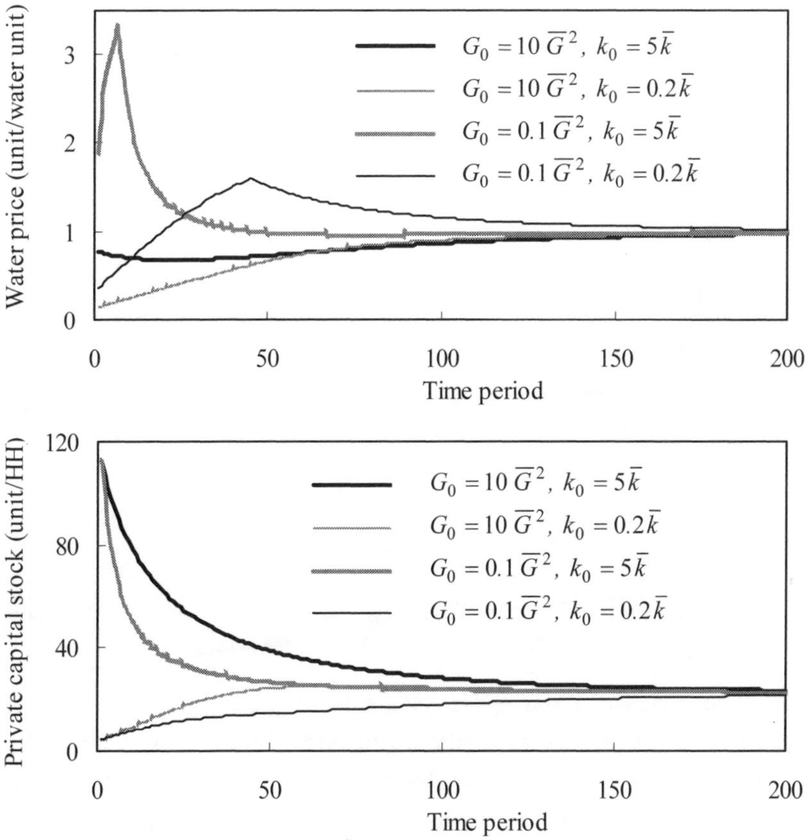

Figure 3.7 Stability of the optimal steady state

These simulation results reveal that the optimal steady state is globally stable, at least in a practical sense. The reservation arises from the fact that convergence to the steady state seems slow compared with the rapid convergence observed in Figure 3.6. Recall that the steady state always has at least one zero real eigenvalue that acts to keep the distance between trajectories and the steady state constant. In this sense the steady state observed here could be asymptotically unstable at the local level, as Proposition 3.6 predicts. Nevertheless, it is clear from Figure 3.7 that the optimal trajectories can be regarded as stable at the global level, and it is at this global level that policy has a role to play in steering the economy towards the optimal path.

Finally, the differences among the three steady states associated with different elasticities of sustainable water production are investigated. Figure

3.8 shows the market-clearing water pricing schedules corresponding to three different optimal steady states.

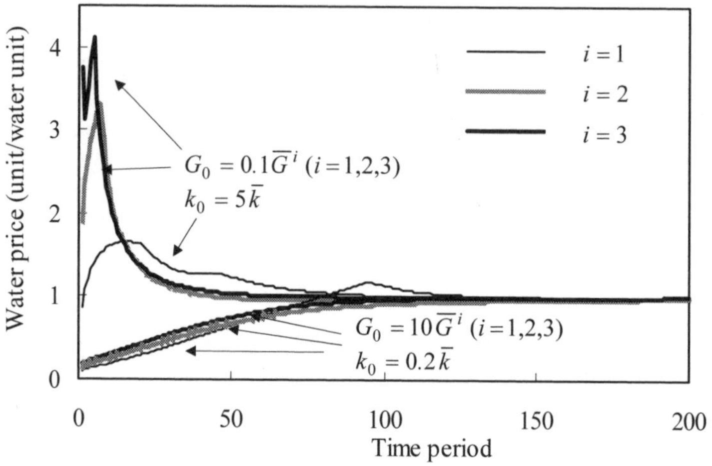

Figure 3.8 Comparison of the different optimal steady states associated with different elasticities of sustainable water production

Contrary to what we may have expected from Proposition 3.6, no structural differences are observed between the pricing schedules associated with $\bar{\varepsilon}_G < 1$ and $\bar{\varepsilon}_G \geq 1$. This observation indicates that local stability analysis is of little relevance where a non-linear system is globally stable in a practical sense but is not asymptotically stable. Here 'globally stable in a practical sense' means that any trajectory converges to the neighbourhood of the steady state but will still remain a certain distance away from a true steady-state solution. This highlights the usefulness and importance of numerical analysis to follow up predictions obtained from theoretical analysis.

3.6 CONCLUSION

In this chapter an analytic model based on the RCK model is developed. It includes two novel specifications for improving the applicability of RCK models for quantitative policy analysis: (1) there is no assumption of perfect foresight assumption in the households' expectation formation; and (2) a two-stage optimisation is undertaken in which the private optimisation and public optimisation processes are separated.

These innovative specifications offer several advantages. The specification of imperfect foresight clarifies the role of expectations in the optimisation process. This is blurred in standard RCK models with a perfect foresight assumption that equates expectations and the optimal solutions. The usefulness of this clarification in model development will be demonstrated further when we introduce various forms of uncertainty in subsequent chapters. The two-stage optimisation setting liberates households from the direct control of the benevolent social planner, which is a synonym for dictatorship in practice. In the two-stage optimisation setting, the first-stage private optimisation is the government's forecast of the responses of households to government policy. This process is free from the normative value judgement of society. In contrast, the second-stage government optimisation is a normative decision-making process in which the objective function must reflect the value judgement of the society. This separation of the social objective function from the private objective function is expected to contribute to sustainable development studies which have often suffered from confusion over value judgement.

With these advantages, this analytic model provides a platform from which an applied model, in the form of a highly aggregated dynamic CGE model, can be constructed. The applied model is explained in the next chapter.

The solution of the first-stage optimisation shows that if there is no supply-side constraint and the water price can be set as the government freely chooses, then the government can induce any level of private capital stock it desires by setting water price (Proposition 3.2), and can thus drive the economy towards the optimal steady state by setting any constant water price (Proposition 3.3).

The solution of the second-stage optimisation (the public optimisation) has several policy implications. The most important result is that there are two candidate optimal water pricing schedules for the optimal solution to the second-stage problem: one is a water pricing schedule determined solely by water market clearance condition, which is termed the 'market-clearing' pricing schedule (Proposition 3.4), and the other corresponds to an interior solution when sustainable water supply capacity exceeds the optimal water demand, which is termed the 'excess-supply' pricing schedule (Proposition 3.5). Derivation of the excess-supply pricing schedule does not require that the sustainability constraint is adhered to, and it is not clear whether this pricing schedule satisfies this constraint or not. On the other hand, it is found that the second-stage optimisation cannot have an interior solution along the market-clearing pricing schedule in practice. Because of these conflicting findings, it is analytically unclear which of two candidate solutions provides the optimal solution to the second-stage problem. It is also found that the excess-supply pricing schedule cannot achieve an optimal steady state, but this fact does not preclude the possibility that this pricing schedule can yield the higher net benefit to society.

Since many theoretical studies of RCK models have derived major conclusions from local stability analysis of the optimal steady state, this study also investigates the local stability of the steady state associated with the market-clearing pricing schedule, mainly for reference purposes. The results show that this steady state exhibits the saddle-path stability which is commonly observed in the RCK model literature. It is found that the stability properties of the market-clearing steady state depend on whether or not the elasticity of sustainable water production with respect to public capital exceeds unity (Proposition 3.6). This result can be explained by the fact that this elasticity captures the impact of water scarcity on the economy.

The most useful insights for policy are provided by numerical simulations. These numerical simulations demonstrate that the market-clearing pricing schedule provides the optimum second-stage solution in practice (Corollary 3.1). This implies that the optimal solution for the problem which will be addressed in the following chapters is likely to be associated with market clearance of publicly supplied goods such as water. This implication introduces a welcome simplification into what would otherwise be the considerably more complicated problem of producing an optimal dynamic solution for a much more complicated applied model. Another interesting result is that the second-stage solution always converges to the neighbourhood of the optimal steady state, although it may remain at a certain small distance from the steady state. This means that the optimal trajectories along the market- clearing pricing schedule are globally stable in a practical sense, a result that is in practice contrary to, but in theory not necessarily inconsistent with, the findings of local stability analysis. These results illustrate the importance of numerical simulations in assessing the practical relevance of policy implications of an analytic model.

NOTES

1. These are the necessary and sufficient conditions since both the objective function and the constraint are concave functions associated with a negative semi-definite Hessian matrix and consequently the Mangasarian Sufficiency Theorem (Mangasarian 1966) holds for this problem.
2. For details of stability analysis methods, see Gandolfo (1997).

APPENDIX 3.1 PROOF OF PROPOSITION 3.1

Recall that the first-order necessary and sufficient conditions for an interior solution are as follows:

$$\frac{\partial H}{\partial c_M}=0 \qquad \Rightarrow \quad \lambda=\varphi\frac{c^{1-\sigma}}{c_M} \tag{A3.1.1}$$

$$\frac{\partial H}{\partial q_H}=0 \qquad \Rightarrow \quad p\lambda=(1-\varphi)\frac{c^{1-\sigma}}{q_H} \tag{A3.1.2}$$

$$\dot{\lambda}-(\rho-v)\lambda=-\frac{\partial H}{\partial m} \quad \Rightarrow \quad \frac{\dot{\lambda}}{\lambda}=-(r-\rho) \tag{A3.1.3}$$

In addition, the transversality condition is $\lim_{s\to\infty}\left[e^{-(\rho-v)(s-t)}\lambda(s)\cdot m(s)\right]=0$.

From the household production function (3.3), (A3.1.1) and (A3.1.2) we derive

$$q_H=\left(\frac{\varphi}{1-\varphi}\right)^{-\varphi}p^{-\varphi}c \tag{A3.1.4}$$

$$c_M=\left(\frac{\varphi}{1-\varphi}\right)^{1-\varphi}p^{1-\varphi}c \tag{A3.1.5}$$

Putting (A3.1.4) into (A3.1.2) we have $\lambda=\varphi^{\varphi}(1-\varphi)^{1-\varphi}p^{-(1-\varphi)}c^{-\sigma}$. Taking time derivatives of both sides with logarithmic transformation, we obtain $\dot{\lambda}/\lambda=-(1-\varphi)\dot{p}/p-\sigma\dot{c}/c$. From this equation and (A3.1.3) we derive the optimal growth rate of consumption as

$$\frac{\dot{c}}{c}=\frac{1}{\sigma}\left\{(r-\rho)-(1-\varphi)\frac{\dot{p}}{p}\right\} \tag{A3.1.6}$$

The following expression for consumption is obtained by solving (A3.1.6) for the period between t and s ($s\geq t$):

$$c(s)=c(t)\left\{\frac{p(t)}{p(s)}\right\}^{\frac{1-\varphi}{\sigma}}exp\left[\frac{1}{\sigma}\int_t^s\{r(\tau)-\rho\}d\tau\right] \tag{A3.1.7}$$

With the optimality conditions (A3.1.4) and (A3.1.5), the equation of motion for the household's assets (3.2) becomes

$$\dot{m} = w + (r - v)m - b_1 p^{1-\varphi} c \tag{A3.1.8}$$

where $b_1 \equiv \varphi^{-\varphi}(1-\varphi)^{-(1-\varphi)} > 0$.

The solution of this differential equation for the period between t and $t+T$ is

$$\begin{aligned} & m(t+T)e^{-\int_t^{t+T}\{r(\tau)-v\}d\tau} \\ & = m(t) + \int_t^{t+T}\left[w(s) - b_1\{p(s)\}^{1-\varphi}c(s)\right]e^{-\int_t^s\{r(\tau)-v\}d\tau}ds \end{aligned} \tag{A3.1.9}$$

When we take the limit as T approaches infinity, the left-hand side becomes zero from the transversality condition as follows.

By solving the differential equation (A3.1.3), we obtain

$$\lambda(t+T) = \lambda(t)e^{-\int_t^{t+T}\{r(\tau)-\rho\}d\tau} \tag{A3.1.10}$$

Putting (A3.1.10) into the transversality condition and replacing s with $t + T$, we have

$$\begin{aligned} & \lim_{t+T\to\infty}\left[e^{-(\rho-v)T}\lambda(t+T)\cdot m(t+T)\right] = \lim_{T\to\infty}\left[e^{-(\rho-v)T}\lambda(t)e^{-\int_t^{t+T}\{r(\tau)-\rho\}d\tau}\cdot m(t+T)\right] \\ & = \lambda(t)\lim_{T\to\infty}\left[e^{-(\rho-v)T}e^{-\int_t^{t+T}r(\tau)d\tau}e^{\rho T}\cdot m(t+T)\right] = \lambda(t)\lim_{T\to\infty}\left[e^{-\int_t^{t+T}r(\tau)d\tau}e^{vT}\cdot m(t+T)\right] \\ & = \lambda(t)\lim_{T\to\infty}\left[m(t+T)e^{-\int_t^{t+T}\{r(\tau)-v\}d\tau}\right] = 0 \end{aligned} \tag{A3.1.11}$$

Since λ(t) represents the shadow price of private capital and takes a positive finite value, (A3.1.11) requires that the term inside the square bracket is zero, which means that the left-hand side of (A3.1.9) becomes zero. Thus, the intertemporal budget constraint becomes

$$\begin{aligned} & b_1\int_t^{\infty}\{p(s)\}^{1-\varphi}c(s)\,e^{-\int_t^s\{r(\tau)-v\}d\tau}ds \\ & = m(t) + \int_t^{\infty}w(s)\,e^{-\int_t^s\{r(\tau)-v\}d\tau}ds \end{aligned} \tag{A3.1.12}$$

Putting (A3.1.7) into (A3.1.12), the consumption function of the 'clairvoyant' household is derived as

$$c(t)=\eta(t)\left[\ m(t)+\int_t^{\infty} w(s)\,e^{-\int_t^s \{r(\tau)-v\}d\tau}ds\right] \tag{A3.1.13}$$

where $\eta(t)\equiv 1\bigg/\left[\ b_1\{p(t)\}^{b_2}\int_t^{\infty}\{p(s)\}^{b_3}e^{\int_t^s \{b_4-b_5 r(\tau)\}d\tau}ds\ \right]$, $b_2\equiv(1-\varphi)/\sigma$, $b_3\equiv(\sigma-1)(1-\varphi)/\sigma$, $b_4\equiv v-\rho/\sigma$ and $b_5\equiv(\sigma-1)/\sigma$.

Here we substitute the true trajectories of exogenous variables w, r and p with households' expectations about them, which we assume constant at the values current in period t. This makes it possible to evaluate time integrals in (A3.1.13) as

$$\begin{aligned}&\int_t^{\infty} w(s)e^{-\int_t^s \{r(s)-v\}d\tau}ds\\&=w(t)\int_t^{\infty} e^{-\{r(t)-v\}(s-t)}ds=w(t)\int_t^{\infty}\frac{d}{ds}\left[\frac{1}{-\{r(t)-v\}}e^{-\{r(t)-v\}(s-t)}\right]ds\\&=-\frac{w(t)}{r(t)-v}\left[e^{-\{r(t)-v\}(s-t)}\right]_t^{\infty}=\frac{w(t)}{r(t)-v}\left[1-\lim_{s\to\infty}e^{-\{r(t)-v\}s}\right]\end{aligned} \tag{A3.1.14}$$

$$\begin{aligned}&b_1\{p(t)\}^{b_2}\int_t^{\infty}\{p(s)\}^{b_3}e^{\int_t^s \{b_4-b_5 r(s)\}d\tau}ds\\&=b_1\{p(t)\}^{b_2+b_3}\int_t^{\infty}e^{\{b_4-b_5 r(t)\}(s-t)}ds=\frac{b_1\{p(t)\}^{1-\varphi}}{b_4-b_5 r(t)}\left[e^{\{b_4-b_5 r(t)\}(s-t)}\right]_t^{\infty}\\&=\frac{b_1\{p(t)\}^{1-\varphi}}{b_5 r(t)-b_4}\left[1-\lim_{s\to\infty}e^{\{b_4-b_5 r(t)\}s}\right]\end{aligned} \tag{A3.1.15}$$

Putting (A3.1.14) and (A3.1.15) into (A3.1.13), the consumption function becomes

$$\begin{aligned}c(t)=&\frac{b_5 r(t)-b_4}{b_1\{p(t)\}^{1-\varphi}\left[1-\lim_{s\to\infty}e^{-\{b_5 r(t)-b_4\}s}\right]}\times\\&\times\left[\ m(t)+w(t)/\{r(t)-v\}\left\{1-\lim_{s\to\infty}e^{-\{r(t)-v\}s}\right\}\right]\end{aligned} \tag{A3.1.16}$$

In order for two limits in (A3.1.16) to converge on zero, the following two conditions are required:

$$r(t)-v>0 \quad\Rightarrow\quad r(t)>v \tag{A3.1.17}$$

$$b_5 r(t)-b_4>0 \quad\Rightarrow\quad r(t)>b_4/b_5=(v\sigma-\rho)/(\sigma-1) \tag{A3.1.18}$$

First we check the relative scale of the two critical values as follows:

$$v - \frac{v\sigma - \rho}{\sigma - 1} = \frac{v(\sigma-1)-(v\sigma-\rho)}{\sigma-1} = \frac{\rho - v}{\sigma - 1} > 0 \qquad \text{(A3.1.19)}$$

Here recall that we previously assumed parameter values such that both the numerator and the denominator of the far right-hand side are positive. When $r > v$, both (A3.1.17) and (A3.1.18) are satisfied. When $b_4/b_5 < r \leq v$ it is obvious that (A3.1.16) cannot take a finite value. If $r = b_4/b_5$ then $c(t)$ becomes positive infinity from (A3.1.16).

For $r < b_4/b_5$ $(< v)$ we need to modify (A3.1.16) into the following form to examine this case:

$$c = \frac{(b_5 r - b_4)m}{b_1 p^{1-\varphi}\left\{1 - \lim_{s\to\infty} e^{-(b_5 r - b_4)s}\right\}} + \frac{w}{b_1 p^{1-\varphi}(r-v)} \lim_{s\to\infty}\left\{\frac{1 - e^{-(r-v)s}}{1 - e^{-(b_5 r - b_4)s}}\right\} \qquad \text{(A3.1.20)}$$

Further, the far right limiting term is modified as

$$\lim_{s\to\infty}\left\{\frac{1 - e^{-(r-v)s}}{1 - e^{-(b_5 r - b_4)s}}\right\} = \lim_{s\to\infty}\left\{\frac{e^{(b_5 r - b_4)s} - e^{(b_5 r - b_4)s-(r-v)s}}{e^{(b_5 r - b_4)s} - 1}\right\}$$

$$= \frac{0 - \lim_{s\to\infty} exp\left\{\frac{1}{\sigma}(\rho - r)s\right\}}{0 - 1} = \lim_{s\to\infty} exp\left\{\frac{1}{\sigma}(\rho - r)s\right\} \qquad \text{(A3.1.21)}$$

Since $r < v$ we have the inequality $\rho - r > \rho - v > 0$. Hence the far right-hand side of (A3.1.21) diverges to positive infinity. Since the first term of (A3.1.16) converges on zero and the second term diverges to positive infinity, $c(t)$ diverges to positive infinity.

To summarise, we require the condition $r > v$ to have a sensible consumption decision. When this condition is satisfied, the optimal consumption level is determined by (3.10).

Q.E.D.

APPENDIX 3.2 PROOF OF PROPOSITION 3.2

By putting (3.18), (3.19) and (3.20) into (3.21), we derive

$$g_k \equiv \frac{\dot{\hat{k}}}{\hat{k}} = \frac{b_6 x^2 - b_7 x + b_8}{\sigma(\beta_K - b_9 x)x}, \quad x \equiv p^{\beta_Q/(1-\beta_Q)} \hat{k}^{\beta_L/(1-\beta_Q)} \tag{A3.2.1}$$

where $b_6 \equiv (\delta + \nu)(\delta + \rho) / \beta_Q{}^{\beta_Q/(1-\beta_Q)} > 0$, $b_7 \equiv (\delta + \nu)\beta_K + (\delta + \rho)(1 - \beta_Q) > 0$, $b_8 \equiv (1 - \beta_Q)\beta_K \beta_Q{}^{\beta_Q/(1-\beta_Q)} > 0$ and $b_9 \equiv (\delta + \nu) / \beta_Q{}^{\beta_Q/(1-\beta_Q)} > 0$.

The condition $r > \nu$ and the equilibrium rate of return to private capital (3.19) determine the domain of x as $0 < x < \beta_K \beta_Q{}^{\frac{\beta_Q}{1-\beta_Q}} / (\delta + \nu) \equiv x_{max}$. For this domain, (A3.2.1) can be expressed as

$$g_k(x) = \frac{\Omega(x)}{\sigma(\beta_K - b_9 x)x} \tag{A3.2.2}$$

where $\Omega(x) \equiv b_6 x^2 - b_7 x + b_8$.

Note that the denominator of the right-hand side of (A3.2.2) is always positive for the given domain. Since the numerator is a quadratic function of x with a positive intercept and the denominator converges on the positive infinitesimal,

$$\lim_{x \to 0+} g_k(x) = \infty \tag{A3.2.3}$$

Now we prove $\lim_{x \to x_{max}-} g_k(x) = -\infty$ as follows. First, rewrite (A3.2.2) as

$$g_k(x) = \frac{(1 - \beta_Q)\beta_K \beta_Q{}^{\beta_Q/(1-\beta_Q)} - \{(\delta + \rho)(1 - \beta_Q) - (\rho - \nu)\beta_K\} x}{\sigma(\beta_K - b_9 x)x} - \frac{\delta + \rho}{\sigma} \tag{A3.2.4}$$

$$\because g_k(x) = \frac{(\delta + \nu)(\delta + \rho)x^2 / \beta_Q{}^{\frac{\beta_Q}{1-\beta_Q}} - \{(\delta + \rho)(1 - \beta_Q) + (\delta + \nu)\beta_K\} x + b_8}{\sigma(\beta_K - b_9 x)x}$$

$$= \frac{(\delta + \rho)(\delta + \nu)x^2 / \beta_Q{}^{\frac{\beta_Q}{1-\beta_Q}} - [(\delta + \rho)(1 - \beta_Q) + \{(\delta + \rho) - (\rho - \nu)\}\beta_K] x + b_8}{\sigma(\beta_K - b_9 x)x}$$

$$= \frac{(\delta+\rho)\left\{(\delta+\nu)x^2 \Big/ \beta_Q^{\frac{\beta_Q}{1-\beta_Q}} - \beta_K x\right\}}{\sigma\left\{\beta_K x - (\delta+\nu)x^2 \Big/ \beta_Q^{\frac{\beta_Q}{1-\beta_Q}}\right\}} + \frac{b_8 - \{(\delta+\rho)(1-\beta_Q)-(\rho-\nu)\beta_K\}x}{\sigma(\beta_K - b_9 x)x}$$

Let $D(x)$ denote the numerator of the left term on the right-hand side of (A3.2.4). The limit of $D(x)$ when x approaches x_{max} from the right side is:

$$\lim_{x \to x_{max}-} D(x) = \beta_K(1-\beta_Q)\beta_Q^{\frac{\beta_Q}{1-\beta_Q}} - \{(\delta+\rho)(1-\beta_Q)-(\rho-\nu)\beta_K\}\frac{\beta_K}{\delta+\nu}\beta_Q^{\frac{\beta_Q}{1-\beta_Q}}$$

$$= \frac{(\delta+\nu)(1-\beta_Q)\beta_K\beta_Q^{\frac{\beta_Q}{1-\beta_Q}} - (\delta+\rho)(1-\beta_Q)\beta_K\beta_Q^{\frac{\beta_Q}{1-\beta_Q}} + (\rho-\nu)\beta_K{}^2\beta_Q^{\frac{\beta_Q}{1-\beta_Q}}}{\delta+\nu}$$

$$= \frac{-(\rho-\nu)(1-\beta_Q)\beta_K\beta_Q^{\frac{\beta_Q}{1-\beta_Q}} + (\rho-\nu)\beta_K{}^2\beta_Q^{\frac{\beta_Q}{1-\beta_Q}}}{\delta+\nu}$$

$$= \frac{-(\rho-\nu)(1-\beta_Q-\beta_K)\beta_K\beta_Q^{\frac{\beta_Q}{1-\beta_Q}}}{\delta+\nu} < 0$$

Since the corresponding denominator is the positive infinitesimal, we have

$$\lim_{x \to x_{max}-} g_k(x) = -\infty \qquad \text{(A3.2.5)}$$

The remaining task is to find x such that $g_k(x) = 0$. Due to the fact that the denominator of (A3.2.2) is positive and the sign of its limit towards its upper bound is negative, it is necessary that $\Omega(x_{max}) < 0$. Since $\Omega(0) = b_8 > 0$, there exists a unique $\bar{x}$ such that $\Omega(\bar{x}) = 0$. Because $\Omega(x)$ is a quadratic function of x with a positive coefficient in the square term, $\bar{x}$ is the smaller root of the equation $\Omega(x) = 0$, that is, $\bar{x} = \left(b_7 - \sqrt{b_7{}^2 - 4b_6 b_8}\right) \Big/ 2b_6 = \beta_K \beta_Q^{\frac{\beta_Q}{1-\beta_Q}} \Big/ (\delta+\rho)$. Since $\rho > \nu$, it is obvious that $\bar{x} < x_{max}$.

$\Omega(x)$ is positive, zero or negative if and only if x is smaller than, equal to or greater than $\bar{x}$, and because the denominator of (A3.2.2) is always positive within the domain, we have proved that

$$g_k(x) \; \begin{matrix} > \\ = \\ < \end{matrix} \; 0 \text{ if and only if } x \; \begin{matrix} < \\ = \\ > \end{matrix} \; \bar{x} \qquad \text{(A3.2.6)}$$

Since $p = x^{(1-\beta_Q)/\beta_Q}\hat{k}^{-\beta_L/\beta_Q}$, $x \begin{smallmatrix} < \\ = \\ > \end{smallmatrix} \bar{x}$ if and only if $p \begin{smallmatrix} < \\ = \\ > \end{smallmatrix} \left(\bar{x}^{1-\beta_Q}\hat{k}^{-\beta_L}\right)^{1/\beta_Q}$.

Moreover, $p = 0$ when $x = 0$, and $p = p_{max} \equiv \left(x_{max}{}^{1-\beta_Q}\hat{k}^{-\beta_L}\right)^{1/\beta_Q}$ when $x = x_{max}$.

From (A3.2.3), (A3.2.5) and (A3.2.6) with the above correspondence between p and x, we have proved that

$$g_k\left(p,\hat{k}\right) \begin{smallmatrix} > \\ = \\ < \end{smallmatrix} 0 \text{ if and only if } p \begin{smallmatrix} < \\ = \\ > \end{smallmatrix} \beta_Q\left(\frac{\beta_K}{\delta+\rho}\right)^{\frac{1-\beta_Q}{\beta_Q}}\left(\frac{1}{\hat{k}}\right)^{\frac{\beta_L}{\beta_Q}}$$

$$\lim_{p\to 0+} g_k\left(p,\hat{k}\right) = \infty \text{ and } \lim_{p\to p_{max}-} g_k\left(p,\hat{k}\right) = -\infty$$

Q.E.D.

APPENDIX 3.3 PROOF OF PROPOSITION 3.3

Assume that the constant water price ($\bar{p}$) corresponds to $x < \bar{x}$. Then (A3.2.6) tells us that $\hat{k}$ grows at a positive rate and consequently that x increases towards $\bar{x}$. On the other hand, if $\bar{p}$ corresponds to $x > \bar{x}$, (A3.2.6) tells us that $\hat{k}$ contracts and consequently x decreases towards $\bar{x}$. Thus the steady state is globally stable within the domain of $g_k(x)$. The steady-state level of private capital stock is obtained from the following relationship:

$$\bar{x} \equiv \beta_K\beta_Q{}^{\beta_Q/(1-\beta_Q)}/(\delta+\rho) = \left(\bar{p}^{\beta_Q}\bar{k}^{\beta_L}\right)^{1/(1-\beta_Q)}$$

Q.E.D.

APPENDIX 3.4 PROOF OF PROPOSITION 3.4

When the market-clearing pricing schedule is determined by the system (3.28), the following rate of growth of water price is obtained by taking the time derivative of the first equation of (3.28) with logarithmic transformation:

$$g_p^{MC} \equiv \dot{p}/p = \frac{\varepsilon_G F^W g_G^{MC} - N_0 e^{\nu t}\left\{\nu(\hat{q}_H + \hat{q}_M) + \hat{k}\left(\partial\hat{q}_H/\partial\hat{k} + \partial\hat{q}_M/\partial\hat{k}\right)\right\}g_k}{N_0 e^{\nu t} p(\partial\hat{q}_H/\partial p + \partial\hat{q}_M/\partial p)} \quad \text{(A3.4.1)}$$

In order to obtain the interior solution along the market-clearing pricing schedule, the Maximum Principle is applied. The current value Lagrangian of the government problem, consisting of the current value Hamiltonian and the sustainability constraint, is:

$$L^G = \left\{\hat{c}\left(\hat{k},p\right)\right\}^{(1-\sigma)}/(1-\sigma) + \mu_G\left[p\left\{\hat{q}_H\left(\hat{k},p\right)+\hat{q}_M\left(\hat{k},p\right)\right\}N_0 e^{\nu t} - \delta G\right]$$
$$+ \mu_k \hat{k} g_k\left(\hat{k},p\right) + \Theta\left[F^W(G) - \left\{\hat{q}_H\left(\hat{k},p\right)+\hat{q}_M\left(\hat{k},p\right)\right\}N_0 e^{\nu t}\right] \quad \text{(A3.4.2)}$$

where μ_G, μ_k and Θ are the Lagrange multipliers associated with G, $\hat{k}$ and the sustainability constraint, respectively.

Assuming an interior solution, the necessary conditions are as follows:

$$\frac{\partial L^G}{\partial p} = 0 \Rightarrow \quad \hat{c}^{-\sigma}\frac{\partial \hat{c}}{\partial p} + \left\{\mu_G\left(\hat{q}_H + \hat{q}_M\right) + \left(p\mu_G - \Theta\right)\left(\frac{\partial \hat{q}_H}{\partial p} + \frac{\partial \hat{q}_M}{\partial p}\right)\right\}N_0 e^{\nu t}$$
$$+ \mu_k \hat{k}\frac{\partial g_k}{\partial p} = 0 \quad \text{(A3.4.3)}$$

$$\dot{\mu}_k - \left(\rho - \nu\right)\mu_k = -\frac{\partial L^G}{\partial \hat{k}} \Rightarrow \quad \dot{\mu}_k = \mu_k\left(\rho - \nu - g_k - \hat{k}\frac{\partial g_k}{\partial \hat{k}}\right) - \hat{c}^{-\sigma}\frac{\partial \hat{c}}{\partial \hat{k}}$$
$$-(p\mu_G - \Theta)\left(\frac{\partial \hat{q}_H}{\partial \hat{k}} + \frac{\partial \hat{q}_M}{\partial \hat{k}}\right)N_0 e^{\nu t} \quad \text{(A3.4.4)}$$

$$\dot{\mu}_G - \left(\rho - \nu\right)\mu_G = -\frac{\partial L^G}{\partial G} \Rightarrow \quad \frac{\dot{\mu}_G}{\mu_G} = \rho + \delta - \nu - \frac{dF^W}{dG}\frac{\Theta}{\mu_G} \quad \text{(A3.4.5)}$$

The Kuhn-Tucker condition for the sustainability constraint is

$$\Theta \geq 0, \; F^W - (\hat{q}_H + \hat{q}_M)N_0 e^{\nu t} \geq 0,$$
$$\Theta\left\{F^W - (\hat{q}_H + \hat{q}_M)N_0 e^{\nu t}\right\} = 0 \quad \text{(A3.4.6)}$$

Θ is zero only if the sustainability constraint is satisfied with strict inequality.

The transversality condition for private capital is automatically satisfied in the first-stage solution, and that for public capital is expressed as

$$\lim_{t\to\infty}\left[e^{-(\rho-\nu)t}\mu_G(t)\cdot G(t)\right] = 0 \quad \text{(A3.4.7)}$$

First, we will investigate the relationship between the Lagrange multipliers. Each Lagrange multiplier represents the shadow price of its corresponding constraint. Since G and $\hat{k}$ are the same good, the ratio of their shadow prices in aggregate terms is unity along the optimal trajectories. Otherwise it would be possible to achieve higher social welfare by allocating more capital investment to the form of capital with the higher shadow price. Hence optimality requires $\mu_G = \mu_k/(N_0 e^{\nu t}) \equiv \mu$.

When the sustainability constraint holds with equality, the relationship $\Theta = p\mu$ holds, since the shadow price of relaxing the sustainability constraint indicates the social benefit of providing additional water in a sustainable manner, and the price of water relative to the capital good is p.

With $\Theta = p\mu$, the above necessary conditions are transformed into

$$\hat{c}^{-\sigma}\frac{\partial \hat{c}}{\partial p} = -\mu\left(F^W + N_0 e^{\nu t}\hat{k}\frac{\partial g_k}{\partial p}\right) \qquad \text{(A3.4.8)}$$

$$\hat{c}^{-\sigma}\frac{\partial \hat{c}}{\partial \hat{k}} = -\mu N_0 e^{\nu t}\left(\delta + \nu - p\frac{dF^W}{dG} + g_k + \hat{k}\frac{\partial g_k}{\partial p}\right) \qquad \text{(A3.4.9)}$$

From these two optimality conditions, we derive the following equation:

$$\frac{\partial \hat{c}/\partial p}{\partial \hat{c}/\partial \hat{k}} - \frac{F^W + N_0 e^{\nu t}\hat{k}\,\partial g_k/\partial p}{N_0 e^{\nu t}\left(\delta + \nu - p\,dF^W/dG + g_k + \hat{k}\,\partial g_k/\partial p\right)} = 0 \qquad \text{(A3.4.10)}$$

Taking time derivative of both sides of (A3.4.10), with logarithmic transformation, gives the following differential equation:

$$\begin{aligned} g_p^{IS} \equiv \frac{\dot{p}}{p} = {} & \frac{(\delta+\rho)\left(F^W + N_0 e^{\nu t}\hat{k}\,\partial g_k/\partial p\right)}{(\hat{c}-\sigma)\varepsilon_p\left(F^W + N_0 e^{\nu t}\hat{k}\,\partial g_k/\partial p\right) - pN_0 e^{\nu t}\hat{k}\left(\partial^2 g_k/\partial p^2\right)} \\ & + \frac{\left(F^W + N_0 e^{\nu t}\hat{k}\frac{\partial g_k}{\partial p}\right)\left(\frac{p\hat{c}}{\hat{k}} - \sigma\right)\varepsilon_k - N_0 e^{\nu t}\hat{k}\left(\frac{\partial g_k}{\partial p} + \hat{k}\frac{\partial^2 g_k}{\partial p^2}\right)g_k}{(\hat{c}-\sigma)\varepsilon_p\left(F^W + N_0 e^{\nu t}\hat{k}\,\partial g_k/\partial p\right) - pN_0 e^{\nu t}\hat{k}\left(\partial^2 g_k/\partial p^2\right)} \\ & + \frac{\left(dF^W/dG\right)\left\{G - p\left(F^W + N_0 e^{\nu t}\hat{k}\,\partial g_k/\partial p\right)\right\}g_G^{MC}}{(\hat{c}-\sigma)\varepsilon_p\left(F^W + N_0 e^{\nu t}\hat{k}\,\partial g_k/\partial p\right) - pN_0 e^{\nu t}\hat{k}\left(\partial^2 g_k/\partial p^2\right)} \end{aligned} \qquad \text{(A3.4.11)}$$

Due to the fact that the interior solution is a special case among market-clearing solutions, the rate of change of the water price must follow the market-clearing pricing schedule. Recall the market-clearing counterpart is (A3.4.1). It is obvious that one of the necessary conditions for $g_p^{IS} = g_p^{MC}$ is that the term $\frac{(\delta+\rho)\left(F^W + N_0 e^{\nu t}\hat{k}\,\partial g_k/\partial p\right)}{(\hat{c}-\sigma)\varepsilon_p\left(F^W + N_0 e^{\nu t}\hat{k}\,\partial g_k/\partial p\right) - pN_0 e^{\nu t}\hat{k}\left(\partial^2 g_k/\partial p^2\right)}$ in (A.3.4.11) must vanish. This requires either $F^W + N_0 e^{\nu t}\hat{k}\,\partial g_k/\partial p = 0$ or $\left|\partial^2 g_k/\partial p^2\right| = \infty$, because it does not make economic sense to associate an infinite value with $\hat{c}$, $\hat{k}$, p or ε_p. If the former is the case then $(\partial\hat{c}/\partial p)/(\partial\hat{c}/\partial\hat{k}) = 0$ is required to satisfy (A3.4.10). This in turn requires that $\partial\hat{c}/\partial p = 0$. If the latter is the case then g_p^{IS} must always be zero and this requires that $g_k = g_G^{MC} = 0$ also because $g_p^{IS} = g_p^{MC}$, which implies a steady state. At the steady state $\partial^2 g_k/\partial p^2\big|_{\bar{k}}$ is evaluated as

$$\frac{\beta_Q(\delta+\rho)\{\rho\beta_K+(\delta+\rho)\beta_L\}}{(1-\beta_Q)\rho\sigma\beta_K p^2}\left[2-\frac{\delta}{\rho}+\frac{2\delta\beta_K}{(1-\beta_Q)\{\rho\beta_K+(\delta+\rho)\beta_L\}}\right]$$

This value cannot be either positive or negative infinite because $p = 0$, which implies infinite water supply capacity, does not make economic sense. As a result, when the sustainability constraint holds with equality, there is no interior solution except for the case $\partial\hat{c}/\partial p = 0$. Although it is possible to have $\partial\hat{c}/\partial p = 0$ through higher water pricing inducing substitution of domestic water consumption with consumption of manufactured goods, this can hold only in the steady state because $\partial\hat{c}/\partial p$ is determined not only by the parameter values but also by the values of the state variables.

Q.E.D.

APPENDIX 3.5 PROOF OF PROPOSITION 3.5

Recall that optimality requires $\mu_G = \mu_k/(N_0 e^{\nu t}) \equiv \mu$. When the sustainability condition holds with strict inequality, $\Theta = 0$ from the Kuhn-Tucker condition (A3.4.6). In this case the optimality condition (A3.4.5) determines the optimal value of μ as $\mu(t) = \mu(0)e^{(\delta-\nu+\rho)t}$. Two optimality conditions (A3.4.3) and (A3.4.4) with $\mu(t) = \mu(0)e^{(\delta-\nu+\rho)t}$ and $\Theta = 0$ become as follows:

$$\hat{c}^{-\sigma}\frac{\partial\hat{c}}{\partial p} = -\mu(0)N_0 e^{(\delta+\rho)t}\left\{(\hat{q}_H+\hat{q}_M)+p\left(\frac{\partial\hat{q}_H}{\partial p}+\frac{\partial\hat{q}_M}{\partial p}\right)+\hat{k}\frac{\partial g_k}{\partial p}\right\} \quad \text{(A3.5.1)}$$

$$\hat{c}^{-\sigma}\frac{\partial\hat{c}}{\partial\hat{k}} = -\mu(0)N_0 e^{(\delta+\rho)t}\left\{p\left(\frac{\partial\hat{q}_H}{\partial\hat{k}}+\frac{\partial\hat{q}_M}{\partial\hat{k}}\right)+g_k+\hat{k}\frac{\partial g_k}{\partial\hat{k}}+\delta+\nu\right\} \quad \text{(A3.5.2)}$$

From these two equations we can derive the following optimality condition,

$$\frac{\partial\hat{c}/\partial p}{\partial\hat{c}/\partial\hat{k}}-\frac{(\hat{q}_H+\hat{q}_M)+p\left(\frac{\partial\hat{q}_H}{\partial p}+\frac{\partial\hat{q}_M}{\partial p}\right)+\hat{k}\frac{\partial g_k}{\partial p}}{p\left(\frac{\partial\hat{q}_H}{\partial\hat{k}}+\frac{\partial\hat{q}_M}{\partial\hat{k}}\right)+g_k+\hat{k}\frac{\partial g_k}{\partial\hat{k}}+\delta+\nu}=0\text{, which is equivalent to}$$

$$\Gamma\left(p,\hat{k}\right)\equiv\frac{\partial\hat{c}/\partial p}{\partial\hat{c}/\partial\hat{k}}-\frac{\partial/\partial p\left\{p(\hat{q}_H+\hat{q}_M)+(g_k+\delta+\nu)\hat{k}\right\}}{\partial/\partial\hat{k}\left\{p(\hat{q}_H+\hat{q}_M)+(g_k+\delta+\nu)\hat{k}\right\}}=0 \qquad \text{(A3.5.3)}$$

This implicit function determines water price $p(t)$, given $\hat{k}(t)$. Once $p(t)$ is determined, the level of $\hat{k}(t)$ at the next moment is determined by the equation of motion, and this then determines the water price at that moment, and so on. At the same time the time path of G is determined by the pricing schedule for water. Hence $\Gamma\left(p,\hat{k}\right)=0$ and the equations of motion for $\hat{k}(t)$ and G collectively determine a unique set of trajectories.

Now let us derive the rate of change of water price along this set of trajectories. By taking time derivatives of equations (A3.5.1) and (A3.5.2), with logarithmic transformation, we produce

$$\frac{\dot{p}}{p}=\frac{\delta+\rho-\left\{p\frac{\partial}{\partial\hat{k}}(\hat{c}-\Lambda)-\sigma\varepsilon_k\right\}g_k}{p\frac{\partial}{\partial p}(\hat{c}-\Lambda)-\sigma\varepsilon_p}\equiv g_p^{ES1}\text{, and} \qquad \text{(A3.5.4)}$$

$$\frac{\dot{p}}{p}=\frac{\delta+\rho-\left\{\hat{k}\frac{\partial}{\partial\hat{k}}(\hat{c}-\Lambda)-\sigma\varepsilon_k\right\}g_k}{\hat{k}\frac{\partial}{\partial p}(\hat{c}-\Lambda)-\sigma\varepsilon_p}\equiv g_p^{ES2} \qquad \text{(A3.5.5)}$$

where $\Lambda\equiv p(\hat{q}_H+\hat{q}_M)+(g_k+\delta+\nu)\hat{k}$.

It is clear that the necessary and sufficient condition for a unique schedule of water pricing is $\hat{c}-\Lambda=0$, and this automatically satisfies $\Gamma\left(p,\hat{k}\right)=0$.

As a result, the following system determines the excess-supply pricing schedule:

$$\begin{cases} \hat{c}(\hat{k},p) - p\left\{\hat{q}_H(\hat{k},p) + \hat{q}_M(\hat{k},p)\right\} - \left\{g_k(\hat{k},p) + \delta + \nu\right\}\hat{k} = 0 \\ \dot{G}/G = (p/G)\left\{\hat{q}_H(\hat{k},p) + \hat{q}_M(\hat{k},p)\right\}N_0 e^{\nu t} - \delta \equiv g_G^{ES}(G,\hat{k},p) \\ \dot{\hat{k}}/\hat{k} = g_k(\hat{k},p) \end{cases} \quad \text{(A3.5.6)}$$

As a consequence, the rate of change of water price can be derived from:

$$\dot{p}/p = -(\delta + \rho + \sigma\varepsilon_k g_k)/\sigma\varepsilon_p \equiv g_p^{ES}(p,\hat{k}) \quad \text{(A3.5.7)}$$

By taking the integral of both sides of the equation of motion for public capital, we obtain

$$G(t) = G_0 e^{-\delta t} + N_0 e^{-\delta t}\int_0^t p(s)\{\hat{q}_H(s) + \hat{q}_M(s)\}e^{(\delta+\nu)s}ds \quad \text{(A3.5.8)}$$

By putting (A3.5.8) and $\mu(t) = \mu(0)e^{(\delta-\nu+\rho)t}$ into the transversality condition, we obtain

$$\lim_{t\to\infty}\left[\mu(0)e^{\delta t}\cdot\left\{G_0 e^{-\delta t} + N_0 e^{-\delta t}\int_0^t p(\hat{q}_H + \hat{q}_M)e^{(\delta+\nu)s}ds\right\}\right]$$

$$= \mu(0)G_0 + \mu(0)N_0\lim_{t\to\infty}\left[\int_0^t p(\hat{q}_H + \hat{q}_M)e^{(\delta+\nu)s}ds\right] = 0 \quad \text{(A3.5.9)}$$

This indicates that the transversality condition cannot be satisfied because the integrand in (A3.5.9) is always non-negative and $\mu(0) = 0$, which means that a zero shadow price of capital at $t = 0$ is economically infeasible in this analysis.

Q.E.D.

APPENDIX 3.6 PROOF OF PROPOSITION 3.6

Let $\bar{p}$, $\bar{k}$ and $\bar{G}$ denote the steady-state values of water price, private capital stock and public capital stock, respectively. As the system (3.34) is autonomous, which means that time does not feature as an explicit argument, the following linearised system near steady state is certainly a uniformly good approximation to the original system around the optimal steady state (Gandolfo 1997):

$$dx/dt = A(x - x^e) \tag{A3.6.1}$$

where $x \equiv \begin{bmatrix} G \\ p \\ \hat{k} \end{bmatrix}$, $x^e \equiv \begin{bmatrix} \overline{G} \\ \overline{p} \\ \overline{k} \end{bmatrix}$ and A is the Jacobian matrix of the original system evaluated at the steady state.

The Jacobian matrix at the steady state is evaluated as follows:

$$A \equiv \begin{bmatrix} \frac{\partial Gg_G^{MC}}{\partial G} & \frac{\partial Gg_G^{MC}}{\partial p} & \frac{\partial Gg_G^{MC}}{\partial \hat{k}} \\ \frac{\partial pg_p^{MC}}{\partial G} & \frac{\partial pg_p^{MC}}{\partial p} & \frac{\partial pg_p^{MC}}{\partial \hat{k}} \\ \frac{\partial \hat{k}g_k}{\partial G} & \frac{\partial \hat{k}g_k}{\partial p} & \frac{\partial \hat{k}g_k}{\partial \hat{k}} \end{bmatrix}_{(x = x^e)} = \begin{bmatrix} A_{11} & A_{12} & 0 \\ A_{21} & A_{22} & A_{23} \\ 0 & A_{32} & A_{33} \end{bmatrix}$$

where $A_{11} \equiv \delta\{\varepsilon_G(\overline{G}) - 1\}$, $A_{12} \equiv \frac{\delta \overline{G}}{\overline{p}}$, $A_{21} \equiv \frac{\delta\{\varepsilon_G(\overline{G}) - 1\}\varepsilon_G(\overline{G})F^W(\overline{G})}{N_0 \overline{G} D_1}$,

$A_{22} \equiv -\frac{\varepsilon_G(\overline{G})\{F^W(\overline{G})\}^2}{N_0 \overline{G} D_1} - \frac{\xi \beta_Q \overline{k} D_2}{(1-\beta_Q)\overline{p} D_1}$, $A_{23} \equiv \frac{-\xi \beta_L D_2}{(1-\beta_Q) D_1}$, $A_{32} \equiv \frac{-\xi \beta_Q \overline{k}}{(1-\beta_Q)\overline{p}}$,

$A_{33} \equiv \frac{-\beta_L b_6}{1-\beta_Q}$, in which $\xi \equiv \frac{(\delta+\rho)\{\rho \beta_K + (\delta+\rho)\beta_L\}}{\rho \sigma \beta_K}$,

$D_1 \equiv -\frac{\partial}{\partial p}(\hat{q}_H + \hat{q}_M)\Big|_{x^e} > 0$ and $D_2 \equiv \frac{\partial}{\partial \hat{k}}(\hat{q}_H + \hat{q}_M)\Big|_{x^e} > 0$.

Let $Z(r)$ denote the characteristic polynomial of A. We have

$$Z(r) \equiv -r^3 + \text{trace}\, A \times r^2 + \Phi(A) \times r + \det A \tag{A3.6.2}$$

where $\text{trace}\, A \equiv A_{11} + A_{22} + A_{33}$, $\Phi(A) \equiv A_{12}A_{21} - A_{11}(A_{22} + A_{33})$ and $\det A \equiv A_{11}(A_{22}A_{33} - A_{23}A_{32}) - A_{12}A_{21}A_{33}$.

The coefficients of $Z(r)$ are evaluated as

$$\text{trace}\, A = \delta\{\varepsilon_G(\overline{G}) - 1\} - \frac{\varepsilon_G(\overline{G})\{F^W(\overline{G})\}^2}{N_0 \overline{G} D_1} - \frac{\xi \beta_Q \overline{k} D_2}{(1-\beta_Q)\overline{p} D_1} - \frac{\xi \beta_L}{1-\beta_Q} \tag{A3.6.3}$$

$$\Phi(A) = \frac{\{\varepsilon_G(\overline{G}) - 1\}}{1-\beta_Q}\left(\frac{\xi \beta_Q \overline{k} D_2}{\overline{p} D_1} + \xi \beta_L\right) \tag{A3.6.4}$$

$$\det A = 0 \tag{A3.6.5}$$

As $\det \boldsymbol{A} = 0$, the characteristic equation $Z(r) = 0$ has one zero real eigenvalue which is unstable. The remaining two eigenvalues are expressed as

$$r = \frac{\text{trace}\,\boldsymbol{A} \pm \sqrt{(\text{trace}\,\boldsymbol{A})^2 + 4\Phi(\boldsymbol{A})}}{2} \tag{A3.6.6}$$

Their signs are determined as follows.

Case 1: $\varepsilon_G(\overline{G}) < 1$

Because both trace $\boldsymbol{A}$ and $\Phi(\boldsymbol{A})$ are strictly negative, the remaining two eigenvalues are either two negative real numbers or two conjugate complex numbers with negative real part. In both cases they are stable eigenvalues.

Case 2: $\varepsilon_G(\overline{G}) > 1$

The sign of $\Phi(\boldsymbol{A})$ is strictly positive and $(\text{trace}\,\boldsymbol{A})^2 + 4\Phi(\boldsymbol{A}) > (\text{trace}\,\boldsymbol{A})^2$ holds regardless of the sign of trace $\boldsymbol{A}$. Thus one of the remaining two eigenvalues is a positive real number and the other is a negative real number, which means that the former is an unstable eigenvalue and the latter is a stable eigenvalue.

Case 3: $\varepsilon_G(\overline{G}) = 1$

Since $\Phi(\boldsymbol{A}) = 0$, the characteristic equation has one zero real eigenvalue and the another eigenvalue for which $r = \text{trace}\,\boldsymbol{A}$ is negative with $\varepsilon_G(\overline{G}) = 1$. Hence this case is associated with one stable and two unstable eigenvalues.

Recall that the linearised system around the steady state is unstable unless the initial values of the same number of state variables as there are unstable eigenvalues can be chosen freely (Gandolfo 1997, Theorem 18.3). Along the market-clearing price schedule, the initial water price is completely determined by the sustainability condition. Therefore, the initial values of the same number of state variables as there are unstable eigenvalues must be chosen freely to achieve the steady state along the market-clearing price schedule.

Q.E.D.

APPENDIX 3.7 PROOF OF PROPOSITION 3.7

The current value Hamiltonian of the household problem in discrete time is

$$H_s = \frac{(c_s)^{1-\sigma}}{1-\sigma} + \frac{1}{1+\rho}\lambda_{s+1}\{w_s + (r-v)m_s - c_s^M - p_s q_s^H\} \qquad \text{(A3.7.1)}$$

The necessary conditions for an interior solution are

$$\frac{\partial H_s}{\partial c_s^M} = 0 \Rightarrow \quad \frac{1}{1+\rho}\lambda_{s+1} = \varphi\frac{(c_s)^{1-\sigma}}{c_s^M} \qquad \text{(A3.7.2)}$$

$$\frac{\partial H_s}{\partial q_s^H} = 0 \Rightarrow \quad \frac{p_s}{1+\rho}\lambda_{s+1} = (1-\varphi)\frac{(c_s)^{1-\sigma}}{q_s^H} \qquad \text{(A3.7.3)}$$

$$\frac{1+v}{1+\rho}\lambda_{s+1} - \lambda_s = -\frac{\partial H_s}{\partial m_s} \Rightarrow \quad \lambda_{s+1} = \frac{1+\rho}{1+r_s}\lambda_s \qquad \text{(A3.7.4)}$$

The transversality condition is

$$\lim_{s\to\infty}\left[\left(\frac{1+v}{1+\rho}\right)^{(s-t)}\lambda_s \cdot m_s\right] = 0 \qquad \text{(A3.7.5)}$$

The following optimal conditions are exactly the same as those in continuous time:

$$c_s^M = \left(\frac{\varphi}{1-\varphi}\right)^{1-\varphi} p_s^{\,1-\varphi} c_s \qquad \text{(A3.7.6)}$$

$$q_s^H = \left(\frac{\varphi}{1-\varphi}\right)^{-\varphi} p_s^{\,-\varphi} c_s \qquad \text{(A3.7.7)}$$

Inserting (A3.7.6) into (A3.7.2) we have $\lambda_{s+1}/(1+\rho) = 1/\left(b_1 p_s^{\,1-\varphi} c_s^{\,\sigma}\right)$ and $\lambda_s/(1+\rho) = 1/\left(b_1 p_{s-1}^{\,1-\varphi} c_{s-1}^{\,\sigma}\right)$ since the same relation must hold in period $s-1$ as well. Inserting these relations into (A3.7.4), we obtain that c_{t+j} = $c_t\left(\frac{p_t}{p_{t+j}}\right)^{\frac{1-\varphi}{\sigma}}\prod_{i=0}^{j-1}\left(\frac{1+r_{t+i}}{1+\rho}\right)^{\frac{1}{\sigma}}$, which becomes the following with the 'imperfect foresight assumption':

$$c_{t+j} = c_t \left(\frac{1+r_t}{1+\rho} \right)^{\frac{j}{\sigma}} \tag{A3.7.8}$$

Recall that the equation of motion of household assets incorporating the relations (A3.7.6) and (A3.7.7) is expressed as

$$m_{s+1} = \frac{1+r_s}{1+\nu} m_s + \frac{1}{1+\nu}\left(w_s - b_1 p_s^{\ 1-\varphi} c_s \right) \tag{A3.7.9}$$

From this with the 'imperfect foresight' assumption, the intertemporal budget constraint from period t to T is derived as follows:

$$m_{t+T}\left(\frac{1+\nu}{1+r_t} \right)^T =$$

$$m_t + \frac{w_t}{1+r_t} \sum_{i=0}^{T-1} \left(\frac{1+\nu}{1+r_t} \right)^i - \frac{b_1 p_t^{\ 1-\varphi} c_t}{1+r_t} \sum_{i=0}^{T-1} \left\{ \left(\frac{1+r_t}{1+\rho} \right)^{1/\sigma} \left(\frac{1+\nu}{1+r_t} \right) \right\}^i \tag{A3.7.10}$$

Recall that the transversality condition with (A3.7.4) becomes

$$\lim_{s\to\infty} \left[\left(\frac{1+\nu}{1+\rho} \right)^{(s-t)} \left(\frac{1+\rho}{1+r_t} \right)^{(s-t)} \lambda_t \cdot m_s \right] = \lambda_t \lim_{s\to\infty} \left[m_s \left(\frac{1+\nu}{1+r_t} \right)^{(s-t)} \right] = 0 \tag{A3.7.11}$$

It means that when T goes to infinity, $m_{t+T}\{(1+\nu)/(1+r_t)\}^T$ becomes zero. Now we can derive the discrete-time optimal consumption function as

$$c_t^* = \eta_t \left\{ m_t + \frac{w_t}{1+r_t} \sum_{i=0}^{\infty} \left(\frac{1+\nu}{1+r_t} \right)^i \right\} \tag{A3.7.12}$$

in which $\eta_t \equiv 1 \Big/ \left[\frac{b_1 p_t^{\ 1-\varphi}}{1+r_t} \sum_{i=0}^{\infty} \left\{ \left(\frac{1+r_t}{1+\rho} \right)^{1/\sigma} \left(\frac{1+\nu}{1+r_t} \right) \right\}^i \right]$.

In order to have sensible optimal consumption, each summation must converge, and this is so when $\left(\frac{1+\nu}{1+r_t} \right) < 1$ and $\left(\frac{1+r_t}{1+\rho} \right)^{1/\sigma} \left(\frac{1+\nu}{1+r_t} \right) < 1$. The necessary and sufficient condition for the former is $r_t > \nu$. The latter, which is equivalent to $r_t > \frac{(1+\nu)^{\sigma/(\sigma-1)}}{(1+\rho)^{1/(\sigma-1)}} - 1$, is automatically satisfied when $r_t > \nu$ due to the fact that $\nu - \left\{ \frac{(1+\nu)^{\sigma/(\sigma-1)}}{(1+\rho)^{1/(\sigma-1)}} - 1 \right\} = (1+\nu)\left\{ 1 - \left(\frac{1+\nu}{1+\rho} \right)^{1/(\sigma-1)} \right\} > 0$.

If $r_t > \nu$, the optimal consumption becomes (3.37). Otherwise, c_t^* cannot be a positive finite value.

Q.E.D.

APPENDIX 3.8 PROOF OF PROPOSITION 3.8

The equation of motion of private capital in discrete time is expressed as $\hat{k}_{s+1} - \hat{k}_s = \{ (r_s^* - \nu)\hat{k}_s + w_s^* - b_1 p_s^{1-\varphi} \hat{c}_s \} / (1+\nu) \equiv \hat{k}_s g_s^k$. Apart from this slight modification, the discrete-time version of the system determining the market-clearing pricing schedule is exactly the same as the continuous-time version.

Now let us consider the excess-supply pricing schedule. The Lagrangian of the government problem in discrete time is

$$L_s^G = \hat{c}_s^{1-\sigma} / (1-\sigma) + \lambda_{s+1}^G \{ p(\hat{q}_s^H + \hat{q}_s^M) N_0 (1+\nu)^s - \delta G_s \} (1+\nu)/(1+\rho) \\ + \lambda_{s+1}^k \hat{k} g_s^k (1+\nu)/(1+\rho) + \Theta_s \{ F^W(G_s) - (\hat{q}_s^H + \hat{q}_s^M) N_0 (1+\nu)^s \} \quad \text{(A3.8.1)}$$

When sustainable water supply capacity exceeds the optimal water demand, $\Theta_s = 0$. In addition, the following relationship among the other two Lagrange multipliers holds:

$$\lambda_{s+1}^G \frac{1+\nu}{1+\rho} = \lambda_s^G = \frac{\lambda_s^k}{N_0 (1+\nu)^s} = \frac{\lambda_{s+1}^k (1+\nu)}{N_0 (1+\rho)(1+\nu)^s} \quad \text{(A3.8.2)}$$

where λ_s^G represents the shadow price of an additional unit of investment in public capital in time s, and λ_s^k represents the shadow price of an additional unit of investment in private capital in time s.

The first equality holds because the shadow price of an additional unit of investment in public capital and the shadow price of allowing an additional unit of public capital in the next time must be the same along the optimal pricing schedule. Note that λ_{s+1}^G represents the value of an additional unit of public capital in $s+1$ from the perspective of time $s+1$. The corresponding value viewed from the perspective of time s is $\lambda_{s+1}^G (1+\nu)/(1+\rho)$. The same logic leads to $\lambda_s^k = \lambda_{s+1}^k (1+\nu)/(1+\rho)$ and the second equality $\lambda_s^G =$

$\lambda_s^k / \{N_0(1+\nu)^s\}$ holds because the same capital good is invested in public capital and private capital and consequently the ratio of their shadow prices along the optimal pricing schedule must be unity, as was explained for the continuous-time case. Define $\lambda_s \equiv \lambda_s^G = \lambda_s^k / \{N_0(1+\nu)^s\}$. The necessary conditions for an interior solution under $\Theta_s = 0$ are

$$\hat{c}_s^{-\sigma} \partial \hat{c}_s / \partial p_s = -N_0(1+\nu)^s \lambda_s \partial / \partial p_s \{\hat{k}_s g_s^k + p_s(\hat{q}_s^H + \hat{q}_s^M)\} \quad \text{(A3.8.3)}$$

$$\hat{c}_s^{-\sigma} \partial \hat{c}_s / \partial \hat{k}_s = -N_0(1+\nu)^s \lambda_s \partial / \partial \hat{k}_s \{\hat{k}_s g_s^k + p_s(\hat{q}_s^H + \hat{q}_s^M)\} - N_0(1+\nu)^s \lambda_s + N_0(1+\nu)^{s-1} \lambda_{s-1}(1+\rho)/(1+\nu) \quad \text{(A3.8.4)}$$

$$\lambda_s - \lambda_{s-1}(1+\rho)/(1+\nu) = \lambda_s \delta \quad \text{(A3.8.5)}$$

The latter two conditions (A3.8.4) and (A3.8.5) are combined into

$$\hat{c}_s^{-\sigma} \frac{\partial \hat{c}_s}{\partial \hat{k}_s} = -N_0(1+\nu)^s \mu_s \left[\frac{\delta+\nu}{1+\nu} + \frac{\partial}{\partial \hat{k}_s}\{\hat{k}_s g_s^k + p_s(\hat{q}_s^H + \hat{q}_s^M)\}\right] \quad \text{(A3.8.6)}$$

From (A3.8.3) and (A3.8.6), the discrete-time version of Γ becomes

$$\Gamma_s \equiv \frac{\partial \hat{c}_s / \partial p_s}{\partial \hat{c}_s / \partial \hat{k}_s} - \frac{\frac{\partial}{\partial p_s}\left\{\hat{k}_s\left(\frac{\delta+\nu}{1+\nu} + g_s^k\right) + p_s(\hat{q}_s^H + \hat{q}_s^M)\right\}}{\frac{\partial}{\partial \hat{k}_s}\left\{\hat{k}_s\left(\frac{\delta+\nu}{1+\nu} + g_s^k\right) + p_s(\hat{q}_s^H + \hat{q}_s^M)\right\}} = 0 \quad \text{(A3.8.7)}$$

By analogy with Appendix 3.5, the discrete-time version of the excess-supply pricing schedule is determined by

$$\hat{c}_s - \left\{\hat{k}_s\left(\frac{\delta+\nu}{1+\nu} + g_s^k\right) + p_s(\hat{q}_s^H + \hat{q}_s^M)\right\} = 0 \quad \text{(A3.8.8)}$$

By substituting $\hat{k}_s g_s^k$ with $\{(r_s^* - \nu)\hat{k}_s + w_s^* - b_1 p_s^{1-\varphi} \hat{c}_s\}/(1+\nu)$, we have

$$\hat{c}_t\left\{1+\nu+\frac{1}{\varphi^\varphi}\left(\frac{p_t}{1-\varphi}\right)^{1-\varphi}\right\} - (1+\nu)p_t(\hat{q}_t^H + \hat{q}_t^M) - (r_t^* + \delta)\hat{k}_t - w_t^* = 0 \quad \text{(A3.8.9)}$$

The remaining equations of motion are self-evident.

Q.E.D.

4. Applied Model of a Water-stressed Developing Economy

4.1 INTRODUCTION

In this chapter an applied model for the policy simulations is constructed by incorporating several key stylised facts of water-stressed developing countries into the analytic model explained in the previous chapter. Furthermore, trade and intermediate goods flows are introduced into the model. The applied model can be regarded as a highly aggregated version of a forward-looking dynamic computable general equilibrium (CGE) model without the assumption of perfect foresight in households' price expectations.

Following this introductory section, Section 4.2 describes the main features of the model and explains how to incorporate the key stylised facts of a water-stressed developing economy. Sections 4.3 and 4.4 explain the first-stage and the second-stage optimisation respectively. In these sections basic model set-up and notation are the same as in the previous chapter. Section 4.5 explains the issues arising from the introduction of trade and taxes. Although the role of trade and taxes in this research is mainly related to calibration and validation of the model, their explicit treatment widens the scope of policy simulations. Section 4.6 summarises the major outcomes and concludes this chapter.

4.2 MODELLING THE KEY STYLISED FACTS

The applied model is based on the analytic model whilst incorporating the following stylised facts commonly observed in water-stressed developing countries:

- Irrigation accounts for the vast majority of total water use, often reaching 80 to 90 per cent (Rosegrant et al. 2002b).
- Production risks in rain-fed agriculture are among the main causes of rural poverty, and consequently of rural–urban migration (Fafchamps et al. 1998).

- Urban unemployment is high with considerable rural–urban migration in spite of priority public investments in the urban modern (or formal) sector (Harris and Todaro 1970; Beladi and Yabuuchi 2001).
- A lack of access to safe water commonly observed in the rural and the urban squatter areas severely undermines social welfare through various pathways: via direct and indirect health risks and higher medical and water expenditure, or via depriving children of educational opportunities (WHO and UNICEF 2000).

The relevance of these stylised facts to the case-study country – Morocco – will be demonstrated in Chapter 5. These key stylised facts are reflected in the applied model as follows.

Firstly, the single private production sector in the analytic model is disaggregated into two rural and one urban production sectors, that is, the rain-fed and the irrigated agricultural sectors and the urban modern sector. The outputs of all production sectors are assumed to be tradeable under the small open economy assumption. On the other hand, labour and capital markets are assumed to be domestic.[1] Rain-fed agriculture is regarded as a household activity that requires only internal resources such as family labour, owned machinery and owned farmland.

Secondly, a multiplicative risk factor with a stochastic distribution is introduced into the rain-fed production function in order to reflect the high production risks of the sector. In fact, the coefficient of variation for annual rainfall variability of rain-fed regions in Morocco is estimated at 0.2, while that for cereal production reaches 0.4 to 0.5 (Karaky and Arndt 2002). Production risks in the irrigated agricultural and the urban modern sectors are assumed to be zero. Although there exists empirical evidence that irrigation does not eliminate agricultural production risk in water-abundant areas (for example, rice production in the Philippines reported by Roumasset 1976), the zero production risk assumption in irrigation helps to highlight the vulnerability of rain-fed agriculture to erratic rainfall patterns in arid and semi-arid regions.

Thirdly, downward rigidity of the urban modern sector wage is assumed, which reflects the minimum wage legislation. The irrigated agricultural sector wage remains flexible. More precisely, it is assumed that the unskilled labour wage in the urban modern sector is fixed at the minimum wage rate despite the presence of surplus labour, whilst flexible wage rates of urban skilled labour and of irrigated agricultural labour clear these two labour markets. This specification generates Harris-Todaro type rural–urban migration in which the wage gap between the rural and the urban sectors induces domestic migration (Todaro 1969; Harris and Todaro 1970).

Fourthly, it is assumed that some fraction of household members who are allocated to rural sectors lack access to safe water and that this fraction is determined by the stock level of public capital in the water supply sector. WHO/UNICEF (2001) estimated access to an improved drinking water source (including 50 per cent of protected spring and well water) at 98 per cent in urban areas and 56 per cent in rural areas of Morocco in 2000. Some other sources estimated that rural access to safe water is much less, due to the use of different definitions of safe water. For instance, WHO/UNICEF (1996) estimated the Moroccan rural access to safe water at 14 per cent. Welfare impacts of a lack of access to safe water are represented by a 'cost' on household members who lack access to safe water. In reality this 'cost' might be direct or indirect health risks, some additional expenditure for bottled water, medical care, the cost of boiling raw water or a reduction in income due to less time allocated to wage labour or to education activities. In the applied model the 'cost' is specified as a reduction in total working time that results in a reduction in wage income.

In order to incorporate the latter two stylised facts into the Ramsey-Cass-Koopmans (RCK) framework, it is assumed that a household's decision is based on household pooled values (pooled income, pooled consumption and so on) in spite of heterogeneity among its members. For example, if one member earns ten units and the other member earns nothing, the household makes decisions as if two members would earn five units each. Though this assumption is a straightforward extension of the conventional view of the household as a single decision-making unit, it appears much stronger in this situation than under an identical individual assumption. Nevertheless, if we were to abandon the assumption that the household is the decision-making unit, we would be forced into an undesirable model specification in which individuals must be indexed based on their migration history and their asset accumulation history.

4.3 FIRST-STAGE OPTIMISATION

4.3.1 Outline

The first-stage optimisation problem consists of the household's utility maximisation problem and the profit maximisation problems of two industrial sectors (the irrigated agricultural sector and the urban modern sector).

Households are not only consuming and saving but are also engaged in rain-fed agricultural activities. Consequently the household's problem is complicated since a household optimises its utility level through: (1) allocating family members to various labour activities; (2) investing into either rain-fed capital or other private capital; and (3) purchasing four types of commodities including water. Furthermore, this applied model allows urban unemployment caused by the urban minimum wage and rural–urban migration.

There are three closed and perfectly competitive markets in the model, that is: (1) for irrigation labour; (2) for urban skilled labour, and (3) for private capital excluding rain-fed capital. The solution of the first-stage optimisation is obtained such that these three markets simultaneously clear.

4.3.2 The Households' Problem

Households' rain-fed agricultural activity problem

It is assumed that the rain-fed agricultural sector is defined as the households' farm activities. There are a fixed number (N) of identical households. The household size (number of members) at $t = 0$ is normalised at unity and grows at a constant rate (ν). In the model 'one person' consists of one labour force age person and his or her dependents, as discussed in Chapter 3. Each household is endowed with the same amount of rain-fed farmland, productivity of which is assumed to be fixed at $\bar{Y}_R$. More precisely, $\bar{Y}_R$ represents the per household maximum productivity of rain-fed farmland with the average rainfall. In the household farm production an important input factor – water – is exogenously and randomly given by rainfall and is represented by a multiplicative risk factor with a stochastic distribution. The rain-fed agricultural production technology is specified as a Leontief function of intermediate goods and aggregate input of labour and capital, and labour–capital aggregate is specified as a Cobb-Douglas function. Hence the per household production function of rain-fed agriculture is

$$Y_t^R = \min\left[\omega_t \bar{Y}_R, \frac{s_t^{RI}}{a^{RI}}, \frac{s_t^{RU}}{a^{RU}}\right], \quad \bar{Y}_R = \tau_R \left(L_t^R\right)^{\beta_{RL}} \left(K_t^R\right)^{\beta_{RK}} \tag{4.1}$$

where Y_t^R: per household yields in year t, ω_t: the production risk factor in year t with expected value $E[\omega_t] = 1$ and variance $Var[\omega_t] = \sigma_\omega^2$, τ_R: technological parameter in rain-fed agriculture, L_t^R: per household family labour input in year t, K_t^R: per household stock of rain-fed capital in year t, s_t^{Rj}: input of intermediate goods produced by the sector j, a_{Rj}: input-output coefficient associated with s_t^{Rj} ($s_t^{Rj} = a_{Rj} Y_t^R$), and β_{RL} and β_{RK}: factor shares of family labour and rain-fed capital with $\beta_{RL} + \beta_{RK} \equiv \beta_R < 1$, which reflects the suppressed fixed factor input – rain-fed farmland.

There is empirical evidence supporting this specification. Rain-fed agricultural production data from Haute Chaouia region in Morocco (de Janvry et al. 1992) reveal no difference between the small and the medium-sized farms' per hectare crop productivity (DH 1453 per ha for the former and DH

1433 per ha for the latter, in which DH stands for dirham) in spite of a threefold difference in per labour productivity (DH 1219 per labour for the former and DH 3572 per labour for the latter), while labour displacement due to mechanisation is ongoing and it causes high rural–urban migration from Haute Chaouia to urban areas such as Casablanca (Zagdouni and Benatya 1990).

When a household optimises profits, the yield is determined by the term $\omega_t \overline{Y}_R$ and the household adjusts the input level of intermediate goods such that equalities between the arguments of the Leontief function hold. Consequently the per household optimal profit from the rain-fed agricultural activity becomes

$$\Pi_t^R = \widehat{p}_t^R \omega_t \overline{Y}_R - p_t^{Uc} I_t^R \quad (\widehat{p}_t^R \equiv p_t^{Rp} - p_t^{Ic} a_{RI} - p_t^{Uc} a_{RU}) \tag{4.2}$$

where $\widehat{p}_t^R$: the net producer price, p_t^{Rp}: the domestic producer price of rain-fed products, p_t^{Uc}: the domestic consumer price of urban products which are used as both consumer goods and production capital, p_t^{Ic}: the domestic consumer price of irrigated agricultural products, and I_t^R: the investment in rain-fed capital.

Note that the numeraire of the applied model is not urban products as in Chapter 3 but local currency. Throughout the remaining chapters of this book p^{ic} denotes a domestic consumer price of good *i*, and p^{ip} denotes a domestic producer price of good *i*. The relationship between producer and consumer prices will be discussed in Section 4.5.

A household allocates a fraction of its members (l_t^i) to labour category *i* where $i = R$: rain-fed agricultural labour, *I*: irrigated agricultural labour, *U*: urban unskilled labour, or *S*: urban skilled labour, and $l_t^R + l_t^I + l_t^U + l_t^S = 1$. Further, the fixed labour allocation to urban skilled labour ($\bar{l}^S$) is assumed. Division of skilled and unskilled labourers is a purely empirical specification without which calibration of the model is made difficult.

To capture the productivity cost of the lack of a water supply, it is assumed that the members without safe water access can supply only $1-\bar{z}$ units of labour services per unit of time instead of one unit with safe water access. The coverage of public water supply, which is determined by the level of public capital stock in terms of water supply facilities, is θ_t in the rural areas and unity in the urban areas. In addition it is assumed that the members without a public water supply collect an amount of water ($\bar{q}_{no}$) without any money transaction.[2] Hence the per capita average water consumption ($\widehat{q}^H$) becomes

$$\widehat{q}_t^H \equiv \left\{l_t^U + \bar{l}^S + \left(1 - l_t^U - \bar{l}^S\right)\theta_t\right\} q_t^H + \left(1 - l_t^U - \bar{l}^S\right)\left(1 - \theta_t\right)\bar{q}_{no} \tag{4.3}$$

where q_t^H is the 'per user' water consumption of publicly supplied water, and the per capita average water expenditure becomes

$$\left\{l_t^U + \bar{l}^S + \left(1 - l_t^U - \bar{l}^S\right)\theta_t\right\} p_t q_t^H \tag{4.4}$$

From these assumptions with (4.1), the labour allocation to the irrigated agriculture is expressed as

$$l_t^I = \left(1 - l_t^U - \bar{l}^S\right) - \frac{1}{\left\{1 - \left(1 - \theta_t\right)\bar{z}\right\}}\left(\frac{1}{1+\nu}\right)^t \left(\bar{Y}_R / \tau_R\right)^{\frac{1}{\beta_{RL}}} \left(1/K_t^R\right)^{\frac{\beta_{RK}}{\beta_{RL}}} \tag{4.5}$$

Modelling rural–urban migration mechanism

The idea that rural–urban migration is determined by the rural–urban expected income differential, rather than the real income differential, was first proposed by Todaro (1969). It was established as one of the most influential rural–urban migration models by Harris and Todaro (1970). The essence of the Harris-Todaro model is endogenous determination of both the urban unemployment rate and the rural wage rate through equilibrating the rural and the urban expected income levels, in the presence of downward rigidity of urban wage rate.

The motivation for migrating would be a higher living standard. The expected wage rate (the real wage rate times the probability of getting a job) is intuitively one of the major determinants of the living standard. If there are other determinants such as access to safe water, it is highly likely that these determinants play a role in the rural–urban migration mechanism. To reflect the influence of the safe water access differential, it is assumed that households optimise their labour allocation between urban unskilled and irrigated agricultural labour, such that allocating a member to either labour category generates the same level of indirect utility derived from the expected wage income. Moreover, the urban unskilled wage rate is assumed to be downwardly rigid at a higher level than the irrigated agriculture wage rate, due to the existence of minimum wage legislation. This model can be regarded as a generalised version of the Harris-Todaro model. In fact, the Harris-Todaro model corresponds to the special case when there is no difference between the rural and the urban areas in terms of public water service. This generalised model has the potential to accommodate any factors differentiating rural–urban living standards.

Let θ_t^E denote the probability for the unskilled member migrating to an urban area of being employed in the urban modern sector. The following proposition gives the equilibrium value of θ_t^E as a result of the household decision.

Proposition 4.1 Assume that θ_t is large enough to satisfy the condition

$$\bar{z}w_t^I(\theta_t)^2 + \left\{(1-\bar{z})w_t^I - p_t\bar{q}_{no}\right\}\theta_t - \overline{w}_t^U(\theta_t)^{1-\varphi_Q} + p_t\bar{q}_{no} \le 0 \qquad (4.6)$$

where w_t^I is the wage rate of the irrigated agricultural labour and $\overline{w}_t^U$ is that of the urban unskilled labour fixed at the legislated minimum rate.

The generalised Harris-Todaro assumption (income-generated indirect utility equalisation assumption) gives the equilibrium value of θ_t^E as

$$\theta_t^{E^*} = (\theta_t)^{\varphi_Q}\left[w_t^I\{1-(1-\theta_t)\bar{z}\} + p_t\bar{q}_{no}(1/\theta_t - 1)\right]\big/\overline{w}_t^U \qquad (4.7)$$

Proof: See Appendix 4.1.

It is easy to check that the Harris-Todaro employment probability, $\theta_t^{E^*} = w_t^I/\overline{w}_t^U$, is obtained by setting $\theta_t = 1$ in (4.7). We expect that the higher θ_t, *ceteris paribus*, the more favourable is the irrigation sector relative to the urban modern sector, which results in the higher $\theta_t^{E^*}$.

The expected sign $\partial\theta_t^{E^*}/\partial\theta_t > 0$ is, however, not automatically established but requires $p_t\bar{q}_{no} < w_t^I\theta_t\left[\varphi_Q + \{\theta_t - (1-\theta_t)\varphi_Q\}\bar{z}\right]\big/\{1-(1-\theta_t)\varphi_Q\}$. This is because the applied model captures the welfare impact of lacking access to safe water as sacrificed labour hours (represented by $\bar{z}$) for fetching subsistence water ($\bar{q}_{no}$) instead of purchasing water at price p_t. Hence the utility generated by saved income by fetching water ($p_t\bar{q}_{no}$) must be smaller than the disutility caused by forgone wage income as well as by limiting water consumption at the subsistence level.

Household budget constraint and utility maximisation problem

Now, the per capita household income incorporating (4.5) is expressed as

$$1/(1+\nu)^t\,\Pi_t^R + r_t p_t^{Uc} m_t + \overline{w}_t^U l_t^{U*}\theta_t^{E*} + w_t^S \bar{l}^S$$
$$+\, w_t^I\left[(1-l_t^{U*}-\bar{l}^S)\{1-(1-\theta_t)\bar{z}\} - \left(\frac{1}{1+\nu}\right)^t\left(\frac{\bar{Y}_R}{\tau_R}\right)^{\frac{1}{\beta_{RL}}}\left(\frac{1}{K_t^R}\right)^{\frac{\beta_{RK}}{\beta_{RL}}}\right] \qquad (4.8)$$

where m_t: household assets (equity shares of private capital), l_t^{U*}: equilibrium labour allocation to the urban unskilled labour, and w_t^S: the wage rate of the urban skilled labour.

Apart from the rain-fed agricultural activity, households purchase and consume market commodities produced by three production sectors as well as publicly supplied water, and invest the rest of their income into equity shares of private capital *m*. The per capita household expenditure, except for the investment in rain-fed capital which is included in the profit function of the rain-fed agriculture, is

$$p_t^{Rc}c_t^R + p_t^{Ic}c_t^I + p_t^{Uc}c_t^U + \left\{\theta_t + \left(l_t^{U*} + \bar{l}^S\right)(1-\theta_t)\right\}p_t q_t^H + p_t^{Uc}I_t \qquad (4.9)$$

where c_t^i: per capita consumption of commodities produced by the sector i (i = R, I, U), and I_t: per capita investment in the equity shares of the private capital.

From the above income and expenditure expressions, the household budget constraint in per capita terms becomes

$$r_t p_t^{Uc}m_t + w_t^I\left(1 - l_t^{U*} - \bar{l}^S\right)\left\{1-\left(1-\theta_t\right)\bar{z}\right\} - \frac{w_t^I}{(1+\nu)^t}\left(\frac{\bar{Y}_R}{\tau_R}\right)^{\frac{1}{\beta_{RL}}}\left(\frac{1}{K_t^R}\right)^{\frac{\beta_{RK}}{\beta_{RL}}}$$
$$+ \bar{w}_t^U l_t^{U*}\theta_t^{E*} + w_t^S\bar{l}^S + \left(\frac{1}{1+\nu}\right)^t\left(\omega_t\hat{p}_t^R\bar{Y}_R - p_t^{Uc}I_t^R\right) = p_t^{Rc}c_t^R + p_t^{Ic}c_t^I + p_t^{Uc}c_t^U$$
$$+\left\{\theta_t + \left(l_t^{U*} + \bar{l}^S\right)(1-\theta_t)\right\}p_t q_t^H + p_t^{Uc}I_t \qquad (4.10)$$

By incorporating this equation into the equation of motion of rain-fed capital $K_{t+1}^R - K_t^R = I_t^R - \delta K_t^R$, in which δ is the depreciation rate, we obtain

$$K_{t+1}^R - K_t^R$$
$$= (1+\nu)^t\left[r_t m_t + \frac{w_t^I}{p_t^{Uc}}\left(1 - l_t^{U*} - \bar{l}^S\right)\left\{1-(1-\theta_t)\bar{z}\right\} + \frac{\bar{w}_t^U}{p_t^{Uc}}\theta_t^{E*}l_t^{U*} + \frac{w_t^S\bar{l}^S}{p_t^{Uc}}\right]$$
$$-\frac{w_t^I}{p_t^{Uc}}\left(\frac{\bar{Y}_R}{\tau_R}\right)^{\frac{1}{\beta_{RL}}}\left(\frac{1}{K_t^R}\right)^{\frac{\beta_{RK}}{\beta_{RL}}} + \frac{\omega_t\hat{p}_t^R\bar{Y}_R}{p_t^{Uc}} - \delta K_t^R - (1+\nu)^t \times$$
$$\times\left[\frac{p_t^{Rc}}{p_t^{Uc}}c_t^R + \frac{p_t^{Ic}}{p_t^{Uc}}c_t^I + c_t^U + \frac{p_t}{p_t^{Uc}}q_t^H\left\{\theta_t + \left(l_t^{U*} + \bar{l}^S\right)(1-\theta_t)\right\} + I_t\right] \qquad (4.11)$$

Another equation of motion is for household assets:

$$m_{t+1} - m_t = \frac{I_t - \nu m_t}{1+\nu} \qquad (4.12)$$

The households' satisfaction production depends on commodity consumption as follows:

$$c_t = \left(c_t^R\right)^{\varphi_R}\left(c_t^I\right)^{\varphi_I}\left(c_t^U\right)^{\varphi_U}\left(\bar{q}_t^H\right)^{\varphi_Q} \tag{4.13}$$

in which $\varphi_i \in (0,1)$ for all i and $\sum_i \varphi_i = 1$.

Assuming a CIES (constant intertemporal elasticity of substitution) function $u(c_t) \equiv (c_t)^{1-\sigma}/(1-\sigma)$ in which σ is the elasticity of marginal felicity with respect to consumption, the representative household's problem at time t is expressed as the following utility maximisation problem, given the household's expectation of exogenous variables:

$$\underset{\{c^I, c^U, q^H, I\}}{Max} \; U_t = \sum_{s=t}^{\infty}\left(\frac{1+\nu}{1+\rho}\right)^s u(c_s) \tag{4.14}$$

subject to two equations of motion (4.11) and (4.12), with the given initial values of K_t^R and m_t. As before, ρ is the rate of pure time preference.

The optimal consumption level

The optimal consumption level is derived with the imperfect foresight assumption in households' expectations. It is assumed that households employ the current value of each exogenous variable in year t as their expectation for its future values for all $s \geq t+1$, for example, $\breve{p}_s = p_t$, $\breve{w}_s^I = w_t^I$, $\breve{r}_s = r_t$ and $\breve{\theta}_s = \theta_t$, except for a random variable ω_t, of which the households' future expectation is some constant $\breve{\omega}$.[3]

The derivation of the optimal consumption is the same as in the case of the analytic model in the previous chapter. The result is summarised in the following proposition.

Proposition 4.2 If $r_t > \nu$ is satisfied, the optimal level of per capita consumption at time t is given as follows:

$$c_t^* = \left(\frac{\varphi_Q}{p_t}\right)^{\varphi_Q} \prod_{i=R,I,U}\left(\frac{\varphi_i}{p_t^{ic}}\right)^{\varphi_i} \times$$

$$\times\left\{1+r_t-(1+\nu)\left(\frac{1+r_t}{1+\rho}\right)^{1/\sigma}\right\}\left[p_t^{Uc} m_t + \frac{1}{r_t-\nu}\left\{\overline{w}_t^U \theta_t^{E*} l_t^{U*}\right.\right.$$

$$+w_t^S\bar{l}^S+w_t^I\left(1-l_t^{U*}-\bar{l}^S\right)(1-(1-\theta_t)\bar{z})+p_t\bar{q}_{no}\left(1-l_t^{U*}-\bar{l}^S\right)(1-\theta_t)\}$$

$$+\left(\frac{1}{1+\nu}\right)^t\frac{\breve{\omega}\hat{p}_t^R\bar{Y}_R}{r_t}-\left(\frac{1}{1+\nu}\right)^t\frac{\beta_R}{r_t(1+r_t)}\left(\frac{\bar{Y}_R}{\tau_R}\right)^{\frac{1}{\beta_R}}\left(\frac{w_t^I}{\beta_{RL}}\right)^{\frac{\beta_{RL}}{\beta_R}}\left\{\frac{p_t^{Uc}(r_t+\delta)}{\beta_{RK}}\right\}^{\frac{\beta_{RK}}{\beta_R}}$$

$$-\left(\frac{1}{1+\nu}\right)^t\frac{1}{1+r_t}\left\{w_t^I\left(\frac{\bar{Y}_R}{\tau_R}\right)^{\frac{1}{\beta_{RL}}}\left(\frac{1}{K_t^R}\right)^{\frac{\beta_{RK}}{\beta_{RL}}}-(1-\delta)p_t^{Uc}K_t^R\right\}\Bigg]\Bigg] \qquad (4.15)$$

Otherwise, c_t^* cannot take positive and finite values.

Proof: See Appendix 4.2.

An important feature of this optimal consumption decision is its independence from the realised production risk factor (ω_t). The optimal consumption decision is deterministic, and the gap between planned and realised income due to the difference between $\breve{\omega}$ and ω_t is assumed to be absorbed by investment (I_t).

To compare Proposition 4.2 with Proposition 3.7, its counterpart in the discrete-time analytic model, the following transformation may be instrumental:

$$c_t^*=\left(\frac{\varphi_Q}{p_t}\right)^{\varphi_Q}\prod_{i=R,I,U}\left(\frac{\varphi_i}{p_t^{ic}}\right)^{\varphi_i}\left\{1+r_t-(1+\nu)\left(\frac{1+r_t}{1+\rho}\right)^{1/\sigma}\right\}\times$$
$$\times\left\{p_t^{Uc}m_t+\frac{1}{r_t-\nu}\widehat{W}_t^{total}-\frac{1}{1+r_t}\left(\frac{1}{1+\nu}\right)^t p_t^{Uc}\hat{I}_t^R\right\} \qquad (4.16)$$

where $\widehat{W}_t^{total}\equiv W_t^{total}-\frac{\nu}{r_t}\left(\frac{1}{1+\nu}\right)^t\breve{\omega}\hat{p}_t^R\bar{Y}_R$, in which

$$W_t^{total}\equiv w_t^I\left[\left(1-l_t^{U*}-\bar{l}^S\right)\{1-(1-\theta_t)\bar{z}\}-\left(\frac{1}{1+\nu}\right)^t\left(\frac{\bar{Y}_R}{\tau_R}\right)^{\frac{1}{\beta_{RL}}}\left(\frac{1}{K_t^R}\right)^{\frac{\beta_{RK}}{\beta_{RL}}}\right]$$

$+\bar{w}_t^U\theta_t^{E*}l_t^{U*}+w_t^S\bar{l}^S+\left(\frac{1}{1+\nu}\right)^t\breve{\omega}\hat{p}_t^R\bar{Y}_R+p_t\bar{q}_{no}\left(1-l_t^{U*}-\bar{l}^S\right)(1-\theta_t)$, and

$$\hat{I}_t^R\equiv I_t^R+\left(\frac{\beta_{RL}r_t+\beta_R\delta}{\beta_{RK}r_t}\right)\left(\frac{\bar{Y}_R}{\tau_R}\right)^{\frac{1}{\beta_R}}\left\{\frac{\beta_{RK}w_t^I}{\beta_{RL}p_t^{Uc}(r_t+\delta)}\right\}^{\frac{\beta_{RL}}{\beta_R}}.$$

In the above expression, $\widehat{W}_t^{total}$ can be interpreted as the present value of expected total per capita labour income (W_t^{total}) which includes rain-fed agricultural profit and income saved by fetching water instead of purchasing publicly supplied water. The former can be regarded as income from rain-fed labour and the latter can be regarded as labour income from fetching water. Similarly, $p_t^{Uc}\widehat{I}_t^R$ can be interpreted as the present value of rain-fed capital investment per household. This transformation makes it clear that the analytic model and the applied model share essentially the same structure.

4.3.3 The Firms' Problem

Irrigated agricultural sector

It is assumed that the production technology of the irrigated agricultural sector may be described by a Leontief function of intermediate goods and a Cobb-Douglas function (with constant returns to scale) of factors of production. Note that a Leontief specification is compatible with the social accounting matrix which will serve as a database of the applied model. A Cobb-Douglas function, which is a CES (constant elasticity of substitution) function with substitution elasticities of unity, is adopted mainly due to its tractability. This specification may overestimate substitutability between water or land and other factors, but the benefit of employing a more elaborate functional specification, a CES function with substitution elasticities of less than unity, does not seem to be enough to compensate for its complexity in this study. The employed production function is

$$Y_t^I = \min\left[F_t^I, \frac{s_t^{IR}}{a_{IR}}, \frac{s_t^{IU}}{a_{IU}}\right], \quad F_t^I = \tau_I \left(A_t^I\right)^{\beta_{IA}} \left(K_t^I\right)^{\beta_{IK}} \left(L_t^I\right)^{\beta_{IL}} \left(Q_t^I\right)^{\beta_{IQ}} \qquad (4.17)$$

where Y_t^I: nationwide aggregate product from this sector in year t, s_t^{Ij}: input of intermediate goods produced by the sector j, a_{Ij}: input-output coefficient associated with s_t^{Ij} ($s_t^{Ij} = a_{Ij}Y_t^I$), τ_I: technological parameter in irrigated agriculture, A_t^I: aggregate irrigated land input in year t, K_t^I: aggregate irrigation capital input in year t, L_t^I: aggregate irrigation labour input in year t, Q_t^I: aggregate irrigation water input in year t, and β_{Ij}: the share of factor input j (j = A, K, L, Q) with $\beta_{Ij} \in (0,1)$ for all j and $\sum_j \beta_{Ij} = 1$.

There is a constraint concerning irrigation land capacity:

$$A_t^I \le \overline{A}_t \equiv \overline{A}\left(G_t^I\right) \qquad (4.18)$$

where $\overline{A}_t$ is the designated land to irrigation in year t determined by the public capital stock in the irrigation sector (G_t^I).

It means that the aggregate irrigation land use cannot exceed the amount of irrigated agricultural land developed by the government. In this study it is assumed that the government sets the irrigated land charge (p_t^A) such that this condition is satisfied.

Aggregate profits in the sector are defined as

$$\Pi_t^I = \widehat{p}_t^I Y_t^I - p_t^A A_t^I - (r_t + \delta) p_t^{Uc} K_t^I - p_t^w Q_t^I - w_t^I L_t^I \qquad (4.19)$$

where $\widehat{p}_t^I \equiv p_t^{Ip} - a_{IR} p_t^{Rc} - a_{IU} p_t^{Uc}$, and p^w is the irrigation water charge.

Aggregate profits are maximised by setting the partial derivatives of Π^I with respect to A^I, K^I, Q^I and L^I at zero, taking all prices as exogenously given, that is, $\widehat{p}_t^I \beta_{IA} Y_t^I = p_t^A A_t^I$, $\widehat{p}_t^I \beta_{IK} Y_t^I = (r_t + \delta) p_t^{Uc} K_t^I$ and so on. From the production function and the optimal conditions, we can rewrite the optimal aggregate profit function as a function of K^I and the exogenous variables:

$$\Pi_t^{I*} = K_t^I \left[\tau_I \widehat{p}_t^I \left(\frac{\beta_{IA}}{p_t^A} \right)^{\beta_{IA}} \left(\frac{\beta_{IQ}}{p_t^w} \right)^{\beta_{IQ}} \left(\frac{\beta_{IL}}{w_t^I} \right)^{\beta_{IL}} \left\{ \frac{\beta_{IK}}{p_t^{Uc}(r_t + \delta)} \right\}^{\beta_{IK}} - 1 \right] \times$$
$$\times\, p_t^{Uc}(r_t + \delta) / \beta_{IK} \qquad (4.20)$$

This expression is a short-run optimal profit function taking the level of capital stock (K^I) and the interest rate (r) as exogenously given. Whether aggregate profits are positive, zero or negative depends on the wage rate of this sector as follows:

$$\Pi_t^{I*} \begin{matrix} > \\ = \\ < \end{matrix} 0 \quad \text{if} \quad w_t^I \begin{matrix} < \\ = \\ > \end{matrix} \beta_{IL} \left[\tau_I \widehat{p}_t^I \left(\frac{\beta_{IA}}{p_t^A} \right)^{\beta_{IA}} \left(\frac{\beta_{IQ}}{p_t^w} \right)^{\beta_{IQ}} \left\{ \frac{\beta_{IK}}{p_t^{Uc}(r_t + \delta)} \right\}^{\beta_{IK}} \right]^{\frac{1}{\beta_{IL}}} \qquad (4.21)$$

Urban modern sector

The production technology of the urban modern sector is assumed to be described by a Leontief function of intermediate goods and a Cobb-Douglas function of factors of production with constant returns to scale.

$$Y_t^U = \min \left[F_t^U, \frac{s_t^{UR}}{a_{UR}}, \frac{s_t^{UI}}{a_{UI}} \right], \quad F_t^U = \tau_U (K_t^U)^{\beta_{UK}} (L_t^U)^{\beta_{UL}} (L_t^S)^{\beta_{US}} \qquad (4.22)$$

where Y^U: nationwide aggregate product from this sector, s_t^{Uj}: input of intermediate goods produced by the sector j, a_{Uj}: input-output coefficient associated with s_t^{Uj} ($s_t^{Uj} = a_{Uj} Y_t^U$), τ_U: technological parameter in urban modern sector, K^U: aggregate urban modern capital, L^U: aggregate unskilled labour input, L^S: aggregate skilled labour input, and β_{Uj}: the share of factor input j ($j = K, L, S$) with $\beta_{Uj} \in (0,1)$ for all j and $\sum_j \beta_{Uj} = 1$.

The sector's aggregate profits are

$$\Pi_t^U = \widehat{p}_t^U Y_t^U - (r_t + \delta) p_t^{Uc} K_t^U - \overline{w}_t^U L_t^U - w_t^S L_t^S \tag{4.23}$$

where $\widehat{p}_t^U \equiv p_t^{Up} - a_{UR} p_t^{Rc} - a_{UI} p_t^{Ic}$.

Aggregate profits are maximised by setting the partial derivatives of Π^U with respect to K^U, L^U and L^S at zero, taking r, $\overline{w}_t^U$ and w^S as exogenously given ($\widehat{p}_t^U \beta_{UK} Y_t^U = (r_t + \delta) p_t^{Uc} K_t^U$, $\widehat{p}_t^U \beta_{UL} Y_t^U = \overline{w}_t^U L_t^U$, $\widehat{p}_t^U \beta_{US} Y_t^U = w_t^S L_t^S$). From the production function and the optimal conditions, we can rewrite the optimal aggregate profit function as a function of L^U and the exogenous variables:

$$\Pi_t^{U*} = \left[\tau_U \widehat{p}_t^U \left\{ \frac{\beta_{UK}}{p_t^{Uc}(r_t + \delta)} \right\}^{\beta_{UK}} \left(\frac{\beta_{UL}}{\overline{w}_t^U} \right)^{\beta_{UL}} \left(\frac{\beta_{US}}{w_t^S} \right)^{\beta_{US}} - 1 \right] \frac{\overline{w}_t^U L_t^U}{\beta_{UL}} \tag{4.24}$$

This expression is a short-run optimal profit function taking the labour input (L^U) and the wage rate of the skilled labour (w^S) as exogenously given. Whether aggregate profits are positive, zero or negative depends on the interest rate (r) as follows:

$$\Pi_t^{U*} \begin{matrix} > \\ = \\ < \end{matrix} 0 \quad \text{if} \quad r_t \begin{matrix} < \\ = \\ > \end{matrix} \frac{\beta_{UK}}{p_t^{Uc}} \left\{ \tau_U \widehat{p}_t^U \left(\frac{\beta_{UL}}{\overline{w}_t^U} \right)^{\beta_{UL}} \left(\frac{\beta_{US}}{w_t^S} \right)^{\beta_{US}} \right\}^{\frac{1}{\beta_{UK}}} - \delta \tag{4.25}$$

4.3.4 Market Equilibrium

In the applied model, the markets for irrigation labour, urban skilled labour and private capital (excluding rain-fed capital) are closed and perfectly competitive. The equilibrium prices in these markets, r^*, w^{I*} and w^{S*}, are determined by three market clearance conditions.

First, competition drives optimal profits of both production sectors towards zero, which results in the following equilibrium price relationships from (4.21) and (4.25):

$$r^*(w_t^S) = \frac{\beta_{UK}}{p_t^{Uc}}\left\{\tau_U \hat{p}_t^U \left(\frac{\beta_{UL}}{\overline{w}_t^U}\right)^{\beta_{UL}}\left(\frac{\beta_{US}}{w_t^S}\right)^{\beta_{US}}\right\}^{\frac{1}{\beta_{UK}}} - \delta \tag{4.26}$$

$$w^{I*}(w_t^S) = \beta_{IL}\left[\tau_I \hat{p}_t^I \left(\frac{\beta_{IA}}{p_t^A}\right)^{\beta_{IA}}\left(\frac{\beta_{IQ}}{p_t^w}\right)^{\beta_{IQ}}\left\{\frac{\beta_{IK}}{p_t^{Uc}(r^*(w_t^S)+\delta)}\right\}^{\beta_{IK}}\right]^{\frac{1}{\beta_{IL}}} \tag{4.27}$$

The remaining equilibrium price (w_t^{S*}) is determined by the following market clearance conditions along with the equilibrium labour allocation to urban unskilled labour (l_t^{U*}).

Capital market clearance

Because of the wage rigidity of urban unskilled labour and the existence of positive urban unemployment, the urban sector has discretion to determine the optimal unskilled labour input (L^{U*}). Given L^{U*}, the optimal urban capital demand is expressed from the optimality condition as follows:

$$K_t^{UD} = \left\{\frac{1}{\tau_U \hat{p}_t^U}\left(\frac{\overline{w}_t^U}{\beta_{UL}}\right)^{1-\beta_{US}}\left(\frac{w_t^S}{\beta_{US}}\right)^{\beta_{US}}\right\}^{\frac{1}{\beta_{UK}}} L_t^{U*} \tag{4.28}$$

Note that the additional superscript '*D*' means the optimal demand and '*S*' means the optimal supply in this subsection.

The supply of private capital is historically given by the household assets held at time *t* (m_t). Hence the capital market clearance requires $K_t^{UD} + K_t^{ID} = N(1+v)^t m_t$, and the equilibrium capital stock in the irrigated agricultural sector is given as

$$K_t^{I*} = N(1+v)^t m_t - \left\{\frac{1}{\tau_U \hat{p}_t^U}\left(\frac{\overline{w}_t^U}{\beta_{UL}}\right)^{1-\beta_{US}}\left(\frac{w_t^S}{\beta_{US}}\right)^{\beta_{US}}\right\}^{\frac{1}{\beta_{UK}}} L_t^{U*} \tag{4.29}$$

Recall the relationship $L_t^U = N(1+v)^t \theta_t^E l_t^U$ and the fact that θ_t^{E*} is a function of w_t^I, the optimal value of which is determined by w_t^S (see equations 4.7 and 4.27). When L^{U*} is given, the labour allocation to urban unskilled labour is equilibrated such that $L_t^{U*} = N(1+v)^t \theta_t^{E*} l_t^{U*}$. With this relationship, the equilibrium level of irrigation capital stock is given as

$$K_t^{I*} = N(1+\nu)^t \left[m_t - \left\{ \frac{1}{\tau_U \hat{p}_t^U} \left(\frac{\overline{w}_t^U}{\beta_{UL}} \right)^{1-\beta_{US}} \left(\frac{w_t^S}{\beta_{US}} \right)^{\beta_{US}} \right\}^{\frac{1}{\beta_{UK}}} \theta^{E*} l_t^{U*} \right] \tag{4.30}$$

Irrigation labour market clearance

From the optimal condition, demand for irrigation labour is given as $L_t^{ID} = K_t^{I*} \beta_{IL} p_t^{Uc} (r_t^* + \delta) / \beta_{IK} w_t^{I*}$, while its supply is

$$L_t^{IS} = N(1+\nu)^t (1 - l_t^{U*} - \bar{l}^S)\{1 - (1-\theta_t)\bar{z}\} - N(\overline{Y}_R / \tau_R)^{\frac{1}{\beta_{RL}}} (1/K_t^R)^{\frac{\beta_{RK}}{\beta_{RL}}} \tag{4.31}$$

The market clearance condition $L_t^{ID} = L_t^{IS}$ requires that the equilibrium labour allocation to urban unskilled labour must satisfy

$$l_t^{U*} = \frac{\{1-(1-\theta_t)\bar{z}\}(1-\bar{l}^S) - \dfrac{\beta_{IL} p_t^{Uc}(r_t^* + \delta)}{\beta_{IK} w_t^{I*}} m_t - \left(\dfrac{1}{1+\nu}\right)^t \left(\dfrac{\overline{Y}_R}{\tau_R}\right)^{\frac{1}{\beta_{RL}}} \left(\dfrac{1}{K_t^R}\right)^{\frac{\beta_{RK}}{\beta_{RL}}}}{\{1-(1-\theta_t)\bar{z}\} - \dfrac{\beta_{IL} p_t^{Uc}(r_t^* + \delta)}{\beta_{IK} w_t^{I*}} \left\{ \dfrac{1}{\tau_U \hat{p}_t^U} \left(\dfrac{\overline{w}_t^U}{\beta_{UL}}\right)^{1-\beta_{US}} \left(\dfrac{w_t^S}{\beta_{US}}\right)^{\beta_{US}} \right\}^{\frac{1}{\beta_{UK}}} \theta_t^{E*}}$$

$$\equiv f_1(w_t^S) \tag{4.32}$$

Urban skilled labour market clearance

The supply of urban skilled labour is given as $L_t^{SS} = N(1+\nu)^t \bar{l}^S$, while the optimal demand is $L_t^{SD} = N(1+\nu)^t \theta_t^{E*} l_t^{U*} \beta_{US} \overline{w}_t^U / \beta_{UL} w_t^S$. The market clearance condition requires

$$l_t^{U*} = \beta_{UL} w_t^S \bar{l}^S / \{ \beta_{US} \overline{w}_t^U \theta^{E*} (w_t^S) \} \equiv f_2(w_t^S) \tag{4.33}$$

Finally, from two expressions of l_t^{U*} (equations 4.32 and 4.33), the equilibrium wage rate of urban skilled labour (w_t^{S*}) is obtained as a solution of an implicit function

$$f_3(w_t^S) = 0 \tag{4.34}$$

where $f_3(w_t^S) \equiv f_1(w_t^S) - f_2(w_t^S) = \dfrac{\Phi_t^1 - \Phi_t^2 (1/w_t^S)^{\frac{\beta_{US}(\beta_{IK}+\beta_{IL})}{\beta_{UK}\beta_{IL}}}}{\Phi_t^3 - \Phi_t^4 (1/w_t^S)^{\frac{\beta_{US}\beta_{IK}}{\beta_{UK}\beta_{IL}}}}$

$- \dfrac{\Phi_t^5 w_t^S}{\Phi_t^6 + \Phi_t^7 (w_t^S)^{\frac{\beta_{US}\beta_{IK}}{\beta_{UK}\beta_{IL}}}}$, in which

$$\Phi_t^1 \equiv \{1-(1-\theta_t)\bar{z}\}(1-\bar{l}^S) - \left(\frac{1}{1+\nu}\right)^t \left(\frac{\bar{Y}_R}{\tau_R}\right)^{\frac{1}{\beta_{RL}}} \left(\frac{1}{K_t^R}\right)^{\frac{\beta_{RK}}{\beta_{RL}}},$$

$$\Phi_t^2 \equiv \left(\frac{1}{1+\nu}\right)^t \frac{\beta_{UK} m_t}{\beta_{IK}} \left\{ \tau_U \hat{p}_t^U \left(\frac{\beta_{UL}}{\overline{w}_t^U}\right)^{\beta_{UL}} \beta_{US}^{\ \beta_{US}} \right\}^{\frac{\beta_{IK}+\beta_{IL}}{\beta_{IL}\beta_{UK}}}$$

$$\times \left\{ \frac{1}{\tau_I \hat{p}_t^I} \left(\frac{p_t^A}{\beta_{IA}}\right)^{\beta_{IA}} \left(\frac{p_t^w}{\beta_{IQ}}\right)^{\beta_{IQ}} \left(\frac{\beta_{UK}}{\beta_{IK}}\right)^{\beta_{IK}} \right\}^{\frac{1}{\beta_{IL}}},$$

$$\Phi_t^3 \equiv \{1-(1-\theta_t)\bar{z}\} \left\{ 1 - \frac{\beta_{UK}\beta_{IL}}{\beta_{UL}\beta_{IK}} (\theta_t)^{\varphi_Q} \right\},$$

$$\Phi_t^4 \equiv \frac{\beta_{UK}}{\beta_{UL}\beta_{IK}} (\theta_t)^{\varphi_Q} p_t \bar{q}_{no} \left(\frac{1}{\theta_t} - 1\right) \left\{ \tau_U \hat{p}_t^U \left(\frac{\beta_{UL}}{\overline{w}_t^U}\right)^{\beta_{UL}} \beta_{US}^{\ \beta_{US}} \right\}^{\frac{\beta_{IK}}{\beta_{IL}\beta_{UK}}}$$

$$\times \left\{ \frac{1}{\tau_I \hat{p}_t^I} \left(\frac{p_t^A}{\beta_{IA}}\right)^{\beta_{IA}} \left(\frac{p_t^w}{\beta_{IQ}}\right)^{\beta_{IQ}} \left(\frac{\beta_{UK}}{\beta_{IK}}\right)^{\beta_{IK}} \right\}^{\frac{1}{\beta_{IL}}}, \quad \Phi_t^5 \equiv \frac{\beta_{UL}\bar{l}^S}{\beta_{US}\overline{w}_t^U},$$

$\Phi_t^6 \equiv (\theta_t)^{\varphi_Q} p_t \bar{q}_{no} (1/\theta_t - 1)/\overline{w}_t^U$ and $\Phi_t^7 \equiv (\theta_t)^{\varphi_Q} \beta_{IL} \{1-(1-\theta_t)\bar{z}\}/\overline{w}_t^U \times$

$$\times \left\{ (\overline{w}_t^U/\beta_{UL})^{\beta_{UL}} (1/\beta_{US})^{\beta_{US}} / (\tau_U \hat{p}_t^U) \right\}^{\frac{\beta_{IK}}{\beta_{IL}\beta_{UK}}} \times$$

$$\times \left\{ \tau_I \hat{p}_t^I (\beta_{IA}/p_t^A)^{\beta_{IA}} (\beta_{IQ}/p_t^w)^{\beta_{IQ}} (\beta_{IK}/\beta_{UK})^{\beta_{IK}} \right\}^{\frac{1}{\beta_{IL}}}.$$

4.3.5 First-Stage Solution

The first-stage solution of the applied model is optimal per capita consumption as a function of the state variables (m and K^R) and the exogenous variables, and the equations of motion for the state variables. It is summarised below.

The optimal expected per capita consumption ($\hat{c}_t$) is obtained by substituting r_t, w_t^I and w_t^S in (4.15) with their equilibrium prices (r_t^*, w_t^{I*} and w_t^{S*}).

Investment is residually determined with absorbing the gap between the planned income and the realised income (note that $\breve{\omega}$ is replaced by ω_t):

$$\hat{I}_t = r_t^* m_t - (\hat{c}_t / p_t^{Uc})(p_t/\varphi_Q)^{\varphi_Q} \prod_{i=R,I,U} (p_t^{ic}/\varphi_i)^{\varphi_i} + (1/p_t^{Uc})[\overline{w}_t^U \theta_t^{E*} l_t^{U*}$$
$$+ w_t^{S*} \bar{l}^S + w_t^I (1 - l_t^{U*} - \bar{l}^S)(1-(1-\theta_t)\bar{z}) + p_t \bar{q}_{no}(1 - l_t^{U*} - \bar{l}^S)(1-\theta_t)]$$
$$+ \left(\frac{1}{1+\nu}\right)^t \frac{\omega_t \,\hat{p}_t^R \overline{Y}_R}{p_t^{Uc}} - \left(\frac{1}{1+\nu}\right)^t \left[\left(\frac{\overline{Y}_R}{\tau_R}\right)^{\frac{1}{\beta_R}} \left\{\frac{\beta_{RK} w_t^{I*}}{\beta_{RL} p_t^{Uc}(r_t^* + \delta)}\right\}^{\frac{\beta_{RL}}{\beta_R}}\right.$$
$$\left. + (w_t^{I*}/p_t^{Uc})(\overline{Y}_R/\tau_R)^{\frac{1}{\beta_{RL}}} (1/K_t^R)^{\frac{\beta_{RK}}{\beta_{RL}}} - (1-\delta)K_t^R \right] \tag{4.35}$$

The equations of motion for m and K^R are

$$\hat{m}_{t+1} = (m_t + \hat{I}_t)/(1+\nu) \tag{4.36}$$

$$\hat{K}_{t+1}^R = \left(\frac{\overline{Y}_R}{\tau_R}\right)^{\frac{1}{\beta_R}} \left\{\frac{\beta_{RK} w_t^{I*}}{\beta_{RL} p_t^{Uc}(r_t^* + \delta)}\right\}^{\frac{\beta_{RL}}{\beta_R}} \tag{4.37}$$

Given the initial values m_0 and K_0^R as well as the exogenous variables, the above system uniquely determines the optimal trajectories of c, m and K^R. The first-stage solutions of the remaining endogenous variables necessary for the second-stage optimisation are as follows:

$$\hat{c}_t^j = (\hat{c}_t \varphi_j / p_t^{jc})(p_t/\varphi_Q)^{\varphi_Q} \prod_{i=R,I,U} (p_t^{ic}/\varphi_i)^{\varphi_i} \quad \text{for } j = R, I, U \tag{4.38}$$

$$\hat{\bar{q}}_t^H = \hat{c}_t (\varphi_Q / p_t)^{1-\varphi_Q} \prod_{i=R,I,U} (p_t^{ic}/\varphi_i)^{\varphi_i} \tag{4.39}$$

$$\hat{q}_t^H = \frac{\hat{\bar{q}}_t^H - \bar{q}_{no}(1 - l_t^{U*} - \bar{l}^S)(1-\theta_t)}{\theta_t + (l_t^{U*} + \bar{l}^S)(1-\theta_t)} \tag{4.40}$$

$$\hat{L}_t^I = N(1+\nu)^t (1 - l_t^{U*} - \bar{l}^S)\{1 - (1-\theta_t)\bar{z}\} - N(\overline{Y}_R/\tau_R)^{\frac{1}{\beta_{RL}}} (1/K_t^R)^{\frac{\beta_{RK}}{\beta_{RL}}} \tag{4.41}$$

$$\hat{Y}_t^I = w_t^{I*} \hat{L}_t^I / (\beta_{IL} \hat{p}_t^I) \tag{4.42}$$

$$\hat{A}_t^I = \beta_{IA} w_t^{I*} \hat{L}_t^I / (\beta_{IL} p_t^A) \tag{4.43}$$

$$\hat{K}_t^I = \beta_{IK} w_t^{I*} \hat{L}_t^I / \{\beta_{IL} p_t^{Uc}(r_t^* + \delta)\} \tag{4.44}$$

$$\hat{Q}_t^I = \beta_{IQ} w_t^{I*} \hat{L}_t^I / (\beta_{IL} p_t^w) \tag{4.45}$$

$$\hat{Y}_t^U = w_t^{S*}\hat{L}_t^S / (\beta_{US}\hat{p}_t^U) \tag{4.46}$$

$$\hat{K}_t^U = \beta_{UK} w_t^{S*}\hat{L}_t^S / \{\beta_{US} p_t^{Uc}(r_t^* + \delta)\} \tag{4.47}$$

$$\hat{L}_t^S = N(1+\nu)^t \bar{l}^S \tag{4.48}$$

Considering the structural similarity between the analytic and the applied models as seen in Proposition 4.2, it is expected that Proposition 3.3, which tells us that the trajectories of the first-stage solution are globally stable under the constant prices of public goods without supply-side constraints, is also valid for the applied model. Properties of the first-stage solution without supply-side constraints are investigated by means of numerical simulations in Chapter 6.

4.4 SECOND-STAGE OPTIMISATION

4.4.1 Outline

In the applied model it is assumed that the budget-neutral government produces two types of water, that is, untreated water (R) which is used as either irrigation water or raw water entering the water treatment facilities, and treated water (Q). Further, the government develops designated irrigation land ($\bar{A}$).

As in the analytic model, each production process is represented by a simple production function. The aggregate untreated water production function is $R_t = F^R(G_t^R)$ where G^R is the stock of public capital for this production. The treated water production function is $Q_t = F_t^D(G_t)$ where G is the stock of public capital associated with water treatment and distribution. The level of this public capital stock (G) determines not only the treated water supply capacity (Q) but also the coverage of public water supply in the rural area (θ). Similarly, the aggregate area of designated land for irrigation is represented by $\bar{A}_t = F^A(G_t^I)$. As in the previous chapter these production functions are constrained by a requirement that production and consumption of goods do not endanger the resilience of ecosystems underpinning life support systems. All production processes involve large-scale facilities and have characteristics of Weitzman's (1970) β sector, as discussed in the previous chapter.

The government collects an irrigation land charge per unit area (p^A) and two types of volumetric water charges; p for domestic water supply and p^W for irrigation water. All the collected charges are invested in either G, G^R or G^I.

4.4.2 The Government Problem

The government revenue from the charges in year t is expressed as

$$M_t^G = p_t \hat{q}_t^H N(1+\nu)^t \{\theta_t + (l_t^{U*} + \bar{l}^S)(1-\theta_t)\} + p_t^w \hat{Q}_t^I + p_t^A \hat{A}_t^I \tag{4.49}$$

The government budget constraint in year t is

$$M_t^G = p_t^{Uc}(I_t^G + I_t^{GR} + I_t^{GI}) \tag{4.50}$$

where I_t^G, I_t^{GR} and I_t^{GI} are public investment in G, G^R and G^I, respectively.

Let θ^G and θ^R denote fractions of the government budget invested in G and G^R, that is, $p_t^{Uc} I_t^G = \theta_t^G M_t^G$ and $p_t^{Uc} I_t^{GR} = \theta_t^R M_t^G$. The public capital accumulation is described by the following three equations of motion:

$$G_{t+1} - G_t = \theta_t^G M_t^G / p_t^{Uc} - \delta G_t \tag{4.51}$$

$$G_{t+1}^R - G_t^R = \theta_t^R M_t^G / p_t^{Uc} - \delta G_t^R \tag{4.52}$$

$$G_{t+1}^I - G_t^I = (1 - \theta_t^G - \theta_t^R) M_t^G / p_t^{Uc} - \delta G_t^I \tag{4.53}$$

The sustainability constraints are

$$\hat{q}_t^H N(1+\nu)^t \{\theta_t + (l_t^{U*} + \bar{l}^S)(1-\theta_t)\} \le Q_t = F^D(G_t) \tag{4.54}$$

$$\hat{q}_t^H N(1+\nu)^t \{\theta_t + (l_t^{U*} + \bar{l}^S)(1-\theta_t)\} + \hat{Q}_t^I \le R_t = F^R(G_t^R) \tag{4.55}$$

$$\hat{A}_t^I \le \bar{A}_t = F^A(G_t^I) \tag{4.56}$$

As in the previous chapter, these are sustainability constraints rather than a mere supply–demand balance. The second sustainability constraint captures a trade-off between the domestic and the irrigation water demands, given raw water production capacity. The objective of the government is to maximise social welfare of the current generation without violating sustainability constraints by choosing the values of policy instruments for the entire planning period. In this chapter the policy instruments are confined to the rates of three public charges and the public investment allocation among G, G^R and G^I. Other candidates such as the urban minimum wage $\overline{w}_t^U$, tariffs or taxes are exogenously fixed. These policy instruments will be discussed in Chapter 6.

Social welfare is defined as the net present value of household utility of the representative household based on the assumption of identical households. Recall the assumption that the household is the decision-making unit despite the heterogeneity among its members, as discussed in Section 4.2.

In this book, the decision-making process of the government is distinguished from that of private agents. The government plans policies for the entire planning period at the planning moment ($t = 0$) based on the expectation of exogenous variables. Households make their consumption plan for the planning moment only and their lack of perfect foresight means that their consumption plan is determined by currently realised information only. This is an important difference. In the government problem, $\hat{c}_t$ for any $t \geq 1$ contains price expectation $\breve{p}_t^{ic}$ and $\breve{p}_t^{ip}$ from the perspective of the planning moment $t = 0$. The employed assumption is that $\breve{p}_t^{ic} = p_0^{ic}$ and $\breve{p}_t^{ip} = p_0^{ip}$, which at face value is exactly the same as the private expectation, but its justification is totally different. For the household problem this 'myopic' expectation is compensated for by the monitoring–feedback decision-making process with which the decision is made based on updated current information. This justification is not valid for the government decision for which a commitment of implementation is required at $t = 0$. Infrastructure development is implemented based on large-scale contracts with private constructors, which require the government's commitment at $t = 0$.

The justification for the government comes from the fact that commodity prices are partially controlled by the government through its foreign exchange policy as well as import taxation. This control is partial because there exist other exogenous external factors affecting these variables. Hence, the government designs policies with the expectation of constant commodity prices since this is one of the government policy targets, but there almost certainly exist gaps between planned and realised commodity prices. This expectation error will differentiate both the planned and the realised revenue and the planned and the actual budget required to implement the investment plan. The policy implementation issues arising from the expectation error will be discussed later in Chapter 6. At this moment we focus on the optimal policy planning.

With the assumption of identical households the government problem can be formally expressed as

$$\underset{\{p, p^w, p^A, \theta^G, \theta^R\}}{Max} \sum_{t=0}^{T} \left(\frac{1+\nu}{1+\rho} \right)^t \frac{\hat{c}_t^{\,1-\sigma}}{1-\sigma} \tag{4.57}$$

subject to equations of motion of two types of private capital stock (4.36) and (4.37), equations of motion of three types of public capital stock (4.51)–(4.53), and three sustainability constraints (4.54)–(4.56), together with the initial and the terminal conditions of each state variable.

Due to the existence of stochastic elements, the solution differs between open-loop optimisation without the feedbacks of the policy outcomes, and closed-loop optimisation adjusted for the realised situation at each time. The commitment to implement the policies at $t = 0$ implies the open-loop solution. A practical implication of this is that the numerical solution is obtained by directly maximising social welfare without stochastic dynamic programming.

4.4.3 Solution of the Second-Stage Optimisation

The government problem formalised in the previous subsection is structurally the same as the one in the analytic model. Its high degree of complexity, however, discourages application of the same technique, the Maximum Principle, to this problem. Furthermore, since the analytic model reveals the non-existence of an interior solution to the government problem, as stated in Proposition 3.8, this may also be expected in the applied model.

The employed solution algorithm to the second-stage optimisation of the applied model heavily relies on the market-clearing pricing schedule as stated in Corollary 3.1. Policy simulations to be explained in Chapter 6 employ the optimisation of public charges along with exogenously given public investment policy, due to difficulty in determining the optimal public charges and the optimal investment allocation simultaneously.

4.5 TRADE AND TAX

4.5.1 General

Until now, issues related to trade and tax have been deliberately avoided. This is because these exogenous variables do not change the model structure or solution. This section incorporates them into the model.

This study employs an assumption of imperfect substitutability between foreign and domestic goods: the so-called Armington assumption (Armington 1969), for both imports and exports. This assumption is very widely employed in applied studies, particularly in the CGE literature.

In addition to import tax and export subsidy, commodity-specific sales tax τ^i ($i = R, I, U$) for producers, and income tax (τ_H) for households, are introduced as they are necessary for model calibration.

To facilitate the following explanation, flows of commodities and money in the economy are schematically illustrated in Figure 4.1. The following notation is common throughout the remaining part of this book:

p^{ip}: Producer price of good i in local currency
p^{ic}: Consumer price of good i in local currency
p^{Di}: Domestic wholesale price of good i in local currency

p^{iW}: World price of good i in international currency
r^e: Real exchange rate, which is defined as a real price of international currency in terms of local currency
E^i: Exports of good i in physical terms
M^i: Imports of good i in physical terms
Y^{Di}: Supply of domestic product i to the domestic wholesale market
D^i: Total demand for import–domestic product composite i
D_j^i: Demand of institution j for composite good i, in which j = H (household), G (government) and S (savings account)
s^{ik}: Intermediate input demand of good k for composite good i
τ^i: Producer tax rate of good i
τ_M^i : Import tax rate of good i
s^i: Export subsidy rate of good i

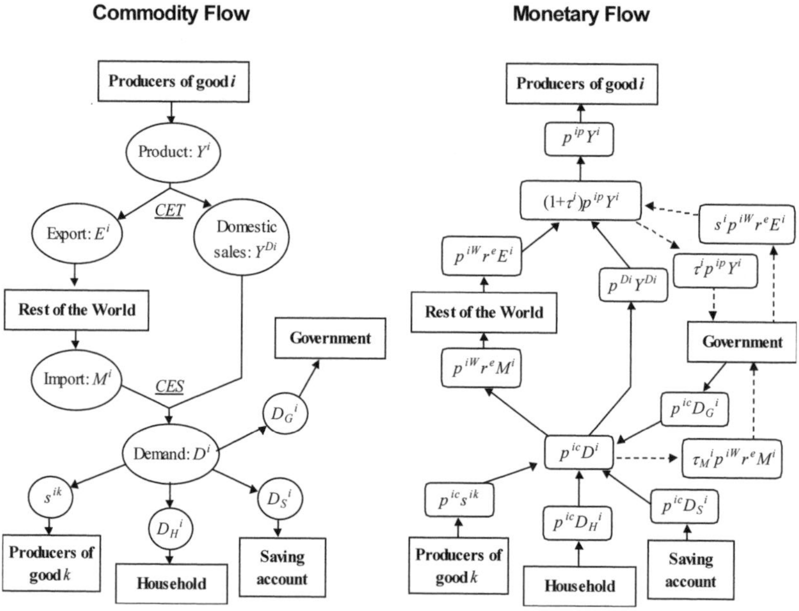

Figure 4.1 Flows of commodities and money with trade and tax

Note that Figure 4.1 does not contain income tax flow from households to the government that has no effect on commodity prices.

4.5.2 Trade Flows and Commodity Prices

Imports

Imperfect substitution between domestically produced and imported goods is specified as the following CES function:

$$D^i = \alpha_M^i \left\{ \delta_M^i \left(M^i\right)^{\frac{\sigma_M^i - 1}{\sigma_M^i}} + \left(1-\delta_M^i\right)\left(Y^{Di}\right)^{\frac{\sigma_M^i - 1}{\sigma_M^i}} \right\}^{\frac{\sigma_M^i}{\sigma_M^i - 1}} \tag{4.58}$$

where α_M^i: scale parameter, δ_M^i: preference parameter of import goods, and σ_M^i: CES elasticity of substitution, with respect to good *i*.

The solution to the consumer's expenditure minimisation problem, given disposable income, results in the optimality condition

$$\frac{M^i}{Y^{Di}} = \left(\frac{\delta_M^i}{1-\delta_M^i}\right)^{\sigma_M^i} \left\{\frac{p^{Di}}{\left(1+\tau_M^i\right)p^{iW} r^e}\right\}^{\sigma_M^i} \tag{4.59}$$

From the commodity and monetary balance conditions, we have

$$D^i = Y^{Di} + M^i \tag{4.60}$$

$$p^{ic} D^i = p^{Di} Y^{Di} + (1+\tau_M^i)\, p^{iW} r^e M^i \tag{4.61}$$

From these four equations (4.58)–(4.61), the following relation among prices is derived:

$$p^{ic} = p^{iW} r^e \left(1+\tau_M^i\right)\eta_M^i \tag{4.62}$$

$$\text{where } \eta_M^i \equiv \frac{\left(\delta_M^i\right)^{\sigma_M^i} + \left(1-\delta_M^i\right)^{\sigma_M^i}\left\{\left(1+\tau_M^i\right)p^{iW} r^e / p^{Di}\right\}^{\sigma_M^i - 1}}{\left(\delta_M^i\right)^{\sigma_M^i} + \left(1-\delta_M^i\right)^{\sigma_M^i}\left\{\left(1+\tau_M^i\right)p^{iW} r^e / p^{Di}\right\}^{\sigma_M^i}}.$$

Exports

Similar to the import case, imperfect substitution between export supply and domestic market supply is specified as the following CET (Constant Elasticity of Transformation) function:

$$Y^i = \alpha_E^i \left\{ \delta_E^i \left(E^i\right)^{\left(\sigma_E^i - 1\right)/\sigma_E^i} + \left(1-\delta_E^i\right)\left(Y^{Di}\right)^{\left(\sigma_E^i - 1\right)/\sigma_E^i} \right\}^{\sigma_E^i/\left(\sigma_E^i - 1\right)} \tag{4.63}$$

where α_E^i: scale parameter, δ_E^i: preference parameter of export goods, and σ_E^i: CET elasticity of substitution, with respect to good *i*.

The solution to the producers' profit maximisation problem, given the quantity of total product, results in the optimality condition

$$\frac{E^i}{Y^{Di}} = \left(\frac{\delta_E^i}{1-\delta_E^i}\right)^{\sigma_E^i} \left\{\frac{p^{Di}}{(1+s^i)p^{iW}r^e}\right\}^{\sigma_E^i} \tag{4.64}$$

From these commodity and monetary balance conditions, we have

$$Y^i = Y^{Di} + E^i \tag{4.65}$$
$$(1+\tau^i)\, p^{ip} Y^i = p^{Di}\, Y^{Di} + (1+s^i)\, p^{iW} r^e E^i \tag{4.66}$$

From these four equations (4.63)–(4.66), the following price relationship is derived:

$$p^{ip} = p^{iW} r^e \left(\frac{1+s^i}{1+\tau^i}\right) \eta_E^i \tag{4.67}$$

where $\eta_E^i \equiv \dfrac{(\delta_E^i)^{\sigma_E^i} + (1-\delta_E^i)^{\sigma_E^i}\{(1+s^i)\, p^{iW} r^e / p^{Di}\}^{\sigma_E^i - 1}}{(\delta_E^i)^{\sigma_E^i} + (1-\delta_E^i)^{\sigma_E^i}\{(1+s^i)\, p^{iW} r^e / p^{Di}\}^{\sigma_E^i}}$.

Determination of domestic wholesale price

The last element to have operational significance for policy simulation is the relationship between the domestic wholesale price and the world price. The employed assumption is that the government subsidises export goods, such that the producers are indifferent as to whether to export their products or to supply them to the domestic wholesale market, while the products can be sold in the rest of the world at the world price. This is because the applied model cannot accommodate multiple products of one industry.[4] This assumption establishes the relationship $p^{Di} = (1+s^i)\, p^{iW} r^e$.

With this relationship, consumer and producer prices are determined as

$$p^{ic} = p^{iW} r^e (1+\tau_M^i)\, \eta_M^i \tag{4.68}$$

where $\eta_M^i \equiv \dfrac{(1+s^i)\left\{(\delta_M^i)^{\sigma_M^i}(1+s^i)^{\sigma_M^i - 1} + (1-\delta_M^i)^{\sigma_M^i}(1+\tau_M^i)^{\sigma_M^i - 1}\right\}}{(\delta_M^i)^{\sigma_M^i}(1+s^i)^{\sigma_M^i} + (1-\delta_M^i)^{\sigma_M^i}(1+\tau_M^i)^{\sigma_M^i}}$, and

$$p^{ip} = p^{iW} r^e \left(1+s^i\right)/\left(1+\tau^i\right) \tag{4.69}$$

as $\eta_E^i = 1$.

Optimal imports and exports can then be derived from the optimality conditions and commodity balance conditions as

$$\hat{E}^i = \Omega_E^i \hat{Y}^i \tag{4.70}$$

where $\Omega_E^i \equiv \left(\delta_E^i\right)^{\sigma_E^i} / \left\{\left(\delta_E^i\right)^{\sigma_E^i} + \left(1-\delta_E^i\right)^{\sigma_E^i}\right\}$, and

$$\hat{M}^i = \left(\frac{1+s^i}{1+\tau_M^i}\right)^{\sigma_M^i} \left(\frac{\delta_M^i}{1-\delta_M^i}\right)^{\sigma_M^i} \left(1-\Omega_E^i\right)\hat{Y}^i \tag{4.71}$$

The former equation indicates that the proportion of exports to total production is constant at Ω_E^i, regardless of tax or subsidy policy. This is an outcome of the assumption that $p^{Di} = (1 + s^i)\, p^{iW} r^e$, which implies that the subsidy rate is automatically determined by the world and the domestic market. The role of the government in this case is purely passive as it merely follows the market signal. The reading of (4.71) must be, therefore, that the government can control the ratio of imports to total production by setting a rate of import tax, but cannot control it through subsidies.

Exports and imports can be simulated based on these equations, once the CES and CET parameters are given.

4.5.3 Income Tax

It is assumed that the government levies a uniform rate tax τ_H on household income. This tax can be incorporated into the household problem by applying the multiplication factor $(1 - \tau_H)$ to all wage rates, the real rate of return (r_t) and the net producer price of rain-fed product ($\widehat{p}_t^R$). As a result, the optimal consumption is modified as follows:.

$$\hat{c}_t = \left(\frac{\varphi_Q}{p_t}\right)^{\varphi_Q} \prod_{i=R,I,U} \left(\frac{\varphi_i}{p_t^{ic}}\right)^{\varphi_i} \left\{1+(1-\tau_H)r_t^* - (1+\nu)\left\{\frac{1+(1-\tau_H)r_t^*}{1+\rho}\right\}^{1/\sigma}\right\} \times$$

$$[p_t^{Uc} m_t + \frac{p_t \bar{q}_{no}\left(1-l_t^{U*}-\bar{l}^S\right)(1-\theta_t)}{(1-\tau_H)r_t^* - \nu} + \left(\frac{1}{1+\nu}\right)^t \frac{\breve{\omega}\,\widehat{p}_t^R \overline{Y}_R}{r_t^*} - \left(\frac{1}{1+\nu}\right)^t \times$$

$$
\times \frac{\beta_R}{(1-\tau_H)r_t^*\{1+(1-\tau_H)r_t^*\}}\left(\frac{\overline{Y}_R}{\tau_R}\right)^{\frac{1}{\beta_R}}\left\{\frac{(1-\tau_H)w_t^{I*}}{\beta_{RL}}\right\}^{\frac{\beta_{RL}}{\beta_R}}\times
$$

$$
\times\left\{\frac{p_t^{Uc}((1-\tau_H)r_t^*+\delta)}{\beta_{RK}}\right\}^{\frac{\beta_{RK}}{\beta_R}}+\frac{1-\tau_H}{(1-\tau_H)r_t^*-\nu}\times
$$

$$
\times\{\overline{w}_t^U\theta_t^{E*}l_t^{U*}+w_t^{S*}\overline{l}^S+w_t^{I*}(1-l_t^{U*}-\overline{l}^S)(1-(1-\theta_t)\overline{z})\}-\left(\frac{1}{1+\nu}\right)^t\times
$$

$$
\times\frac{1}{1+(1-\tau_H)r_t^*}\left\{(1-\tau_H)w_t^{I*}\left(\frac{\overline{Y}_R}{\tau_R}\right)^{\frac{1}{\beta_{RL}}}\left(\frac{1}{K_t^R}\right)^{\frac{\beta_{RK}}{\beta_{RL}}}-(1-\delta)p_t^{Uc}K_t^R\right\}\Bigg]\Bigg] \quad (4.72)
$$

The equation of motion of private assets is also modified as

$$
m_{t+1}=\frac{1+(1-\tau_H)r_t^*}{1+\nu}m_t-\frac{1}{(1+\nu)p_t^{Uc}}\left(\frac{p_t}{\varphi_Q}\right)^{\varphi_Q}\prod_{i=R,I,U}\left(\frac{p_t^{ic}}{\varphi_i}\right)^{\varphi_i}\hat{c}_t
$$

$$
+\frac{1-\tau_H}{(1+\nu)p_t^{Uc}}\left[w_t^{I*}(1-l_t^{U*}-\overline{l}^S)\{1-(1-\theta_t)\overline{z}\}+\overline{w}_t^U\theta_t^{E*}l_t^{U*}+w_t^{S*}\overline{l}^S\right]
$$

$$
+\frac{p_t\overline{q}_{no}(1-l_t^{U*}-\overline{l}^S)(1-\theta_t)}{(1+\nu)p_t^{Uc}}+\left(\frac{1}{1+\nu}\right)^t\frac{\omega_t(1-\tau_H)\hat{p}_t^R\overline{Y}_R}{(1+\nu)p_t^{Uc}}
$$

$$
-\left(\frac{1}{1+\nu}\right)^{t+1}\frac{(1-\tau_H)w_t^{I*}}{p_t^{Uc}}\left(\frac{\overline{Y}_R}{\tau_R}\right)^{\frac{1}{\beta_{RL}}}\left(\frac{1}{K_t^R}\right)^{\frac{\beta_{RK}}{\beta_{RL}}}-\left(\frac{1}{1+\nu}\right)^{t+1}\times
$$

$$
\times\left[\left(\frac{\overline{Y}_R}{\tau_R}\right)^{\frac{1}{\beta_R}}\left\{\frac{\beta_{RK}(1-\tau_H)w_t^{I*}}{\beta_{RL}p_t^{Uc}((1-\tau_H)r_t^*+\delta)}\right\}^{\frac{\beta_{RL}}{\beta_R}}-(1-\delta)K_t^R\right] \quad (4.73)
$$

It should be noted that household decisions are summarised in these two equations. The effects of income tax are, thus, fully covered by the above modification.

4.6 CONCLUSION

This chapter has addressed a way to incorporate the stylised facts of water-stressed developing countries into the analytic model developed in the previous chapter. Four key stylised facts are taken into account: (1) dominant share of water use by irrigated agriculture; (2) vulnerability of rain-fed agriculture; (3) a high urban unemployment rate; and (4) poor access to safe water in the rural areas. For this purpose the analytic model is modified in the following way.

Firstly, the production sector is disaggregated into three sectors: rain-fed agricultural, irrigated agricultural and urban modern sectors. This specification allows the model not only to address irrigation–rain-fed issues but also to pave a way to modelling the rural–urban migration mechanism. Production risk is introduced in the rain-fed agriculture sector only in order to reflect its inherent environmental vulnerability. Note that the household problem is specified as a utility maximisation, given household expectations of specific variables, instead of expected utility maximisation. This is because it is difficult to regard household expectations about prices and public policy variables as stochastic. The expected utility model is not suitable to deal with this case.

Secondly, a labour market equilibrium for unskilled labourers is introduced. It is assumed that a household allocates its unskilled members to either irrigated agricultural or urban modern sectors, such that indirect utility derived from the expected wage income is indifferent in either case. The obtained equilibrium can be regarded as a generalised version of the Harris-Todaro model. Indeed, when the public water supply coverage is 100 per cent in a rural area, this model is reduced to the Harris-Todaro model.

Thirdly, poor access to safe water in the rural area is modelled through a 'cost', which generates disutility for household members who lack access to safe water. This cost is represented as a reduction of labour supply which can be interpreted as a reduction of net wage income. This reflects the opportunity cost of forgone wage income from fetching water and additional expenditure, for example, on medical care caused by water-borne diseases. An idea to capture this cost by a higher price of water, such as the price of bottled water, is abandoned because it requires introducing an additional production sector, the private water sector, into this general equilibrium framework.

These modifications are implemented without losing tractability. It should be noted that this is underpinned by a crucial assumption that the representative household is a single decision-making unit in spite of the heterogeneity of household members in terms of occupation and safe water access. This assumption is at odds with distributional issues, which are among the key aspects of sustainable development, but without this assumption we were forced to index all individuals based on their migration and asset accumulation history in the applied model.

It has been confirmed that the applied model maintains essentially the same structure as the analytic model despite its drastically increased complexity. However, an introduction of stochastic elements makes necessary a much more careful treatment of the government problem. In this chapter an explicit treatment of government expectations, which must be distinguished from households' expectations, is introduced. Issues of policy implementation under uncertainty are discussed in Chapter 6.

Insights provided by the analytic model are used to establish a solution algorithm. The employed solution algorithm optimises public charges, but does not optimise public investment. Instead, several patterns of public investment policy are exogenously set as policy scenarios, which is discussed in Chapter 6.

Issues arising from incorporating trade flows and taxes into the model have also been discussed. Obtained results are highly important to calibrating and validating the model. Moreover, an explicit treatment of trade flows and taxes enables the model to consider more policy scenarios.

NOTES

1. The share of foreign direct investment in gross fixed capital formation was around 3 per cent between 1960 and 1990 and 9 per cent during the 1990s. However, the latter high share was largely due to privatisation of Maroc Telecom (Bouoiyour 2003).
2. An introduction of money transaction for 'private water' such as bottled water necessarily results in an introduction of a private water sector in this general equilibrium setting, which costs the analytical tractability of the applied model.
3. The notation ' ˘ ' denotes expectations of exogenous variables.
4. For the case when differentiation between export goods and domestically sold goods is allowed, see Sadoulet and de Janvry (1995, pp. 204–5).

APPENDIX 4.1 PROOF OF PROPOSITION 4.1

Let M_t^U denote the expected wage income derived from allocating one unskilled labourer to an urban area, and M_t^I denote that derived from allocating one unskilled labourer to the irrigation agriculture sector, respectively. Let θ_t^E denote the probability for an unskilled worker migrating to an urban area of gaining employment in the urban modern sector. We have $M_t^U = \theta_t^E \overline{w}_U$ and $M_t^I = w_t^I\{1-(1-\theta_t)\overline{z}\}$.

Due to the poor access to safe water in rural areas, expected water consumption is expressed as $\widehat{q}_t^{HU} = q_t^H$ for urban residents and $\widehat{q}_t^{HI} = \theta_t q_t^H + (1-\theta_t)\,\overline{q}_{no}$ for irrigation labourers.

Let V_t^U denote the indirect felicity derived from expected income wage when one unskilled labourer is allocated to an urban area and V_t^I denote that derived from expected income wage when one unskilled labourer is allocated to the irrigation agriculture sector. The indirect felicity is derived by solving the following felicity maximisation problem:

$$\underset{\{c^R,c^I,c^U,q^H\}}{Max} u(c_t), \quad c_t = \left(c_t^R\right)^{\varphi_R}\left(c_t^I\right)^{\varphi_I}\left(c_t^U\right)^{\varphi_U}\left(\widehat{q}_t^H\right)^{\varphi_Q} \tag{A4.1.1}$$

subject to the budget constraint $p_t^R c_t^R + p_t^I c_t^I + p_t^U c_t^U + p_t q_t^{Hi} \le M_t^i$ for $i = U, I$.

For the purpose of this analysis we can apply any positive monotonic transformation to the felicity function. Thus we use the simplest case, $u(c) = c$.

Assuming an interior solution, we derive the Marshallian demands and consequently the following indirect felicity for each case:

$$V_t^U = \theta_t^E \overline{w}_t^U \prod_{i=R,I,U,Q}\left(\frac{\varphi_i}{p_t^i}\right)^{\varphi_i} \tag{A4.1.2}$$

$$V_t^I = (\theta_t)^{\varphi_Q}\left[w_t^I\{1-(1-\theta_t)\overline{z}\} + p_t\overline{q}_{no}\left(\frac{1}{\theta_t}-1\right)\right]\prod_{i=R,I,U,Q}\left(\frac{\varphi_i}{p_t^i}\right)^{\varphi_i} \tag{A4.1.3}$$

The following equilibrium probability θ_t^{E*} is easily obtained by solving $V_t^U = V_t^I$:

$$\theta_t^{E*} = \frac{(\theta_t)^{\varphi_Q}}{\overline{w}_t^U}\left[w_t^I\{1-(1-\theta_t)\overline{z}\} + p_t\overline{q}_{no}\left(\frac{1}{\theta_t}-1\right)\right] \tag{A4.1.4}$$

In addition, there is a restriction that $0 < \theta_t^{E*} \leq 1$, which imposes a condition

$$\bar{z} w_t^I (\theta_t)^2 + \{(1-\bar{z}) w_t^I - p_t \bar{q}_{no}\} \theta_t - \overline{w}_t^U (\theta_t)^{1-\varphi_Q} + p_t \bar{q}_{no} \leq 0 \tag{A4.1.5}$$

Q.E.D.

APPENDIX 4.2 PROOF OF PROPOSITION 4.2

The current value Hamiltonian for the household's problem is

$$\begin{aligned} H_s = \frac{{c_s}^{1-\sigma}}{1-\sigma} + \lambda_{s+1}^R \frac{(1+\nu)^{s+1}}{1+\rho} \Bigg[\breve{r}_s m_s + \frac{\breve{w}_s^I}{\breve{p}_s^{Uc}} (1 - l_s^{U*} - \bar{l}^S) \{1 - (1 - \breve{\theta}_s) \bar{z}\} \\ + \frac{\overline{w}_s^U}{\breve{p}_s^{Uc}} \theta_s^{E*} l_s^{U*} + \frac{\breve{w}_s^S \bar{l}^S}{\breve{p}_s^{Uc}} + \left(\frac{1}{1+\nu} \right)^s \Bigg\{ \frac{\breve{\omega}_s \overline{Y}_R}{\breve{p}_s^{Uc}} (\breve{p}_s^{Rp} - a_{RI} \breve{p}_s^{Ic} - a_{RU} \breve{p}_s^{Uc}) \\ - \frac{\breve{w}_s^I}{\breve{p}_s^{Uc}} \left(\frac{\overline{Y}_R}{\tau_R} \right)^{\frac{1}{\beta_{RL}}} \left(\frac{1}{K_s^R} \right)^{\frac{\beta_{RK}}{\beta_{RL}}} - \delta K_s^R \Bigg\} - \frac{\breve{p}_s^{Rc}}{\breve{p}_s^{Uc}} c_s^R - \frac{\breve{p}_s^{Ic}}{\breve{p}_s^{Uc}} c_s^I - c_s^U \\ - \frac{\breve{p}_s}{\breve{p}_s^{Uc}} q_s^H \{ \breve{\theta}_s + (l_s^{U*} + \bar{l}^S)(1 - \breve{\theta}_s) \} - I_s \Bigg] + \lambda_{s+1}^m \frac{I_s - \nu m_s}{1+\rho} \end{aligned} \tag{A4.2.1}$$

where λ^R and λ^m are the Lagrange multipliers.

Assuming an interior solution, the necessary conditions are as follows:

$$\frac{\partial H_s}{\partial c_s^i} = 0 \Rightarrow \qquad {c_s}^{1-\sigma} \frac{\varphi_i}{c_s^i} = \frac{(1+\nu)^{s+1}}{1+\rho} \lambda_{s+1}^R \frac{\breve{p}_s^{ic}}{\breve{p}_s^{Uc}} \text{ for } i = R, I, U. \tag{A4.2.2}$$

$$\frac{\partial H_s}{\partial q_s^H} = 0 \Rightarrow \qquad {c_s}^{1-\sigma} \frac{\varphi_Q}{\bar{q}_s^H} = \frac{(1+\nu)^{s+1}}{1+\rho} \lambda_{s+1}^R \frac{\breve{p}_s}{\breve{p}_s^{Uc}} \tag{A4.2.3}$$

$$\frac{\partial H_s}{\partial I_s} = 0 \Rightarrow \qquad \lambda_{s+1}^R (1+\nu)^{s+1} = \lambda_{s+1}^m \tag{A4.2.4}$$

$$\frac{1+\nu}{1+\rho} \lambda_{s+1}^R - \lambda_s^R = -\frac{\partial H_s}{\partial K_s^R} \Rightarrow$$

$$\frac{\lambda_s^R}{\lambda_{s+1}^R} = \frac{(1-\delta)(1+\nu)}{1+\rho} + \frac{\breve{w}_s^I}{\breve{p}_s^{Uc}} \left(\frac{1+\nu}{1+\rho} \right) \frac{\beta_{RK}}{\beta_{RL}} \left(\frac{\overline{Y}_R}{\tau_R} \right)^{\frac{1}{\beta_{RL}}} \left(\frac{1}{K_s^R} \right)^{\frac{\beta_R}{\beta_{RL}}} \tag{A4.2.5}$$

$$\frac{1+\nu}{1+\rho} \lambda_{s+1}^m - \lambda_s^m = -\frac{\partial H_s}{\partial m_s} \Rightarrow \frac{\lambda_s^m}{\lambda_{s+1}^m} = \frac{1}{1+\rho} + \frac{\lambda_{s+1}^R (1+\nu)^{s+1}}{\lambda_{s+1}^m} \left(\frac{\breve{r}_s}{1+\rho} \right) \tag{A4.2.6}$$

In addition, the transversality conditions are

$$\lim_{s\to\infty}\left[\left(\frac{1}{1+\rho}\right)^{(s-t)}\lambda_s^R\cdot K_s^R\right]=0 \tag{A4.2.7}$$

$$\lim_{s\to\infty}\left[\left(\frac{1+\nu}{1+\rho}\right)^{(s-t)}\lambda_s^m\cdot m_s\right]=0 \tag{A4.2.8}$$

The derivation of the optimal consumption growth rate is similar to that in the analytic model. From (A4.2.2)–(A4.2.5) with household satisfaction production function (4.13), we obtain

$$c_s^i=c_s\frac{\varphi_i}{\breve{p}_s^{ic}}\left(\frac{\breve{p}_s}{\varphi_Q}\right)^{\varphi_Q}\prod_{k=R,I,U}\left(\frac{\breve{p}_s^{kc}}{\varphi_k}\right)^{\varphi_k}\quad\text{for } i=R,I,U, \tag{A4.2.9}$$

$$\widehat{q}_s^H=c_s\frac{\varphi_Q}{\breve{p}_s}\left(\frac{\breve{p}_s}{\varphi_Q}\right)^{\varphi_Q}\prod_{k=R,I,U}\left(\frac{\breve{p}_s^{kc}}{\varphi_k}\right)^{\varphi_k} \tag{A4.2.10}$$

By substituting (A4.2.9) into (A4.2.2) we have

$$\frac{(1+\nu)^{s+1}}{1+\rho}\lambda_{s+1}^R=\breve{p}_s^{Uc}\left(\frac{1}{c_s}\right)^{\sigma}\left(\frac{\varphi_Q}{\breve{p}_s}\right)^{\varphi_Q}\prod_{i=R,I,U}\left(\frac{\varphi_i}{\breve{p}_s^{ic}}\right)^{\varphi_i} \tag{A4.2.11}$$

(A4.2.4) and (A4.2.6) are combined to produce

$$\lambda_s^R=\frac{(1+\nu)(1+\breve{r}_s)}{1+\rho}\lambda_{s+1}^R \tag{A4.2.12}$$

From (A4.2.11) and (A4.2.12) with some algebraic manipulation, we obtain the following equation for optimal per capita consumption:

$$c_{t+T}^*=c_t^*\left\{\frac{\breve{p}_{t+T}^{Uc}}{\breve{p}_t^{Uc}}\left(\frac{\breve{p}_t}{\breve{p}_{t+T}}\right)^{\varphi_Q}\prod_{i=R,I,U}\left(\frac{\breve{p}_t^{ic}}{\breve{p}_{t+T}^{ic}}\right)^{\varphi_i}\prod_{j=0}^{T-1}\left(\frac{1+\breve{r}_{t+1+j}}{1+\rho}\right)\right\}^{\frac{1}{\sigma}} \tag{A4.2.13}$$

Similarly, from (A4.2.5) and (A4.2.12) we obtain

$$K_s^{R*}=\left(\frac{\overline{Y}_R}{\tau_R}\right)^{\frac{1}{\beta_R}}\left\{\frac{\beta_{RK}\breve{w}_s^I}{\beta_{RL}\breve{p}_s^{Uc}(\breve{r}_s+\delta)}\right\}^{\frac{\beta_{RL}}{\beta_R}} \tag{A4.2.14}$$

Here the 'imperfect foresight' assumption is applied. This assumption makes K_s^{R*} constant for all $s \geq t+1$. Therefore the optimal level of household investment in K^R is given by

$$I_s^{R*} = K_{s+1}^{R*} - (1-\delta)K_s^{R*} = \\ = \begin{cases} \left(\dfrac{\overline{Y}_R}{\tau_R}\right)^{\frac{1}{\beta_R}} \left\{\dfrac{\beta_{RK} w_t^I}{\beta_{RL} p_t^{Uc}(r_t+\delta)}\right\}^{\frac{\beta_{RL}}{\beta_R}} - (1-\delta)K_t^R & \text{for } s = t, \text{and} \\ \delta\left(\dfrac{\overline{Y}_R}{\tau_R}\right)^{\frac{1}{\beta_R}} \left\{\dfrac{\beta_{RK} w_t^I}{\beta_{RL} p_t^{Uc}(r_t+\delta)}\right\}^{\frac{\beta_{RL}}{\beta_R}} & \text{for } s \geq t+1. \end{cases} \tag{A4.2.15}$$

Moreover, this assumption makes l_s^{U*} and θ_s^{E*} constant and equal to l_t^{U*} and θ_t^{E*}, respectively. With these results, the equation of motion for household assets becomes:

$$m_{t+1} = \frac{1+r_t}{1+v} m_t - B_1 c_t^* + B_2 + \left(\frac{1}{1+v}\right)^t B_3 \\ - \left(\frac{1}{1+v}\right)^{t+1} \frac{w_t^I}{p_t^{Uc}} \left(\frac{\overline{Y}_R}{\tau_R}\right)^{\frac{1}{\beta_{RL}}} \left(\frac{1}{K_t^R}\right)^{\frac{\beta_{RK}}{\beta_{RL}}} - \left(\frac{1}{1+v}\right)^{t+1} \times \\ \times \left[\left(\frac{\overline{Y}_R}{\tau_R}\right)^{\frac{1}{\beta_R}} \left\{\frac{\beta_{RK} w_t^I}{\beta_{RL} p_t^{Uc}(r_t+\delta)}\right\}^{\frac{\beta_{RL}}{\beta_R}} - (1-\delta)K_t^R\right] \quad \text{for } s = t \tag{A4.2.16}$$

$$m_{s+1} = \frac{1+r_t}{1+v} m_s - B_1 c_s^* + B_2 + \left(\frac{1}{1+v}\right)^s (B_3 - B_4) \quad \text{for } s \geq t+1 \tag{A4.2.17}$$

where $B_1 \equiv \dfrac{1}{(1+v)p_t^{Uc}} \left(\dfrac{p_t}{\varphi_Q}\right)^{\varphi_Q} \prod_{i=R,I,U} \left(\dfrac{p_t^{ic}}{\varphi_i}\right)^{\varphi_i}$, $B_2 \equiv \dfrac{1}{(1+v)p_t^{Uc}}[\, \overline{w}_t^U \theta_t^{E*} l_t^{U*}$
$+ w_t^I(1-l_t^{U*}-\overline{l}^S)\{1-(1-\theta_t)\overline{z}\} + w_t^S \overline{l}^S + p_t \overline{q}_{no}(1-l_t^{U*}-\overline{l}^S)(1-\theta_t)]$,

$B_3 \equiv \dfrac{\breve{\omega}\, \widehat{p}_t^R \overline{Y}_R}{(1+v)p_t^{Uc}}$ and $B_4 \equiv \dfrac{1}{1+v}\left(\dfrac{\overline{Y}_R}{\tau_R}\right)^{\frac{1}{\beta_R}} \left\{\dfrac{\beta_{RK} w_t^I}{\beta_{RL} p_t^{Uc}(r_t+\delta)}\right\}^{\frac{\beta_{RL}}{\beta_R}} \left(\dfrac{\beta_{RL} r_t + \beta_R \delta}{\beta_{RK}}\right)$.

The optimal consumption in year $t+T$ with the constant price expectation is obtained from (A4.2.13) as follows:

$$c_{t+T}^* = c_t^* \left(\frac{1+r_t}{1+\rho}\right)^{T/\sigma} \tag{A4.2.18}$$

From (A4.2.17) and (A4.2.18), we obtain the intertemporal budget constraint between years $t+1$ and $t+1+T$ as follows

$$m_{t+1+T}\left(\frac{1+\nu}{1+r_t}\right)^T = m_{t+1} - B_1 c_t^* \sum_{i=1}^{T} \beta_1^{\,i} + B_2 \sum_{i=1}^{T} \beta_2^{\,i}$$

$$+\left(\frac{1}{1+\nu}\right)^t (B_3 - B_4) \sum_{i=1}^{T} \beta_3^{\,i} \qquad \text{(A4.2.19)}$$

where $\beta_1 \equiv \frac{1+\nu}{1+r_t}\left(\frac{1+r_t}{1+\rho}\right)^{1/\sigma}$, $\beta_2 \equiv \frac{1+\nu}{1+r_t}$ and $\beta_3 \equiv \frac{1}{1+r_t}$.

When T approaches infinity, the left-hand side becomes zero from the transversality condition as follows.

First, we have $\lambda_{s+1}^m = \lambda_s^m \left(\frac{1+\rho}{1+\breve{r}_s}\right)$ from (A4.2.4) and (A4.2.6), and the 'imperfect foresight' assumption results in $\lambda_{t+T}^m = \lambda_t^m \left(\frac{1+\rho}{1+r_t}\right)^T$. Inserting this into the second transversality condition (A4.2.8), we have

$$\lim_{T\to\infty}\left[\left(\frac{1+\nu}{1+\rho}\right)^T \cdot \lambda_{t+T}^m \cdot m_{t+T}\right] = \lim_{T\to\infty}\left[\left(\frac{1+\nu}{1+\rho}\right)^T \cdot \lambda_t^m \left(\frac{1+\rho}{1+r_t}\right)^T \cdot m_{t+T}\right]$$

$$= \lambda_t^m \lim_{T\to\infty}\left[m_{t+T}\left(\frac{1+\nu}{1+r_t}\right)^T\right] = 0 \qquad \text{(A4.2.20)}$$

As λ_t^m represents the shadow price of household assets which must be a positive value, (A4.2.20) requires $\lim_{T\to\infty}\left[m_{t+T}\{(1+\nu)/(1+r_t)\}^T\right] = 0$.

At the same time the boundedness of the right-hand side requires that all the common ratios (βs) must be less than unity. The necessary and sufficient condition for $\beta_2 < 1$ and $\beta_3 < 1$ is $r_t > \nu \geq 0$, while $\beta_1 < 1$, which is equivalent to $r_t > \frac{(1+\nu)^{\sigma/(\sigma-1)}}{(1+\rho)^{1/(\sigma-1)}} - 1$, is automatically satisfied when $r_t > \nu$ due to the fact that $\nu - \left\{\frac{(1+\nu)^{\sigma/(\sigma-1)}}{(1+\rho)^{1/(\sigma-1)}} - 1\right\} = (1+\nu)\left\{1 - \left(\frac{1+\nu}{1+\rho}\right)^{1/(\sigma-1)}\right\} > 0$.

When $r_t > \nu$, (A4.2.19) becomes

$$m_{t+1} = B_1 c_t^* \frac{\beta_1}{1-\beta_1} - B_2 \frac{\beta_2}{1-\beta_2} - \left(\frac{1}{1+v}\right)^t (B_3 - B_4) \frac{\beta_3}{1-\beta_3} \qquad \text{(A4.2.21)}$$

Finally, (A4.2.21) is incorporated into (A4.2.16) and the optimal consumption in year t becomes (4.15). If $r_t \leq v$, c_t^* cannot be a finite positive value.

Q.E.D.

5. Calibration and Validation of the Applied Model

5.1 INTRODUCTION

Modelling requires, by definition, abstraction from certain aspects of reality. For this purpose some aspects relevant to research objectives are specified in some depth while other aspects are rather grossly simplified or ignored by assumption. If a model fails to be a useful and relevant tool for addressing research questions, this is not necessarily because of the simplification or ignorance of reality itself, as is often suggested, but may be because of its inability to replicate those aspects of reality relevant to the research. This can be evaluated only by model validation. Therefore, conducting simulations without model validation cannot provide reliable answers to empirical questions.

This chapter reports the results of calibration and validation of the applied model along with detailed data description. Section 5.2 introduces Morocco as the case-study country. Section 5.3 describes the data and explains construction of an aggregate version of the social accounting matrix (SAM) based on a published Moroccan SAM for the year 1994. The aggregate version of SAM serves as the principal database of the applied model. Note that it is desirable to calibrate the model based on a not very recent dataset for the purpose of dynamic model validation using time-series data. In our case, the model was calibrated for the year 1994 and validated for the period between 1995 and 2002. Section 5.4 explains the calibration process and reports the results, and Section 5.5 does the same for validation. In Section 5.6 sustainable production functions of water and irrigation land are constructed, and Section 5.7 concludes this chapter.

5.2 CASE-STUDY COUNTRY: MOROCCO

The applied model constructed in Chapter 4 is calibrated and validated based on Moroccan data. Morocco is chosen as the case-study country for the following two reasons:

- Morocco is a water-stressed developing country where all the key stylised facts incorporated into the applied model are observed.
- There exist several datasets on Morocco that are highly relevant to this study. In particular, a Moroccan social accounting matrix for the year 1994 (Löfgren et al. 1999) provides an ideal dataset for this study.

5.2.1 Geography and Climate

Morocco is located in North Africa bordered by both the Atlantic Ocean and the Mediterranean Sea. The total land area is 71 million hectares, including the Western Sahara, and is characterised by a high degree of geographical heterogeneity that is well illustrated by the fact that both the broadest plains and the highest mountains in North Africa lie in Morocco.

As a consequence, climatic conditions vary across the country. In general, the plains regions along the Mediterranean and Atlantic coasts are associated with annual precipitation levels of 400–750 mm, while the annual precipitation level frequently exceeds 750 mm in the High and the Middle Atlas regions which form a north-east part of the Atlas mountains. By contrast the Saharan regions often have less than 100 mm precipitation per year. On average, total precipitation for the entire Moroccan territory is estimated at 150 billion m^3 per year (World Bank 1995), which is equivalent to 211 mm per year. Table 5.1 shows spatial variation of mean precipitation in Morocco and Figure 5.1 provides a map of the country.

Table 5.1 Annual mean precipitations in Morocco (mm per year)

City	Region	75–79	80–84	85–89	90–94	95–99	75–99
Tangier	North	839.1	600.9	676.1	624.3	804.0	708.9
Fes	North	572.2	407.3	468.2	391.7	401.8	448.2
Ifrane	North	1034.3	785.9	944.8	774.9	968.2	901.6
Rabat	North	632.2	453.0	494.8	347.7	511.1	487.8
Casablanca	North	431.9	302.1	396.2	316.3	442.0	377.7
Marrakech	Central	223.8	197.7	228.2	198.0	277.5	225.0
Ouarzazate	Central east	92.7	77.1	188.5	116.9	96.4	115.1
Agadir	South	214.7	260.1	322.8	156.7	328.9	256.6
Laayoune	South	63.0	45.2	78.1	73.4	–	63.5

Source: Royaume du Maroc (1982–85, 1990–2003)

During 1980s and 1990s drought has occurred every two years on average, which is significantly higher than the average for the past 100 years (every ten years). Recent drought years are 1992, 1993, 1995, 1999 and 2000. Although it is inconclusive whether or not this higher frequency of droughts is caused by anthropogenic factors such as greenhouse gas emissions, several climate change researchers predict a further decrease of precipitation in this region.

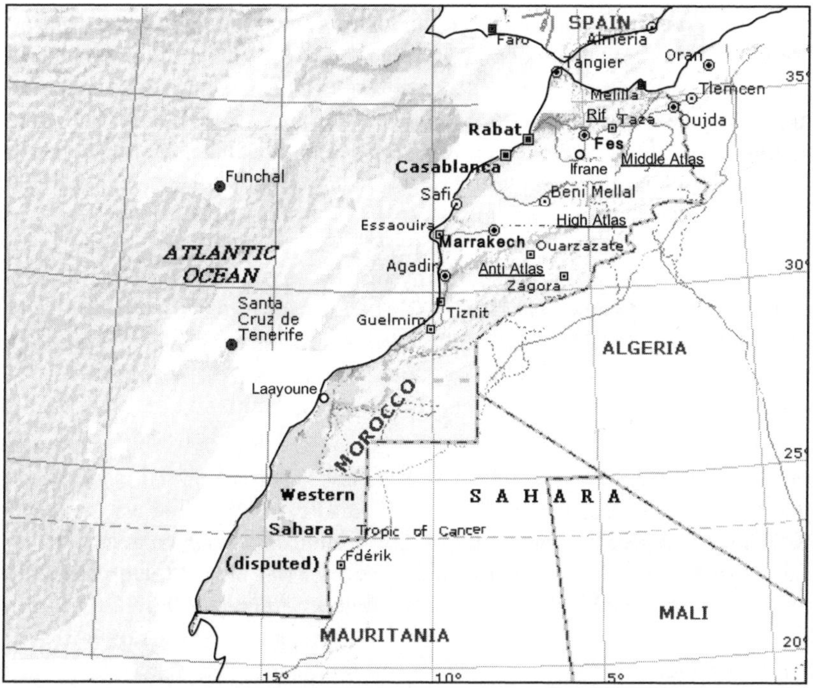

Figure 5.1 Country map of Morocco

Hulme et al. (1995) derive future climate change scenarios for Africa using an energy-balance model and general circulation models (GCMs). Although their scenarios show a huge range of possible future rainfall from a decrease of tens of percent to an increase of similar magnitude from the current level, they conclude that 'it does appear that northern Africa may experience a further reduction in rainfall amounts over coming decades' (p. 16). Knippertz et al. (2003) statistically investigate the effects of the large-scale atmospheric circulation parameters, especially synoptic and baroclinic activities, on precipitation in Morocco based on monthly precipitation data of the Global Historical Climatology Network (GHCN). Their analysis consistently predicts a negative influence of increasing greenhouse gas emissions on precipitation in the regions along the Atlantic and the Mediterranean coasts, but it cannot provide a conclusive prediction of precipitation in the regions south of the Atlas mountains where local and orographic influences are dominating.

5.2.2 Demography

The total population of Morocco was estimated at 29.6 million in 2002. The population growth rate has dropped gradually from 2 per cent per year during the 1980s to 1.6 per cent per year during the 1990s. This drop in population growth is clearly reflected in the decreasing percentage of the youth population (under 15 years) from 39.8 per cent in 1990 to 32.3 per cent in 2000 (Royaume du Maroc 1982–85, 1990–2003). Table 5.2 summarises the demographic data.

Table 5.2 Demographics of Morocco

Year	1975	1980*	1985	1990	1995	2000
Total population (million persons)	17.2	20.1	22.1	24.5	26.4	28.7
Youth share of age under 15 group (%)	46.0	44.4	41.6	39.8	36.2	32.3
10-year mean annual growth rate (%)	2.6	2.8	2.5	2.0	1.8	1.6

Note: * Interpolation based on 1979 and 1982 data.

Source: Royaume du Maroc (1982–85, 1990–2003), and World Bank (1998).

Note that Morocco is one of the major labour exporting countries to the European Union. The net emigration rate in 2004 was estimated at 0.98 persons per thousand people (Central Intelligence Agency 2005).

5.2.3 Economy

The Moroccan economy has been transformed from a French colonial economy, which exported agricultural products and phosphate rocks, into a more diversified economy in which the service sector plays a key role at least in the urban areas. Although Morocco is still a leading producer of phosphates, the role of the mining industry in exports has reduced drastically from 32 per cent of the total value of exports in 1981 to 8 per cent in 1991, due to both the diversification of economic activity and the declining world price of phosphates (World Bank 1995).

Morocco is an upper-middle-income country with a gross domestic product of US$32.9 billion, or US$3597 per capita based on purchasing power parity (PPP) in 2000 (Economist Intelligence Unit 2002). Based on the Human Development Index, Morocco was 112th among 162 countries in 1999 and 126th out of 175 countries in 2001 (UNDP 2000, 2003).

Agricultural sector

The role of agriculture has become more and more limited in terms of GDP share (18.5 per cent in 1994) but is still highly significant in terms of labour absorption – it provided 45 per cent of total employment in the same year. The rural economy provides nearly 80 per cent of total rural employment and produces 60 per cent of total rural value-added (Löfgren et al. 1999).

Furthermore, it has been observed that the high vulnerability of rain-fed agriculture to drought has sometimes severely hampered nationwide economic development. Figure 5.2 shows the relationship between year-to-year variation of nationwide real GDP and rain-fed agricultural production in physical terms. Rain-fed agricultural production is approximated by total non-industrial crop production.

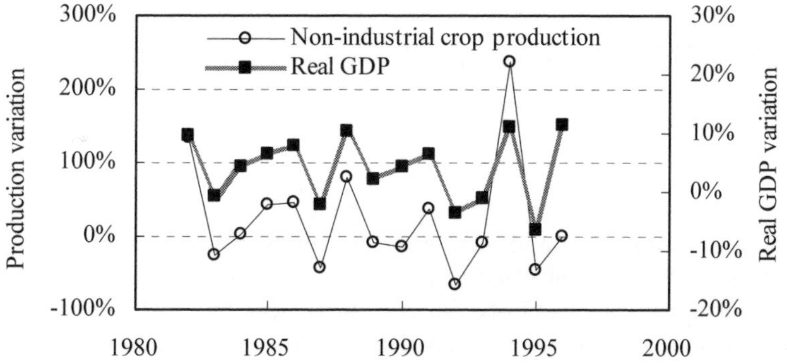

Source: Royaume du Maroc (1982–85, 1990–2003).

Figure 5.2 Variation of rain-fed agricultural production and real GDP

It is obviously tough for the farmers to cope with such huge production fluctuation. Furthermore, several climate change researchers predict a higher frequency of extreme climatic events which may significantly augment this fluctuation (Hulme et al. 1995; Parish and Funnell 1999).

Against this background the Moroccan government has focused on irrigation infrastructure development as the core of its rural development strategy. The government has allocated more than 60 per cent of public investment in agriculture to irrigation development since 1965 (Kadi 2002). It is estimated that the large-scale and medium-scale irrigation areas administered by the government have increased from 0.64 million hectares in 1984 to 0.86 million hectares in 1994 (Académie du Royaume du Maroc 2000). Although the share of irrigation areas is estimated at 10–15 per cent of the total cultivated land, including small-scale private irrigation areas, irrigated agriculture currently contributes around 45 per cent of the agricultural value-added and 75 per cent of agricultural exports (Kadi 2002).

Urban unemployment

One of the major challenges of the Moroccan economy is a chronically high rate of urban unemployment, underpinned by significant rural–urban migration. This migration-induced urban unemployment mechanism is observed by the large difference in unemployment rates between rural and urban areas, as shown in Table 5.3.

Table 5.3 Urban and rural unemployment rates

	1995	1999	2000	2002
Urban unemployment rate (%)	22.3	21.8	21.2	18.2
Rural unemployment rate (%)	7.6	5.0	4.6	3.6

Source: Royaume du Maroc (1996, 2000–2003).

The main driving force of rural–urban migration is not only lower income or higher poverty incidence in the rural areas, but also poorer public services in the rural areas mainly in terms of safe water, electricity and education (Löfgren et al. 1999). The World Bank (1995) reported that a lack of access to safe water remains 'the primary cause of ill-health in the rural areas' (p. 2). These findings are consistent with the generalised Harris-Todaro model described in Proposition 4.1.

Trade and foreign direct investment

The trade balance of Morocco is chronically negative with the ratio of exports to imports at around 70–80 per cent. Recently the leading export goods are textiles followed by food products, in particular fish products, while the leading import goods are machinery and equipment for industrial purposes (Economic Intelligence Unit 2002). The government has conducted a trade liberalisation programme since the early 1980s under the Structural Adjustment Program led by the International Monetary Fund. Since then, trade liberalisation has gradually been implemented through the elimination of quantitative restrictions and reductions of import tariffs (Löfgren et al. 1999). There still remains, however, a high degree of trade protection for domestic agriculture.

The government maintains a relatively tight foreign exchange rate control scheme as a principal policy tool to deal with inflation, despite increasing pressure, mainly from exporters, to devalue. The Moroccan local currency – the dirham (DH) – is regarded as overvalued, which obviously contributes to the chronic trade deficit.

The share of foreign direct investment to gross fixed capital formation is small. It was estimated at 3.2 per cent in the 1980s and 9.7 per cent in the 1990s, and a large part of the latter is associated with the privatisation of Maroc Telecom (Bouoiyour 2003).

5.2.4 Water Sector and Water Policy

The major part of the water sector in Morocco is directly controlled by the government. Key players are DGH (the Direction Générale de l'Hydraulique), ONEP (the Office National de l'Eau Potable) and ORMVA (the Office Régional de Mise en Valeur Agricole). DGH is responsible for water resource development, including mobilising raw water for large-scale irrigation areas. ONEP is mainly responsible for drinking water supplies including planning, constructing and managing water treatment and supply facilities, except for the large cities where autonomous water providers (Régies) supply drinking water. ORMVA is responsible for management of the major irrigation areas. Nine ORMVAs exist: Loukkos, Moulouya, Gharb, Doukkala, Tadla, Haouz, Souss-Massa, Ouarzazate and Tafilalet. Overall management of the national water policy is provided by the National Water and Climate Council (World Bank 1995).

Water resource development

Of 150 billion m^3 of the average annual nationwide rainfall, about 120 billion m^3 is evaporated and 30 billion m^3 remains as a potential water resource, of which 22.5 billion m^3 flows as surface water and 7.5 billion m^3 replenishes groundwater (World Bank 1995).

The rainy season is between December and February and most surface flow is concentrated in this period. Due to this highly seasonal nature of the hydrological cycle, surface water resource development in Morocco has relied heavily on dam construction. The Moroccan water resource development plan anticipates that the annual mobilisation of surface water will be increased from 8.26 billion m^3 in 1990 to 13.78 billion m^3 in 2020, of which 2.78 billion m^3 is to be supplied by the Al Wahida dam and the remaining 2.74 billion m^3 will be supplied by the other 51 dams (World Bank 1995).

Of the 7.5 billion m^3 annual groundwater recharge, the total renewable groundwater resource available for use is estimated at between 3 and 4.5 billion m^3. Due to the very uneven spatial distribution of the renewable groundwater (the Middle and the High Atlas regions are endowed with 70 per cent of the renewable groundwater resources) mining of non-renewable groundwater is undertaken in some regions. Nationwide total extraction is estimated at 2.73 billion m^3, which is less than the total renewable groundwater resources available for use. The groundwater resource development plan anticipates a 10 per cent increase in groundwater harvest to 2.99 billion m^3 in 2020.

Other potential water sources, such as the desalination of seawater or the recycling of wastewater, are rarely utilised in Morocco. For instance, desalinisation and demineralisation facilities in the southern regions currently produce 0.015 billion m^3 as a whole, which is merely 0.01 per cent of total domestic water supply (World Bank 1995).

The World Bank (1995) reported that the average total public investment in dams and transfers for the period between 1990 and 1994 was DH 0.7 billion per year, and was expected to reach DH 3 billion per year for the period from 1995 to 2000. Throughout the remaining part of this chapter, the dirham is at the 1993 price, unless otherwise indicated.

Water use

Nationwide water use is dominated by irrigation, whose share was estimated at 85 per cent in 1990 (World Bank 1995) and 88 per cent in the early 2000s (Kadi 2002). The former estimate is based on an assumption that some part of the return flow from irrigation (irrigation water returning to aquifers) could be recycled. Based on a more conventional estimate of gross consumptive use, the share of irrigation water in the same year was estimated at 92 per cent (World Bank 1995). The shares of domestic and industrial water use were estimated at 8 per cent and 4 per cent respectively in the early 2000s (Kadi 2002).

Water consumption in 1990 is estimated at 9190 million m^3 for irrigation use and 1210 million m^3 for domestic and industrial uses. The government has traditionally attached high priority to satisfying domestic and industrial water demand. The future projection of water demand is thus based on estimations of the future domestic and industrial water demand, and the difference between projected water supply capacity and the forecasted demand is defined as the irrigation water supply potential. The combined future domestic and industrial water demand in 2020 is forecasted at 2720 million m^3, which is equivalent to 2.7 per cent annual growth, based on the following assumptions:[1]

- Per capita domestic consumption rises gradually from the current estimate of 100–150 litre per capita per day (lcd) in the urban areas and from the current estimate of 7.5–40 lcd in the rural areas.
- Industrial demand grows annually at a rate of 4 per cent.
- Population grows annually at a rate of 2.5 per cent in the urban areas and 1.5 per cent in the rural areas, taking rural–urban migration into account.
- Water supply delivery loss drops from the current level of 30 per cent to 20 per cent.

As a result, with an additional assumption that 310 million m^3 must be kept in water courses to flush solid waste and other debris to the sea, the potential irrigation water supply is forecast at 13610 million m^3, which is equivalent to

1.3 per cent annual growth. This potential irrigation water supply accounts for 81 per cent of the forecast water supply capacity in 2020 (World Bank 1995).

Irrigation infrastructure development

As mentioned before, irrigation infrastructure development has been given high priority in the government's rural development strategy. The Moroccan government prepared the irrigation investment plan as the National Irrigation Programme (Plan National d'Irrigation) in 1992, of which the main goal is to expand irrigation areas to exceed 1 million hectares by 2000 and reach 1.2 million hectares by the year 2010. The total expenditure under the National Irrigation Programme is estimated at over DH 40 billion including the capital costs of new facilities, the rehabilitation costs of existing facilities, operation and maintenance costs, recurrent costs and debt service. The required annual public spending is estimated at around DH 2 billion over the period 1995–2000, which is approximately twice more than the investment level over the period 1988–1994 of DH 0.9 billion (World Bank 1995).

Löfgren et al. (1997) provided more detailed information about the National Irrigation Programme for the period between 1993 and 2001, as shown in Table 5.4.

Table 5.4 National Irrigation Programme

	1993	1994	1995	1996	1997	1998	1999	2000	2001	Total
Investment (billion 1994 DH)	0.51	0.58	1.30	1.98	2.46	1.32	0.66	0.62	0.45	9.88
Perimeter area (thousand ha)	–	10.0	16.6	15.4	25.5	5.9	20.1	–	–	93.5
Irrigation water (million m^3)	–	–	68	73	151	46	148	–	–	486

According to this table, the forecast irrigation expansion is 0.09 million hectares during this period, which is too small to achieve the original goal. This discrepancy seems mainly due to the exclusion of low probability future projects of which total costs are estimated at DH 8 billion at the 1994 price (1994 DH).

Löfgren et al. (1997) revealed that the National Irrigation Programme envisages unchanged per hectare irrigation water use. The forecast irrigation water supply potential requires, however, significant reduction in per hectare irrigation water use. The World Bank (1995) reported that the expected irrigation area expansion to 0.83 million hectares of large-scale irrigation areas and 0.47 million hectares of small- to medium-scale irrigation areas will result in a reduction of available irrigation water from 14 140 m^3 per hectare in 1990 to 10 000 m^3 per hectare in 2020. Such a reduction seems to be 'not likely to be feasible with current technology and has important consequences for future investment and for water management' (p. 15).

Access to safe water

While most statistics agree that there is almost 100 per cent coverage of public water service in the Moroccan urban areas, the estimate in the rural areas varies significantly. For instance, Löfgren et al. (1999) referred to an estimate that only 4 per cent of rural households had access to safe water in 1994, while the World Bank (1995) employed an estimate that 14 per cent of rural households had secured water supplies in 1990, 2 per cent being household connection, 6 per cent standpipes and 6 per cent modernised wells.

The present research employs the estimates reported by WHO/UNICEFF (2001) that compiled the results of the Moroccan Demographic and Health Survey conducted in 1987, 1992 and 1995 as well as those of Global Water Supply and Sanitation Assessment 2000 conducted by WHO in 1999. Table 5.5 summarises the estimates in WHO/UNICEFF (2001).

Table 5.5 Access to safe water and improved sanitation in Morocco

	Year	1987	1992	1995	1999
Urban	Safe water access	87.2	94.1	96.8	100.0
	- Private tap	*69.7*	*76.4*	*85.6*	*84.0*
	- Standpipe	*17.5*	*17.7*	*11.2*	*16.0**
	Improved sanitation	91.0	83.0	90.0	100.0
Rural	Safe water access	25.4	17.5	19.8	38.0
	- Private tap	*7.9*	*9.1*	*10.6*	*6.0*
	- Standpipe	*17.5*	*8.4*	*9.2*	*32.0**
	Improved sanitation	28.0	31.0	39.0	36.0

Note: * Defined as population with reasonable access to a public water point.

According to the World Bank (1995), the average total public investment for the period between 1990 and 1994 was DH 0.2 billion per year in domestic water distribution and DH 0.15 billion per year in sanitation and sewerage, and was forecast to reach DH 1 billion per year each in domestic water distribution and in sanitation and sewerage for the period from 1995 to 2000.

Water and irrigation land pricing

In Morocco, volumetric domestic water charge schemes with multiple price ranges (or tiers) have been implemented for cost recovery of the domestic water service providers (Régies), and the rates of domestic water charges significantly vary among the Régies. These rates have been revised on an almost annual basis. Table 5.6 shows a time series of real-term domestic water tariffs of the average of ten cities among 12 cities reported in the national statistical yearbooks (Royaume du Maroc 1982–85, 1990–2003).[2]

Table 5.6 Average of real water tariff of ten cities in Morocco

Year	1985	1990	1995	2000
1st range rate (1994 DH/m³)	1.14	1.18	1.75	1.71
5-year mean annual change (%)	-2.9	0.6	8.3	-0.5
2nd range rate (1994 DH/m³)	2.25	2.41	3.60	4.88
5-year mean annual change (%)	3.4	1.4	8.3	6.3
3rd range rate (1994 DH/m³)	3.07	3.33	4.97	7.13
5-year mean annual change (%)	10.1	1.6	8.4	7.5
1st range	0 – 30 m³	0 – 24 m³		0 – 8 m³
2nd range	30 – 60 m³	24 – 60 m³		8 – 20 m³
3rd range	> 60 m³	> 60 m³		20 – 40 m³
4th range	–	–		> 40 m³

Although the recent drastic real-price escalation of domestic water appears surprising, it is consistent with the Moroccan government policy to achieve full cost recovery of the urban water distribution systems as well as the operation and maintenance costs of the sewerage systems by the year 2000 (World Bank 1995, p. 31).

According to Kadi (2002), irrigation land and water pricing for the large-scale irrigation areas is legislated by the Code of Agricultural Investment (1969) as follows:

- Irrigation land charge (land improvement tax), which can be paid by yearly instalments for 17 years with 4 per cent annual interest rate, covers 30 per cent of capital investment costs. The first 5 hectares are exempted for the farmers with less than 20 hectares of land holdings.
- Volumetric irrigation water charge covers 10 per cent of capital investment costs, full operation and maintenance costs plus 40 per cent of replacement costs.

In addition, irrigation farmers are responsible for the energy costs for pumping, if necessary. The government is responsible for the remaining capital investment and replacement costs. In practice, however, volumetric water charges are set far below the legislated level, usually only 25–50 per cent of the level calculated based on the Code. The main reason is the necessity for the government both to encourage farmers to irrigate and to equalise the rate of volumetric charges across different irrigation areas. The cost recovery through irrigation land charges is worse due to the fact that 80 per cent of farmers hold less than 5 hectares of land each.

Coping with this reality, the revision of the pricing scheme for irrigation land and water are ongoing (Kadi 2002). Despite a lack of reliable nationwide statistics for the irrigation land and water charges, there is little doubt that rates are rising drastically as in the case of domestic water charges.

5.3 DATA DESCRIPTION

5.3.1 Data Sources

The input datasets for calibration and validation of the applied model are constructed based on the following data and information.

Moroccan social accounting matrix for the year 1994

Löfgren et al. (1999) constructed a disaggregated social accounting matrix (SAM), a 104 × 104 matrix, for the year 1994.[3] Because this SAM is designed to capture both the rural–urban and the rain-fed–irrigated agriculture dichotomies, it is an ideal and indispensable database for this study in which these dichotomies play important roles.

Several studies have provided Moroccan SAMs for different years. They include: Sadoulet and de Janvry (1995) for the year 1980; Mateus (1988), Goldin and Roland-Holst (1995), Martens (1995) and Decaluwé et al. (1999) for the year 1985; and Roland-Holst (1996) for the years 1990 and 1994. They are not used in this study because none of them contain the information necessary to divide rain-fed and irrigation agriculture in a satisfactory manner.

Moroccan national statistical yearbook

The following data are collected from a series of Moroccan national statistical yearbooks (Annuaire Statistique du Maroc):

- Demography
- Climatic conditions
- Crop production
- Minimum wage rates
- Domestic water tariffs
- Urban and rural labour force and employment.

International Financial Statistics (IFS)

The following data are collected from a series of International Financial Statistics:

- Nominal effective exchange rates
- Total value of exports
- Total value of imports
- GDP deflators for Morocco and USA.

Others
The other data sources are as follows:

- The real interest rate data are collected from a series of World Development Indicators (WDI).
- Nationwide total irrigation area data are from Académie du Royaume du Maroc (2000).
- Public capital investment is based on data from the World Bank (1995).
- Proportion of skilled labour in 1994 is from Löfgren et al. (1999).

5.3.2 Construction of Aggregate Social Accounting Matrix

The applied model requires a SAM consisting of:

- five factors – land, capital, unskilled labour, skilled labour and irrigation water;
- the government and a homogeneous group of households;
- the rest of the world and a savings account;
- three private production sectors – rain-fed agriculture, irrigation agriculture and urban modern sectors; and
- the accounts representing taxes and subsidies.

This aggregate SAM is constructed based on the 104 × 104 Moroccan SAM developed by Löfgren et al. (1999) as follows. In this subsection the *k*th account in the original 104 × 104 Moroccan SAM is referred to as [*k*].

Reclassification by summation
Most parts of aggregation can easily be done by summation of the accounts that can be regarded as breakdowns of an account. By this method the original SAM is reclassified as follows (note that codes within round brackets are used in the aggregate SAM):

- Unskilled labour (L): a sum of [1]–[4]. Note that rural skilled labour, which represents 8.7 per cent of the labour force, is classified into this category due to the assumption that all rural labour is unskilled.
- Farm land (A): a sum of [6]–[8].
- Private capital (K): a sum of [10]–[14].

- Household (HH): a sum of [16]–[19].
- Rest of the World (ROW): either [21] or a sum of [22] and [23], because the original SAM sometimes breaks down the rest of the world into EU [22] and non-EU [23] countries.
- Irrigation agricultural sector (I): a sum of [25]–[39], [53]–[55] and [59]–[61], which represents all the rural production activities except for the rain-fed agricultural activities, which includes rural manufacturing, rural construction and so on. Recall that the purpose of the rain-fed–irrigation division in the applied model is to capture the vulnerability of rain-fed agriculture. Hence irrigation agriculture stands for non-rain-fed rural activities.
- Rain-fed agricultural sector (R): a sum of [40]–[52].
- Urban modern sector (U): a sum of [56]–[58] and [62]–[65].
- Direct and indirect taxes (TAX): a sum of [100] and [101].
- Tariffs and non-tariff barriers (TNT): a sum of [15], [103] and [104].

Skilled labour (S) [5], irrigation water (Q) [9], government (GOV) [20], savings account (SAV) [24] and subsidies (SUB) [102] are unchanged.

Mapping commodity accounts to production activity accounts

The original 104 × 104 Moroccan SAM employs a commodity-by-industry account framework to represent private production activities, which allows better treatment of secondary products of production activities (Miller and Blair 1985). In the commodity-by-industry framework, consumers purchase commodities supplied by various industries (production activities) as well as by imports. Despite its advantage of representing the actual economic transactions, this framework is not compatible with the applied model in which each production sector produces only one type of commodity. To have compatibility it is necessary to map each of 34 commodities recorded in the original SAM to one of three private production sectors in the applied model. This mapping has been done based on an assumption that a composition of a commodity output in terms of each industry's product supply is fixed, which is often referred to as the industry-based technology assumption (Miller and Blair 1985, p. 165).[4]

The mapping processes are as follows (see Miller and Blair 1985). First, the following matrix notation is introduced:

- The make matrix ($\boldsymbol{V}$): a 3 × 34 matrix of which rows are production activities and columns are commodities.
- The use matrix ($\boldsymbol{U}$): a 34 × 3 matrix of which rows are commodities and the columns are production activities.

- The final commodity demand matrix (***E***): a 34 × 5 matrix of which rows are commodities and the columns are institutions. Note that the subsidy account, which pays money to commodity accounts, is treated as an institution in addition to the household, government, rest of the world and savings accounts.
- The vectors of commodity-based trade-and-tax ($\boldsymbol{C}_i$): row vectors with 34 elements represent transactions from each commodity account to *i*th account, where i = ROW, TAX, SUB and TNT.

All of these matrices and vectors are immediately obtained from the reclassified SAM as its parts.

Let v_{ij} denote *i*th row and *j*th column of ***V***. The vector of total production of commodity (***Q***) is obtained as a row vector with 34 elements which represent total output of commodities, that is, $q_j = \sum_i v_{ij}$. Similarly, the vector of industry total input (***X***) is obtained as a row vector with three elements representing total input of production activities, that is, x_j is a column sum of all elements of *j*th production activity account of the reclassified SAM.

Now we can derive the following two matrices which serve as mapping operators between commodities and industries. Note that in this subsection the superimposed hat (^) indicates a diagonal matrix of a vector.

$\boldsymbol{B} = \boldsymbol{U}\hat{\boldsymbol{X}}^{-1}$: a 34 × 3 matrix represents the value of commodity required as intermediate input to produce one unit value of output of industry.
$\boldsymbol{D} = \boldsymbol{V}\hat{\boldsymbol{Q}}^{-1}$: a 3 × 34 matrix represents a fraction of output value of industry to produce one unit value of commodity.

It can be interpreted that the ***D*** matrix is an operator to map commodity demand to industry demand and the ***B*** matrix is the commodity-by-industry version of the technological matrix. These operators provide all the necessary information. First, $\boldsymbol{A} \equiv \boldsymbol{DB}$, a 3 × 3 matrix, functions as a conventional technological matrix which represents the value of industrial output as intermediate input to produce one unit value of industries' output. Similar to the conventional input- output table, the intermediate goods flow among industries are given as $\boldsymbol{Z} = \boldsymbol{A}\hat{\boldsymbol{X}}$ (3 × 3). The final industry product demand matrix is derived as $\boldsymbol{Y} = \boldsymbol{DE}$ (3 × 5).

Transactions from each industry account to the *i*th account, where i = ROW, TAX, SUB and TNT, are derived as $F_i^{\mathrm{T}} = \boldsymbol{D}C_i^{\mathrm{T}}$ in which superscript T denotes transposed vectors. The derived F_i is a three-element row vector. Note that indirect taxes appear in both production activity and commodity accounts in the original SAM and these two accounts must be combined after this mapping operation.

The aggregate version SAM

The aggregate version SAM is shown in Table 5.7, in which intra-sectoral intermediate goods flows (such as a transaction from R to R) are eliminated.

Table 5.7 Aggregate version of Moroccan SAM for 1994 (billion 1994 DH)

	L	S	A	Q	K	HH	GOV	ROW	SAV	R	I	U	TAX	SUB	TNT	Total
L										6.8	17.9	17.4				42.1
S												74.0				74.0
A										15.4	2.9					18.3
Q											2.4					2.4
K										6.2	16.1	71.2				93.5
HH	42.1	74.0	18.3	2.4	88.0		7.7	21.4							8.0	262.1
GOV					5.4	2.1							38.9		20.4	66.8
ROW					0.1	5.6	7.0	25.3		3.2	13.7	69.4				124.1
SAV						45.0	8.0	6.7								59.7
R						23.4		1.4			7.6	18.4				50.8
I						47.1		11.1	14.4	7.5		35.9		0.7		116.7
U						123.7	40.8	58.2	45.3	8.5	43.9			2.5		322.9
TAX						15.2					2.8	20.9				38.9
SUB							3.2									3.2
TNT										3.2	9.2	15.9				28.4
Total	42.1	74.0	18.3	2.4	93.5	262.1	66.8	124.1	59.7	50.8	116.7	322.9	38.9	3.2	28.4	

5.3.3 Other Datasets

All the other input data for the model calibration are as follows.

- Total population [person]: 26 590 000
- Rural labour force [person]: 5 024 400
- Urban unskilled employment [person]: 2 279 666
- Urban skilled employment [person]: 1 590 734
- Urban unemployment rate in 1995 [per cent]: 22.3
- Public water service coverage in rural areas in 1995 [per cent]: 20
- Water delivery loss in domestic water supply [per cent]: 30
- Real interest rate [per cent per year]: 9.55
- Irrigation water charge [1994 DH/m^3]: 0.347
- Irrigation area [ha]: 863800
- Total water supply [million m^3 /year]: 11 377

In addition, the following exogenous data are collected for the model validation.

Real exchange rates are obtained based on the nominal exchange rates with eliminating inflation of both the local currency (dirham) and the international currency (US dollars) using GDP deflators.

Production risk factors are given as a proportion of each year's non-industrial crop production in physical terms to its average for 1975–2002.

Urban minimum wage rates are based on the actual rates with deflating by the GDP deflator.

Number of working hours per year is assumed to be constant at the value estimated by dividing calibrated annual minimum wage (to be explained later) by the actual minimum wage rate in 1994.

Domestic water charge is estimated by assuming per capita domestic water consumption of 120 lcd during the 1990s and 100 lcd since 2000 and applying an average of ten cities' water tariffs in real terms. The value in 1994 is calibrated as explained later. It is assumed that a drastic (more than 70 per cent) price rise in 2000 induces reduction of domestic water consumption.

Irrigation water charge in the base year is assumed to be the same as the estimated total irrigation water cost by Löfgren et al. (1997). A 5 per cent annual price escalation is then applied.

Irrigation land charge in the base year is estimated by dividing irrigation land factor payment recorded in SAM by the estimate of total irrigation area of 0.864 million hectares. A 5 per cent annual price escalation is then applied.

Domestic water service coverage is estimated using the calibrated production function such that the value becomes 20 per cent in 1994 and 38 per cent in 1999.

All the exogenous input data for the model validation are shown in Table 5.8.

Table 5.8 Exogenous input data for model validation

Year	1994	1995	1996	1997	1998	1999	2000	2001	2002
Real exchange rate (1994 DH/1994 USD)	9.20	9.00	9.14	10.02	10.03	10.14	10.92	11.55	11.14
Production risk factor (average of '75 – '02 = 1)	1.60	0.44	1.71	0.85	1.13	0.75	0.38	0.90	1.08
Urban minimum wage (1994 DH/year)	7626	7098	7634	7549	7522	7481	8108	7966	7919
Domestic water charge (1994 DH/m^3)	2.50	2.58	2.55	2.50	2.88	2.98	5.20	5.11	5.08
Irrigation water charge (1994 DH/m^3)	0.347	0.364	0.383	0.402	0.422	0.443	0.465	0.488	0.513
Irrigation land charge (1994 DH/m^3)	3373	3542	3719	3905	4100	4305	4520	4746	4983
Domestic water service coverage (%)	20.0	24.0	27.7	31.3	34.7	37.9	41.0	43.9	46.7

The observed data for the model validation are shown in Table 5.9.

Table 5.9 Observed data for validation

Year	1994	1995	1996	1997	1998	1999	2000	2001	2002
Real interest rate (% per year)	9.6	–	9.6	–	–	12.5	11.6	10.5	12.5
Urban unemployment rate (%)	–	22.3	17.8	16.7	–	21.8	21.2	–	18.2
Total value of export (FOB) (bil. 1994 DH)	51.0	54.6	55.0	60.3	61.5	65.6	69.2	69.6	74.1
Total value of import (FOB) (bil. 1994 DH)	70.4	74.3	72.6	76.3	81.4	87.0	99.4	99.1	103.0

5.4 MODEL CALIBRATION

5.4.1 Overall Procedure

The applied model has been calibrated based on the above data for the year 1994, the base year of this study. It should be noted that only the first-stage optimisation is subject to calibration since the government decision does not require any calibration. This is another advantage of separating the decision-making process of the government from that of the private agents. Calibration requires an assumption that the observed decisions satisfy optimality conditions, which seems much less strong for the private agents' decisions than for those of the government. The calibration procedure for this model requires particular attention to the following two issues.

First, 'one person' in the model represents one working-age person and his or her dependents. This means that the number of households N is not equal to the total population in the base year, even though initial household size is normalised at unity. Moreover, this is important to set, or to judge the relevance of, per capita values, particularly per capita consumption.

Second is the physical unit of commodity or, as its dual concept, the price of commodity. One unit of, say, urban modern sector product in the model is defined as a composite of highly heterogeneous commodities such as cars, houses, business consulting services and so on. Obviously there is no information about the price of such a composite commodity, but there must be a particular relationship between the price and the physical unit of commodity that can be compatible with the model. In the applied model this relationship is represented by the technological parameters in the production function. For each commodity, the technological parameter is calibrated given an arbitrarily set commodity price.

The overall calibration procedure is as follows. Calibration equations are derived from either the optimal conditions or the optimal solutions of the first-stage optimisation explained in Chapter 4. In the explanation SAM(*i*, *j*) denotes the *i*th row and *j*th column of the aggregate SAM, and the superimposed hat (^) indicates either observed or calibrated values.

Step 1: Calibrate the number of households and urban labour allocation:

$$\hat{N} = \hat{L}^{rural} + \left(\hat{L}^{U} + \hat{L}^{S}\right)/\left(1-\hat{\theta}^{U}\right) \tag{5.1}$$

in which $L^{rural} \equiv L^{R} + L^{I}$, $\hat{\theta}^{E} = \left(1-\hat{\theta}^{U}\right)\hat{L}^{U}/\left(\hat{L}^{U}+\hat{\theta}^{U}\hat{L}^{S}\right)$, $\hat{l}^{S} = \hat{L}^{S}/\hat{N}$ and $\hat{l}^{U} = \hat{L}^{U}/\left(\hat{N}\hat{\theta}^{E}\right)$.

Step 2: Calibrate 'per user' domestic water consumption $\hat{q}^{H}$ and average per capita water consumption $\hat{\bar{q}}^{H}$:[5]

$$\hat{q}^{H} = \frac{\alpha^{Q} SAM(\text{GOV},\text{HH})}{\hat{p}\hat{N}\left\{\hat{\theta}+\left(\hat{l}^{U}+\hat{l}^{S}\right)\left(1-\hat{\theta}\right)\right\}} \tag{5.2}$$

in which α^{Q} is a fraction of water expenditure to total transaction from HH to GOV, and

$$\hat{\bar{q}}^{H} = \hat{q}^{H}\left\{\hat{\theta}+\left(\hat{l}^{U}+\hat{l}^{S}\right)\left(1-\hat{\theta}\right)\right\} + \bar{q}_{no}\left(1-\hat{l}^{U}-\hat{l}^{S}\right)\left(1-\hat{\theta}\right) \tag{5.3}$$

An underlying assumption is that the fraction α^{Q} of the transaction from the household account to the government account in the SAM represents domestic water expenditure. α^{Q} will be calibrated in Step 8 by trial and error.

Step 3: Calibrate parameters φ_i and β_{ik}:

$$\hat{\varphi}_{i} = \frac{SAM(i,\text{HH})}{\sum_{k=\text{R,I,U}} SAM(k,\text{HH}) + \eta^{Q} SAM(\text{GOV},\text{HH})} \quad \text{for } i = \text{R, I, U} \tag{5.4}$$

where $\eta^{Q} \equiv \dfrac{\hat{\bar{q}}^{H}}{\hat{q}^{H}\left\{\hat{\theta}+\left(\hat{l}^{U}+\hat{l}^{S}\right)\left(1-\hat{\theta}\right)\right\}}$.

$$\hat{\varphi}_Q = \frac{\eta^Q SAM(\text{GOV},\text{HH})}{\sum_{k=\text{R,I,U}} SAM(k,\text{HH}) + \eta^Q SAM(\text{GOV},\text{HH})} \tag{5.5}$$

$$\hat{\beta}_{ik} = \frac{SAM(k,i)}{\sum_{j=Factor} SAM(j,i)} \quad \text{for } i = \text{R, I, U} \tag{5.6}$$

in which *Factor* = L, S, K, A, Q.

Step 4: Calibrate wage rates and rural labour allocation:

$$\hat{w}^U = SAM(\text{L,U})/\hat{L}^U \tag{5.7}$$

$$\hat{w}^S = SAM(\text{S,U})/\hat{L}^S \tag{5.8}$$

$$\hat{w}^I = \frac{\hat{\theta}^E \hat{w}^U / \hat{\theta}^{\hat{\varphi}_Q} - \hat{p}\bar{q}_{no}\left(\hat{N}_{pop}/\hat{N}\right)\left(1/\hat{\theta} - 1\right)}{1 - \left(1 - \hat{\theta}\right)\bar{z}} \tag{5.9}$$

$$\hat{l}^I = SAM(\text{L,I})/\hat{N}\hat{w}^I \tag{5.10}$$

$$\hat{l}^R = \hat{L}^{rural}/\hat{N} - \hat{l}^I \tag{5.11}$$

where N_{pop} is total population, and $\bar{q}_{no}$ = 3.65 (m^3/person/year), which is equivalent to 10 (lcd), and $\bar{z} = 0.2$ are chosen. The subsistence amount of water $\bar{q}_{no}$ = 10 lcd seems reasonable judging from the fact that the rural domestic water demand was estimated at 7.5 lcd for 1990 (World Bank 1995, p. 55).

Note that not only a labour force age person but also his or her dependent is counted as 'one capita' for the figures measured in terms of lcd. 'Cost parameter' of 0.2 is a rough guess.

Step 5: Calibrate the rates of the import, product and income taxes and the export subsidy:

$$\hat{\tau}_M^i = \frac{SAM(\text{TNT},i)}{SAM(\text{ROW},i)} \quad \text{and} \quad \hat{\tau}^i = \frac{SAM(\text{TAX},i)}{\sum_{j=Prod} SAM(j,i)} \quad \text{for } i = \text{R, I, U} \tag{5.12}$$

where *Prod* = L, S, K, A, Q, R, I, U.

$$\hat{s}^i = \frac{SAM(i,\text{SUB})}{SAM(i,\text{ROW})} \quad \text{for } i = \text{I, U} \tag{5.13}$$

$$\hat{\tau}_H = \frac{SAM(\text{TAX}, \text{HH})}{\sum_{\forall i} SAM(i, \text{HH}) - SAM(\text{TAX}, \text{HH})} \tag{5.14}$$

Step 6: Calibrate trade parameters (see Section 5.4.2).

Step 7: Calibrate technological parameters (see Section 5.4.3).

Step 8: Calibrate remaining parameters such as σ, ρ and rates of water loss, as well as domestic water consumption and so on (see Section 5.4.4).

Below, the last three steps are explained.

5.4.2 Calibration of Trade Parameters

Recall the optimal imports and exports derived in Chapter 4:

$$\hat{E}^i = \Omega_E^i \hat{Y}^i \text{ and } \hat{M}^i = \left(\frac{1+s_i}{1+\tau_M^i}\right)^{\sigma_M^i} \left(\frac{\delta_M^i}{1+\delta_M^i}\right)^{\sigma_M^i} \left(1-\Omega_E^i\right)\hat{Y}^i \tag{5.15}$$

where $\Omega_E^i = \frac{\hat{E}^i}{\hat{Y}^i} = \frac{SAM(i,\text{ROW})}{\sum_{k=Prod} SAM(k,i)} \left(\frac{1+\hat{s}^i}{1+\hat{\tau}^i}\right)$.

The parameters of the CES function for import composite goods are then calibrated as

$$\hat{\delta}_M^i = \Omega_M^i / \left(1+\Omega_M^i\right) \tag{5.16}$$

where $\Omega_M^i \equiv \left(\frac{1+\hat{\tau}_M^i}{1+\hat{s}^i}\right) \frac{\{SAM(\text{ROW},i)\}^{1/\sigma_M^i}}{\left\{\left(\frac{1+\hat{\tau}^i}{1+\hat{s}^i}\right) \sum_{k=Prod} SAM(k,i) - SAM(i,\text{ROW})\right\}^{1/\sigma_M^i}}$.

CES elasticity of substitution σ_M are determined as $\hat{\sigma}_M^R = 2.0$, $\hat{\sigma}_M^I = 3.0$ and $\hat{\sigma}_M^U = 5.0$ using: (1) values reported in literature; and (2) the proportion of imports to commodity production (7.1 per cent for rain-fed agriculture, 15.1 per cent for irrigation agriculture and 32.5 per cent for urban modern products) as a proxy of substitutability between traded and domestically produced goods.[6]

5.4.3 Calibration of Technological Parameters in Production Functions

It is assumed that the world price of each commodity in terms of 1994 US dollars (p^{iW}) is constant. Since the choice of these commodity prices does not affect the simulation results, they are normalised at unity. Note that the unit of these prices is 1994 US dollars per physical unit of commodity i, in which $i = R, I, U$.

Given the world commodity prices, the rates of import and product taxes and export subsidy as well as trade parameters, the technological parameters are calibrated as follows. Note that the capital depreciation rate is set at 0.07 based on the previous works. For example, King and Levine (1994) employed $\delta = 0.07$ to construct a cross-country dataset of physical capital stock. Agénor and Aynaoui (2003) chose $\delta = 0.08$ for Moroccan private capital.

First, notice the producer and net producer prices are calibrated as

$$\hat{p}^{ip} = \left(\frac{1+\hat{s}^i}{1+\hat{\tau}^i}\right)\hat{p}^{iW}\hat{r}^e \text{ and } \hat{\bar{p}}^i = \frac{\sum_{k=Factor} SAM(k,i)}{\sum_{j=Prod} SAM(j,i)}\hat{p}^{ip} \tag{5.17}$$

where *Factor* = L, S, K, A, Q, and *Prod* = L, S, K, A, Q, R, I, U, as before.

Similarly, the consumer prices are calibrated as

$$\hat{p}^{ic} = \eta_M^i\left(1+\hat{\tau}_M^i\right)\hat{p}^{iW}\hat{r}^e \tag{5.18}$$

where $\eta_M^i = \dfrac{(1+\hat{s}_i)\left\{(\delta_M^i)^{\sigma_M^i}(1+\hat{s}_i)^{\sigma_M^i-1} + (1-\delta_M^i)^{\sigma_M^i}(1+\hat{\tau}_M^i)^{\sigma_M^i-1}\right\}}{(\delta_M^i)^{\sigma_M^i}(1+\hat{s}_i)^{\sigma_M^i} + (1-\delta_M^i)^{\sigma_M^i}(1+\hat{\tau}_M^i)^{\sigma_M^i}}$.

From these price expressions, the equilibrium real interest rate expression (4.26) is modified into

$$\hat{r} + \hat{\delta} = \frac{\hat{\beta}_{UK}}{\hat{p}^{Uc}}\left\{\tau_U\hat{\bar{p}}^U\left(\frac{\hat{\beta}_{UL}}{\hat{w}^U}\right)^{\hat{\beta}_{UL}}\left(\frac{\hat{\beta}_{US}}{\hat{w}^S}\right)^{\hat{\beta}_{US}}\right\}^{1/\hat{\beta}_{UK}} \tag{5.19}$$

This gives the calibration equation of τ_U as

$$\hat{\tau}_U = \frac{1}{\hat{\bar{p}}^U}\left\{\frac{\hat{p}^{Uc}(\hat{r}+\hat{\delta})}{\hat{\beta}_{UK}}\right\}^{\hat{\beta}_{UK}}\left(\frac{\hat{w}^U}{\hat{\beta}_{UL}}\right)^{\hat{\beta}_{UL}}\left(\frac{\hat{w}^S}{\hat{\beta}_{US}}\right)^{\hat{\beta}_{US}} \tag{5.20}$$

Similarly, τ_I and τ_R are calibrated by the following equations derived from the equilibrium irrigation sector wage and urban unskilled labour allocation:

$$\hat{\tau}_I = \frac{1}{\hat{\bar{p}}^I}\left(\frac{\hat{p}^A}{\hat{\beta}_{IA}}\right)^{\hat{\beta}_{IA}}\left\{\frac{\hat{p}^{Uc}(\hat{r}+\hat{\delta})}{\hat{\beta}_{IK}}\right\}^{\hat{\beta}_{IK}}\left(\frac{\hat{w}^I}{\hat{\beta}_{IL}}\right)^{\hat{\beta}_{IL}}\left(\frac{\hat{p}^w}{\hat{\beta}_{IQ}}\right)^{\hat{\beta}_{IQ}} \tag{5.21}$$

$$\hat{\tau}_R = \frac{\sum_{i=Factor} SAM(i,\mathrm{R})}{\hat{N}\hat{p}^{Rp}}\left\{\frac{\hat{N}(\hat{r}+\hat{\delta})}{SAM(\mathrm{K},\mathrm{R})}\right\}^{\hat{\beta}_{RK}}\Big/ D^{\tau_R} \tag{5.22}$$

in which $D^{\tau_R} \equiv \left[\left\{1-(1-\hat{\theta})\bar{z}\right\}\left(1-\hat{\imath}^U-\hat{\imath}^S\right)-\frac{\hat{\beta}_{IL}\{SAM(\mathrm{K},\mathrm{U})+SAM(\mathrm{K},\mathrm{I})\}}{\hat{\beta}_{IK}\hat{w}^I\hat{N}}\right.$

$$\left.+\frac{\hat{\beta}_{IL}\hat{p}^{Uc}(\hat{r}+\hat{\delta})\hat{L}^U}{\hat{\beta}_{IK}\hat{w}^I\hat{N}}\left\{\frac{1}{\hat{\tau}_U\hat{\bar{p}}^U}\left(\frac{\hat{w}^U}{\hat{\beta}_{UL}}\right)^{1-\hat{\beta}_{US}}\left(\frac{\hat{w}^S}{\hat{\beta}_{US}}\right)^{\hat{\beta}_{US}}\right\}^{\hat{\beta}_{UK}}\right]^{\hat{\beta}_{RK}}.$$

5.4.4 Calibration of Remaining Parameters

The last step in the calibration of the model deals with all the remaining parameters ($\breve{\omega}$, ρ and σ) as well as the rates of domestic water charge, water expenditure fraction α^Q, and water delivery loss in irrigation. They are calibrated such that: (1) the computed optimal household expenditure and total water supply are close to the observed values; and (2) the computed per user domestic water consumption is close to an estimate based on which the rate of domestic water charge is determined. The latter may require some explanation. Recall that the domestic water tariffs in Morocco employ a tiered structure in which unit water price differs depending on water consumption. Consumption levels of, say, 100 lcd and 150 lcd result in different rates of domestic water charge, which in turn affect the computed value of optimal domestic water consumption. Therefore this last step in the calibration has been done by trial and error. Once preference parameters and the rate of water charge are calibrated, total water supply is adjusted to coincide with the observed value by calibrating water delivery loss in irrigation.

Regarding the last step of the calibration process, two caveats must be made. One is the treatment of household income that is not covered by the model. The SAM records transactions from GOV, ROW and TNT to the household account and they account 14.2 per cent of total household income. It cannot be excluded since it definitely affects households' decisions on the optimal consumption. This extra income is thus treated, in both the calibration and validation, as a part of household income subject to the imperfect foresight household expectations, but it is excluded from policy simulations. The other is the fact that the computed optimal household expenditure with plausible values of $\breve{\omega}$ and other preference parameters is bound to underestimate the observed value. One possible explanation is that the households' expectation of rain-fed production would be significantly affected by current production. Remember that the base year (1994) was one of the best crop years with $\omega_t = 1.6$. Nevertheless, the assumption of risk- averse forward-looking farmers, which is represented by $\breve{\omega} < 1$, is maintained. The degree of underestimation, 6.4 per cent in the base case, seems acceptable judging from the complexity of the model.

5.4.5 Calibration Results

The employed parameter values and the results of the calibration are as follows:

- Number of households: $N = 9\ 621\ 410$
- Pure rate of time preference: $\rho = 0.075$
- Depreciation rate: $\delta = 0.07$
- Elasticity of marginal felicity: $\sigma = 10$
- Expected value of production risk factor: $\breve{\omega} = 0.9$
- Commodity weight in satisfaction production: $\varphi_R = 0.119$, $\varphi_I = 0.240$, $\varphi_U = 0.631$, $\varphi_Q = 0.010$
- Factor share of production function: $\beta_{RK} = 0.348$, $\beta_{RL} = 0.383$, $\beta_{IK} = 0.409$, $\beta_{IL} = 0.455$, $\beta_{IA} = 0.074$, $\beta_{IQ} = 0.061$, $\beta_{UK} = 0.438$, $\beta_{UL} = 0.107$, $\beta_{US} = 0.455$
- Technological parameters: $\tau_R = 140.5$, $\tau_I = 63.3$, $\tau_U = 70.1$
- Input-output coefficient: $a_{RI} = 0.146$, $a_{RU} = 0.174$, $a_{IR} = 0.080$, $a_{IU} = 0.453$, $a_{UR} = 0.075$, $a_{UI} = 0.136$
- Consumer commodity price (1994 DH/unit): $p^{Rc} = 9.849$, $p^{Ic} = 10.617$, $p^{Uc} = 10.097$
- Producer commodity price (1994 DH/unit): $p^{Rp} = 9.203$, $p^{Ip} = 9.469$, $p^{Up} = 8.758$
- Initial levels of private capital stock (unit): $m_0 = 5445.3$, $K^R{}_0 = 385.7$
- Rates of income tax: $\tau_H = 0.062$
- Rates of product tax: $\tau^R = 0$, $\tau^I = 0.031$, $\tau^U = 0.096$
- Rates of import tax: $\tau_M^R = 1.024$, $\tau_M^I = 0.675$, $\tau_M^U = 0.229$
- Rates of export subsidy: $s^R = 0$, $s^I = 0.061$, $s^U = 0.043$
- CES elasticity of substitution: $\sigma_M^R = 2.0$, $\sigma_M^I = 3.0$, $\sigma_M^U = 5.0$
- CES import preference parameter: $\delta_M^R = 0.354$, $\delta_M^I = 0.470$, $\delta_M^U = 0.496$

- Fraction of water expenditure to SAM(GOV, HH): $\alpha^{Q} = 0.86$
- Domestic water charge rate (1994 DH/m^3): $p = 2.497$
- Irrigation water charge rate (1994 DH/m^3): $p^{w} = 0.347$
- Irrigation land charge rate (1994 DH/ha): $p^{A} = 3373$
- Per user domestic water consumption (lcd): $q^{H} = 120$
- Water delivery loss in domestic water supply (%): 30
- Water delivery loss in irrigation (%): 32.6

5.5 VALIDATION

5.5.1 Base Case

The model calibration described in the previous section was based on data and information in a single year. The statically calibrated model is then dynamically validated with time-series data of the following variables as exogenous input:[7]

- Production risk factor
- Real exchange rate
- Urban minimum wage
- Rates of public charges (domestic and irrigation water, irrigation land)
- Public water service coverage in the rural areas.

The following four variables are selected as validation criteria and their observed values and the simulated values will be compared:

- Total value of exports
- Total value of imports
- Real interest rate
- Urban unemployment rate.

Trade data reported in IFS are significantly smaller than those recorded in the SAM (export: 28 per cent, import: 18 per cent). These data are proportionally scaled up such that the absolute level of trade data in 1994 coincides. Taxes, subsidies and import taxes are fixed at the 1994 level.

As the base case, a 5 per cent annual price escalation of irrigation water and land charges in real terms is introduced. Judging from the revision of the domestic water tariff table in 2000 and the government policy towards full-cost recovery in irrigation agriculture, this assumption is not unrealistic. The base case results are shown in Figure 5.3.

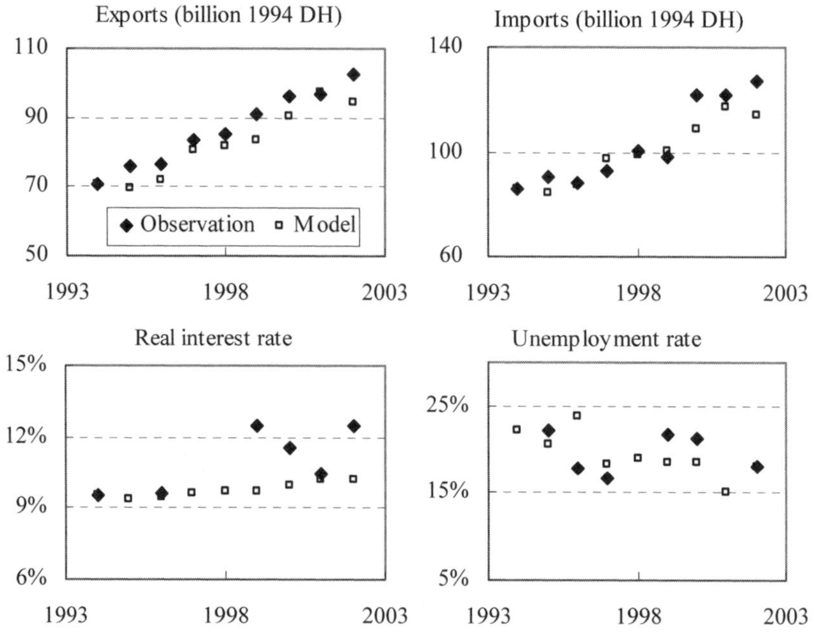

Figure 5.3 Validation results: Base case

Except for the failure to capture fluctuation of real interest rates, the simulated values reproduce the observed trends quite well. Considering the rather wide scope and consequent complexity of the model, the validation seems quite successful.

5.5.2 Sensitivity Analysis

The robustness against parameter values is tested by sensitivity analysis in which each parameter value is changed upward and downward by 50 per cent. One of the most important endogenous variables, the optimal consumption of satisfaction that determines the social welfare, is added into the sensitivity analysis.

The results of sensitivity analysis are summarised in Table 5.10. These results show the robustness of the model against the variation of parameter values. The most parameter-sensitive variable seems to be the urban unemployment rate, in particular against ρ and the price escalation rate of irrigation water and land charges.

Table 5.10 Results of sensitivity analysis in terms of percentage change of mean value from the base case

Parameter	Scenario	c	r	θ^U	E and M
Rate of price rise	50% Low	0.4 %	1.0 %	−7.3 %	0.4 %
	50% High	−0.4 %	−0.9 %	7.1 %	−0.4 %
$\breve{\omega}$	50% Low	−1.8 %	−2.9 %	−4.2 %	1.8 %
	50% High	1.8 %	3.2 %	4.3 %	−1.8 %
σ	50% Low	−1.3 %	−1.9 %	−2.8 %	1.2 %
	50% High	0.5 %	0.7 %	1.0 %	−0.4 %
ρ	50% Low	−3.6 %	−5.4 %	−7.9 %	3.3 %
	50% High	2.8 %	5.3 %	7.2 %	−3.0 %
δ	50% Low	5.6 %	0.1 %	1.2 %	−0.5 %
	50% High	−3.6 %	−0.4 %	−1.1 %	0.4 %

Note: c: consumption of satisfaction, r: real interest rate, θ^U: urban unemployment rate, E: total value export, and M: total value import. E and M are both proportional to total product and respond exactly the same way.

It might be worth mentioning that each sensitivity run affects the simulated trajectories in a way that the trajectories pivot around the initial point. Figure 5.4 illustrates this fact.

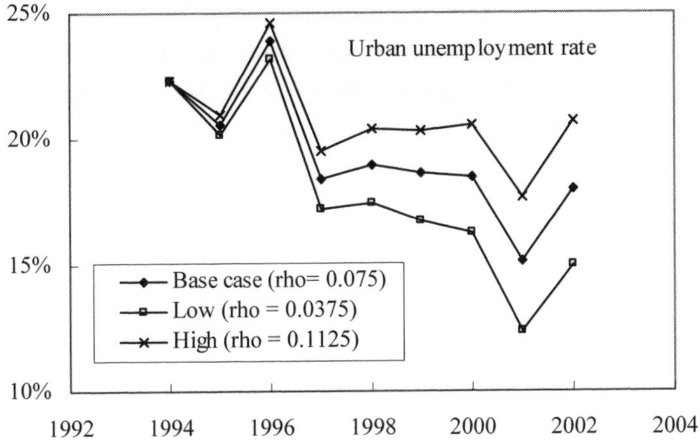

Figure 5.4 Illustration of effects of changing parameter values

As a whole, the rate of pure time preference ρ is the most influential parameter. The importance of ρ in dynamic optimisation is understandable. The welfare improvement effect of higher ρ, which means more myopic preference, is simply due to the short period of validation of only eight years. It is expected that for the longer period higher ρ will result in lower welfare as shown in Figure 5.5.

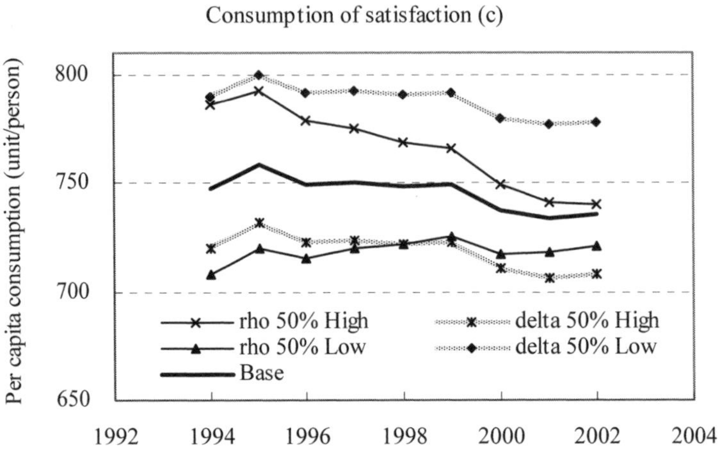

Figure 5.5 Welfare impacts of changing values of ρ and δ

The observed relatively significant impact of changing the depreciation rate on consumption level illuminates the importance of private capital stock as a determinant of welfare. This shift is expected to hold for the entire planning horizon.

5.6 CONSTRUCTION OF SUSTAINABLE PRODUCTION FUNCTIONS

5.6.1 Concept of Sustainable Production Function

As explained in Chapter 3, the public sector production functions represent the relationship between public capital stock and production capacity on condition that production and consumption of publicly supplied goods do not endanger the resilience of ecosystems that underpin life support systems. What is demonstrated here is admittedly rudimentary application of this concept, but the potential of this approach should not be underestimated. Construction of sustainable production functions in a reliable and operational manner requires knowledge of the impacts of production activity on ecosystem resilience, consensus on safe minimum standards to maintain the resilience, and technological and engineering knowledge to achieve it. This challenge provides an excellent opportunity to implement a truly interdisciplinary study in which each discipline plays a distinct and indispensable role.

In this book sustainable production functions are constructed by multiplying the required level of capital stock based on the present engineering practice by a factor termed the 'sustainability coefficient'. Even such a simplified method could provide some useful insight about sustainable development policy.

5.6.2 Sustainable Raw Water Production Function

The World Bank (1995) reported the expected public expenditure in the water sector and the detailed information of dams in Morocco (pp. 56–8). Based on this information a time series of both raw water supply capacity and public capital stock in raw water production is constructed as shown in Table 5.11.

Table 5.11 Raw water production development (1990–2019)

Yr	Supply capacity (mil.m^3)	Incre-ment (mil.m^3)	Capital stock (bil.DH)	Invest-ment (bil.DH)	Yr	Supply capacity (mil.m^3)	Incre-ment (mil.m^3)	Capital stock (bil.DH)	Invest-ment (bil.DH)
90	11 072	71.5	6.00	0.7	05	14 740	8.0	25.61	3.0
91	11 272	200.9	6.28	0.7	06	14 841	100.6	26.82	5.0
92	11 279	6.4	6.54	0.7	07	14 968	127.4	29.94	5.0
93	11 291	12.1	6.78	0.7	08	15 107	138.5	32.84	5.0
94	11 464	173.3	7.01	0.7	09	15 313	206.5	35.54	5.0
95	11 764	300.0	7.22	3.0	10	15 370	57.0	38.06	5.0
96	11 816	52.0	9.71	3.0	11	15 573	203.0	40.39	5.0
97	13 565	1 749.1	12.03	3.0	12	15 593	20.0	42.56	5.0
98	13 573	8.2	14.19	3.0	13	15 730	137.0	44.58	5.0
99	13 954	380.7	16.20	3.0	14	15 730	0.0	46.46	5.0
00	14 043	88.9	18.06	3.0	15	16 069	339.0	48.21	5.0
01	14 182	139.0	19.80	3.0	16	16 069	0.0	49.84	5.0
02	14 267	85.0	21.41	3.0	17	16 102	32.5	51.35	5.0
03	14 440	172.5	22.91	3.0	18	16 102	0.0	52.75	5.0
04	14 732	292.5	24.31	3.0	19	16 244	142.0	54.06	5.0

Source: Adopted from World Bank (1995).

The annual depreciation rate is assumed to be 7 per cent, the same as for the private capital stock, and the value of initial capital stock is assumed to be DH 6 billion such that public capital stock does not decrease between 1990 and 1995. Annual public investments in raw water production are based on the

World Bank (1995) up to the year 2000, and those after the year 2000 are assumed to be DH 3 billion until 2005 and DH 5 billion from 2006.

Based on this table, public capital stock in monetary terms is converted into physical terms based on the calibrated consumer price of capital good, and a sustainability coefficient of 1.3 is applied based on a crude assumption that raw water supply development without losing ecosystem resilience requires 30 per cent more capital stock input than the present engineering practice. This assumption makes, for example, the sustainable production capacity in 1994 be 90 per cent of the observed production capacity with the present engineering practice. The model sensitivity to sustainability coefficients is tested in Chapter 6. The sustainable production function is calibrated as shown in Figure 5.6.

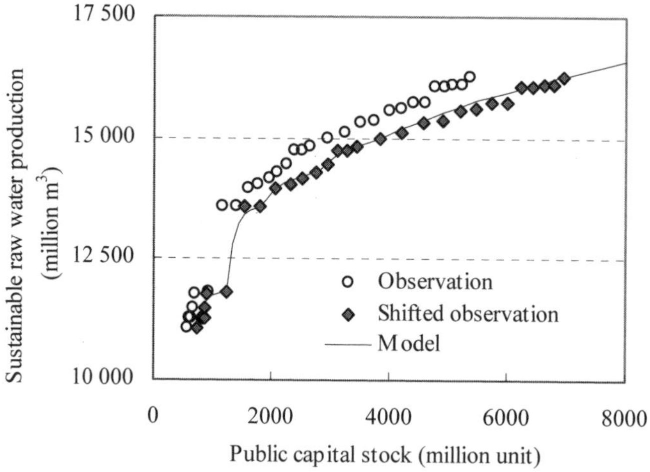

Figure 5.6 Sustainable raw water production function

The calibrated sustainable production function consists of the following set of equations:

$$\begin{cases} R_t = 11829.2 \times \left(1 - 45.53e^{-0.0085G_t^R}\right) \text{ for } G_t^R < 1250 \\ R_t = 13591.0 \times \left(1 - 2{,}876.45e^{-0.008G_t^R}\right) \text{ for } 1250 \leq G_t^R < 1827 \\ R_t = 14342.2 \times \left(1 - 5.16e^{-0.0025G_t^R}\right) \text{ for } 1827 \leq G_t^R < 2757 \\ R_t = 15135.3 \times \left(1 - 3.59e^{-0.0015G_t^R}\right) \text{for } 2757 \leq G_t^R < 3855 \\ R_t = 17020.9 \times \left(1 - 0.38e^{-0.0003G_t^R}\right) \text{for } 3855 \leq G_t^R < 6417 \\ R_t = 9911.2 \times \left(G_t^R\right)^{0.1} - 7746.36 \text{ for } G_t^R \geq 6417 \end{cases} \tag{5.23}$$

where R_t: sustainable raw water production (million m^3/year), and G_t^R : public capital stock in raw water production (million unit).

5.6.3 Sustainable Treated Water Production Function

Based on treated water production data in the national statistical yearbooks, with treated water supply public expenditure reported in the World Bank (1995), a time series of treated water supply capacity and public capital stock in treated water production is constructed as shown in Table 5.12, with assumptions that the annual depreciation rate is 7 per cent and that the value of initial capital stock is DH 1 billion. Delivery loss is assumed to be 30 per cent in 1990 and to decrease 0.5 per cent per year when the annual investment is DH 0.2 billion and 1.35 per cent per year after 1995.

Table 5.12 Treated water production development (1985–2001)

Yr	Water production (mil. m^3) ONEP	Regies	Delivery loss	Total supply (million m^3)	Capital stock (billion DH)	Investment (billion DH)
85	387.0	107.0	32.5%	333.5	1.00	0.2
86	393.0	109.0	32.0%	341.4	1.13	0.2
87	423.0	116.0	31.5%	369.2	1.25	0.2
88	461.0	117.0	31.0%	398.8	1.36	0.2
89	478.0	122.0	30.5%	417.0	1.47	0.2
90	525.0	128.0	30.0%	457.1	1.57	0.2
91	562.0	127.0	29.5%	485.7	1.66	0.2
92	587.0	140.0	29.0%	516.2	1.74	0.2
93	560.0	126.0	28.5%	490.5	1.82	0.2
94	593.0	119.0	28.0%	512.6	1.89	0.2
95	583.0	96.0	26.7%	497.9	1.96	1.0
96	611.0	91.0	25.3%	524.2	2.82	1.0
97	615.0	114.0	24.0%	554.0	3.62	1.0
98	630.0	111.0	22.7%	573.0	4.37	1.0
99	649.0	105.0	21.3%	593.1	5.06	1.0
00	650.0	120.0	20.0%	616.0	5.71	1.0
01	658.0	127.0	18.7%	638.5	6.31	1.0

Source: Royaume du Maroc (1985, 1990–2003) and World Bank (1995).

Based on this table, public capital stock in monetary terms is converted into physical terms based on the calibrated consumer price of capital good, and a sustainability coefficient of 1.8 is applied based on a crude assumption that the sustainable supply of treated water including a high level of wastewater treatment requires 80 per cent more capital stock input than the present engineering practice. Remember that the Moroccan government plans to invest DH 1 billion annually for the sewerage facilities in addition to DH 1 billion investment for the drinking water supply system between 1994 and 2000 (World Bank 1995), and that the current sewerage service is far from satisfactory. This assumption makes, for example, the sustainable production capacity in 1994 be 69 per cent of the observed production capacity with the present engineering practice. The calibrated sustainable production function is shown in Figure 5.7.

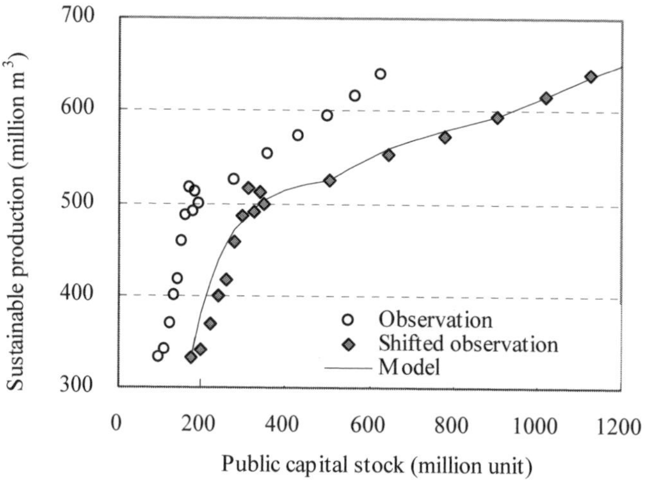

Figure 5.7 Sustainable treated water production function

The calibrated sustainable production function consists of the following set of equations:

$$\begin{cases} Q_t = 528.1 \times \left(1 - 3.13e^{-0.012G_t}\right) \text{ for } G_t < 503 \\ Q_t = 622.9 \times \left(1 - 0.72e^{-0.003G_t}\right) \text{ for } 503 \leq G_t < 903 \\ Q_t = 82.9(G_t)^{0.3} - 45.29 \quad \text{for } G_t \geq 903 \end{cases} \tag{5.24}$$

where Q_t: sustainable treated water production (million m^3/year), and G_t: public capital stock in treated water production (million unit).

In addition, it is assumed that both the public water supply service coverage in the rural areas and the delivery loss of treated water are determined by the following function of public capital stock G:

$$\theta_t = 1 - 0.93e^{-0.0008G_t} \tag{5.25}$$

$$Loss\text{-}H_t = 0.08 + 0.25\,e^{-0.0013G_t} \tag{5.26}$$

where θ_t : rural water service coverage, and $Loss\text{-}H_t$: domestic water delivery loss.

These functions are calibrated such that delivery loss rates of 30 per cent and 20 per cent correspond to the capital stock in 1990 and 2000 respectively, and such that rural water service coverage of 20 per cent and 38 per cent corresponds to the capital stock in 1994 and 1999.

5.6.4 Sustainable Irrigation Land Production Function

Based on irrigation land data (Académie du Royaume du Maroc 2000) with the National Irrigation Programme (Löfgren et al. 1997) for the irrigation area expansion after the year 1996 and public expenditure data in irrigation infrastructure (World Bank 1995), a time series of irrigation area and public capital stock in irrigation infrastructure is constructed, as shown in Table 5.13, with assumptions that the annual depreciation rate is 7 per cent and that the value of initial capital stock is DH 3.5 billion.

Table 5.13 Irrigation land development (1980–99)

Yr	Irrigation area (1000 ha)	Capital stock (bil. DH)	Invest-ment (bil. DH)	Yr	Irrigation area (1000 ha)	Capital stock (bil. DH)	Invest-ment (bil. DH)
80	578	3.5	0.5	90	763	6.2	0.9
81	596	3.8	0.5	91	802	6.6	0.9
82	612	4.0	0.5	92	835	7.1	0.9
83	620	4.2	0.5	93	856	7.5	0.9
84	644	4.4	0.5	94	864	7.8	0.9
85	653	4.6	0.5	95	875	8.2	2.0
86	670	4.8	0.5	96	891	9.6	2.0
87	693	5.0	0.5	97	916	10.9	2.0
88	709	5.1	0.9	98	922	12.2	2.0
89	734	5.6	0.9	99	942	13.3	2.0

Source: Académie du Royaume du Maroc (2000), Löfgren et al. (1997) and World Bank (1995).

Based on this table, public capital stock in monetary terms is converted into physical terms based on the calibrated consumer price of capital good, and a sustainability coefficient of 1.5 is applied based on a crude assumption that sustainable supply of irrigation land requires 50 per cent more capital stock input than the present engineering practice. This assumption makes, for example, the sustainable production capacity in 1994 be around 78 per cent of the observed production capacity with the present engineering practice. The calibrated sustainable production function is shown in Figure 5.8.

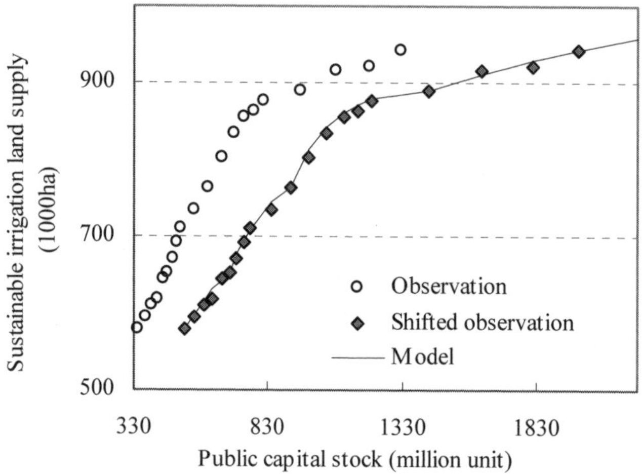

Figure 5.8 Sustainable irrigation land production function

The calibrated sustainable production function consists of the following set of equations:

$$\begin{cases} A_t = 770.1 \times \left(1 - 1.19e^{-0.003G_t^I}\right) \text{ for } G_t^I < 685 \\ A_t = 790.9 \times \left(1 - 21.09e^{-0.007G_t^I}\right) \text{ for } 685 \leq G_t^I < 914 \\ A_t = 894.1 \times \left(1 - 87.95e^{-0.007G_t^I}\right) \text{ for } 914 \leq G_t^I < 1429 \\ A_t = 751.5\left(G_t^I\right)^{0.1} - 663.4 \text{ for } G_t^I \geq 1429 \end{cases} \tag{5.27}$$

in which A_t: sustainable irrigation land provision (1000 ha/year), and G_t^I: public capital stock in irrigation land production (million unit).

In addition, the following relationship between public capital stock G^I and delivery loss of irrigation water is assumed:

$$Loss\text{-}IR_t = 0.15 + 0.3043\, e^{-0.0007G_t^I} \tag{5.28}$$

where $Loss\text{-}IR_t$ is irrigation water conveyance loss.

5.7 CONCLUSION

This chapter provides the necessary information to conduct policy simulations. The case-study country – Morocco – is introduced with care taken to explain the specification and key assumptions of the applied model.

The employed data and model calibration procedure is explained in depth in order to ensure reproducibility of this research. Although a calibration procedure itself is highly study-specific in nature, a detailed explanation of this process, which is rarely found in literature, may be useful for other researchers.

The result of model validation seems successful. Sensitivity analysis reveals parameter-robustness of the applied model. The effects of changes in parameter values are consistent with economic theory as well as our intuition.

Finally, sustainable production functions that play a key role in policy simulations are constructed based on a time series of public capital accumulation and supply capacity development that represents the relationship between supply capacity and public capital stock with present engineering practice that is not necessarily sustainable. Therefore sustainability coefficients, which are rather arbitrarily chosen for illustrative purpose and are subject to sensitivity analysis, are multiplied to the required level of public capital stock.

NOTES

1. This forecast is corresponding to the base case, and the lower- and upper-bound cases are also prepared by changing the assumptions, for example lower or higher industrial demand growth, status quo delivery loss or further reduction to 10 per cent, and so on. The lower-bound forecast is 1949 million m^3 and the upper-bound is 6276 million m^3 (World Bank 1995, p. 14).
2. The ten cities are; Agadir, El Jadida, Essaouira, Fes, Kenitra, Marrakech, Meknes, Safi, Tangier and Tetouan. Casablanca and Rabat are excluded due to a lack of data since 2000. The rate of the fourth range is slightly higher than that of the third range, for example 7.81 versus 7.76 current DH/m^3 in Fes in 2000.
3. The International Food Policy Research Institute (IFPRI) provides this SAM on request.
4. The alternative assumption is that a composition of an industry's product in terms of commodity input is fixed, which is referred to as the commodity-based technology assumption. For the discussion on choice between these two technology assumptions, see p. 166 of Miller and Blair (1985), which is based on Stone (1961).
5. The distinction between 'per user' and 'per capita' is important throughout calibration and validation processes. A part of population is not covered by public water supply service.
6. Löfgren et al. (1999) assign values between 2 and 7 to σ_M of each disaggregated commodity, with higher values for grains. Agénor and Aynaoui (2003) employ $\sigma_M = 0.8$ for agricultural products and $\sigma_M = 1.0$ for urban products.
7. Berentsen et al. (1996) distinguish three types of model validation process: technical validation which covers logical consistency, data selection and methodological issues; operational validation which concerns reproducibility of reality; and dynamic validation which concerns durability of the model through its life cycle. This section explains operational validation of the applied model.

6. Policy Simulations

6.1 INTRODUCTION

This chapter reports the methodology and results of the policy simulations. This study proposes a policy analysis procedure with a clear distinction between the planning and the implementation of policies. Policies are planned based on expectations of uncertain exogenous variables, but they must be implemented with realised values of those variables that do not, in general, satisfy these expectations. The policy-making process must accommodate uncertainty not only in planning the optimal policy but also in simulating the policy implementation process when the expectations are not satisfied. This study explicitly incorporates uncertainty into both parts of the policy-making process, using the Monte Carlo simulation technique. This approach allows policy simulations to deal with uncertainty in a more flexible and practical way than the stochastic dynamic optimisation approach.

This chapter is organised as follows. First, properties of the first-stage solution without supply-side constraints are investigated in Section 6.2. This section illuminates both similarities and differences between the analytic and the applied models. Section 6.3 establishes the simulation procedure with a detailed explanation of the policy implementation process under uncertainty. Section 6.4 formulates policy scenarios. Each policy scenario represents a particular combination of policy variables with a particular environment. The main objectives of the policy simulations are: (1) to demonstrate the potential of the proposed methodology; and (2) to provide a rough idea of policy implications, rather than to provide practical policy advice. In this sense the applied model of this study is not a fully applied model, but a platform to construct such a model. Section 6.5 reports the simulation results, and discussion on the results is provided in Section 6.6.

6.2 NUMERICAL SIMULATION WITHOUT SUPPLY-SIDE CONSTRAINTS

The numerical simulation model in this section consists of only the first-stage optimisation with constant rates of public charges. The model is almost identical to that for validation explained in Chapter 5, except that the following exogenous inputs are given:

- Public charges are fixed at the 1994 levels and rural water service coverage is set at 100 per cent.
- Urban minimum wage is fixed at the 1994 level.
- Production risk factors and foreign exchange rates are randomly disturbed around their expected values with standard deviations of 0.366 for the production risk factor and 0.09 for the real exchange rate. These values are exactly the same in the remaining policy simulations and their justification is provided in Section 6.3.2.
- Three levels of initial private capital stock are given by multiplying the calibrated private capital stocks in 1994 by 1, 0.5 and 2.

In order to investigate the convergence property of the trajectories, the planning period is set at 100 years. Taking random factors into account, Monte Carlo simulations with five trials are employed and the mean values are evaluated. The simulations were conducted using the GAMS.

Figure 6.1 shows the simulated trajectories of consumption and capital stock levels.

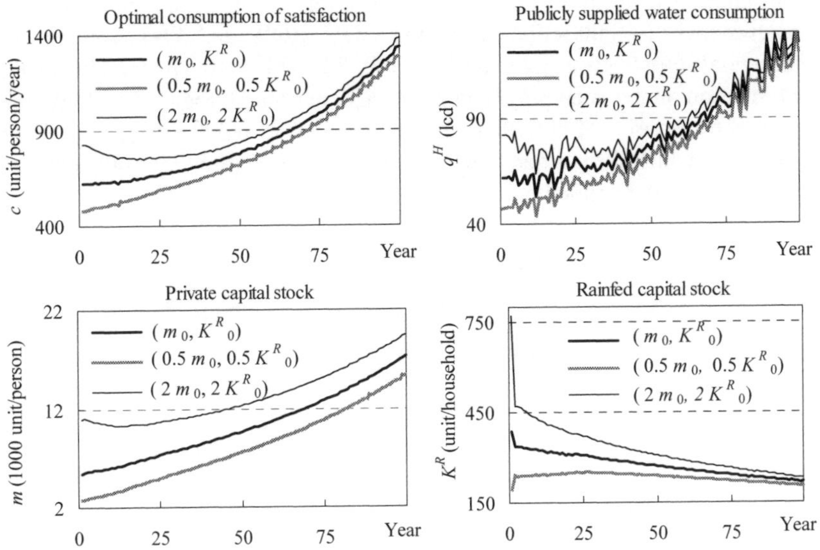

Figure 6.1 Optimal trajectories without supply-side constraints

These trajectories clearly exhibit a convergence tendency, as observed in the analytic model. This convergence property, which precludes the existence of threshold values of initial capital stock below which the economy is driven into a poverty trap, is the most important similarity between the analytic and the applied models. By analogy it is expected that the introduction of supply-side constraints does not change this convergence tendency.

A distinct difference between the analytic and the applied models is the lack of steady states in the applied model, which reflects the fact that the nationwide productivity of rain-fed agriculture in the applied model is fixed and its per capita value decreases with population growth.

It appears, on the surface, surprising that consumption levels of publicly supplied water, of which the price is constant at unity, are disturbed by random shocks more severely than the level of satisfaction consumption. This is because it is the relative prices, not the nominal prices, of commodities that directly affect the optimal consumption levels. In terms of relative prices, the price of publicly supplied water fluctuates the most because the other three commodity prices follow the same fluctuation of real exchange rates.

From the viewpoint of social welfare, positive growth of per capita consumption level as shown in Figure 6.1 contributes to welfare improvement. Despite the perfect access to safe water, the mean level of satisfaction consumption in the first year is nearly 20 per cent less than the calibrated consumption level in 1994. This is mainly due to the elimination of extra income such as transactions from the GOV, ROW and TNT accounts to households (see Section 5.4.4 in Chapter 5). To complete the picture, however, information on the unemployment rate is also important. Figure 6.2 shows the optimal trajectories of the urban unemployment rate and the irrigation labour wage rate, which further demonstrate the convergence property of the optimal trajectories of the applied model.

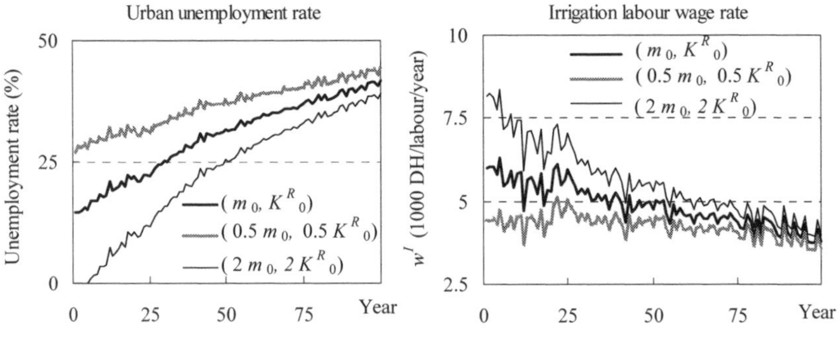

Figure 6.2 Urban unemployment rate and irrigation labour wage rate

Figure 6.2 reveals a negative aspect of optimal development trajectories when there is no public investment. A steady rise in urban unemployment rates reflects a decline in irrigation labour wage rates that is a consequence of an absence of public investment in the irrigated agricultural sector.

6.3 SIMULATION PROCEDURE

6.3.1 Policy Implementation under Uncertainties

The policy-making process of the government in the applied model involves uncertainty in terms of both the production risk factor and commodity prices. When the government makes policies based on certain expectations of uncertain exogenous variables, some implementation rules, or in other words some adjustment mechanisms against expectation errors, must be prepared at the same time. For example, if the government implements pricing schedules for public charges and investment schedules for public capital stocks, neither the expected revenue nor the expected investment (purchased amount of capital goods) can be achieved due to the expectation errors. Furthermore, there is no guarantee of satisfying the sustainability constraints. On the other hand, if the pricing schedule is such that the sustainability constraints are satisfied with equality, the realised prices are different from the planned ones and there is no guarantee that the collected charges are enough to implement the planned investment schedules. Needless to say there is no policy implementation rule that can simultaneously satisfy all the conditions used in the policy planning stage. What the government can do is to predetermine which policies it commits to implement and how it will absorb the expectation errors.

Among many alternatives, the following implementation rule is assumed. The government commits to implement the planned pricing schedules for public charges and to invest (accumulate) the planned amount of public capital in physical terms. This policy implementation rule aims at capturing the inflexible aspects of public pricing and infrastructure investment policies in practice.

The gap between the plan and the reality is absorbed by introducing safety margins for both the supply capacity and the financial position of the government. In the policy planning process the sustainability constraints and the equations of motion for public capital are modified into, for instance:

$$\hat{Q}_t^I + \hat{q}_t^H N(1+\nu)^t \left\{\theta_t + \left(l_t^{U*} + \bar{l}^S\right)(1-\theta_t)\right\} = \chi^{SC} F^R\left(G_t^R\right) \tag{6.1}$$

$$G_{t+1}^R - G_t^R = \chi^{GB} \theta_t^R M_t^R / p_0^{Uc} - \delta G_t^R \tag{6.2}$$

where $\chi^{SC} \in (0,1]$ and $\chi^{GB} \in (0,1]$ are safety factors regarding the sustainability constraints and the government budget, respectively. Needless to say, in the simulation of the policy implementation process the original equations of motion without safety factors are used.

The lower values of the safety factors are associated with the larger safety margins. There is a trade-off between satisfying the sustainability constraints or keeping a positive budget balance and the attainable social welfare. The larger safety margins are associated with the lower probability of violating the sustainability constraints or running a budget deficit but with lower social welfare. This study could capture this trade-off by introducing the Monte Carlo method for the policy implementation simulations.[1]

6.3.2 Simulation Procedure

The established simulation procedure is as follows:

1. Set the public investment allocation as well as the exogenous policy variables such as tax rates.
2. Based on the government's expectations of production risk factors and foreign exchange rates, endogenously determine the optimal rates of public charges p_t, p_t^w and p_t^A, as well as consequent levels of public investment I_t^G, I_t^{GR} and I_t^{GI} by solving the government optimisation problem. This optimisation problem is solved as a mixed complementarity problem (MCP) using the GAMS modelling software.
3. Introduce random disturbances around the expected value of the production risk factor and foreign exchange rates, which are given as normally distributed random numbers generated by GAMS. Standard deviations are set at 0.366 for the production risk factor based on a coefficient of variation of non-industrial crop production between 1975 and 2002, and 0.09 for the real exchange rate based on a coefficient of variation of real exchange rates for the decade after 1993 when the Structural Adjustment Program finished.
4. Conduct Monte Carlo simulations of policy implementation process using GAMS, given randomly disturbed production risk factors and foreign exchange rates. In addition to all the exogenous policy variables, the optimal pricing and investment schedules determined in (2) are given exogenously.

In order to absorb the gap between the revenue and the expenditure of the government, it is assumed that the government has a savings account in which the surplus budget is saved and the deficit is covered by, if possible, dissaving. Only years in which the government savings account runs a deficit are regarded as budget deficit years. Based on preliminary Monte Carlo simulations with this assumption, safety factors are set at $\chi^{SC} = 0.85$ and $\chi^{GB} = 0.98$ such that the probability of violating sustainability constraints and running a government budget deficit come to around 10 to 15 per cent for the former and around 5 per cent for the latter under the current environment. Preliminary simulations reveal that the reduction of the probability of violating the sustainability constraints to less than 10 per cent requires a very low χ^{SC}.

In addition, it is assumed that 20 per cent of the import tax revenue is earmarked for water sector public investment. 1994 SAM records DH 28.4 billion of import tax revenue. Judging from the fact that the total public expenditure for the water sector during the period 1995–2000 is roughly DH 7 billion according to the World Bank (1995), this assumption seems reasonable. This specification tries to capture the relatively high dependence of the revenue of the Moroccan government on trade taxes (Economist Intelligence Unit 2002). Without taking into account the negative effects of trade liberalisation in terms of a reduction in the disposable budget, any trade liberalisation proposals are hardly convincing for the policy makers. For example, Goldin and Roland-Holst (1995) conducted policy simulations of trade liberalisation without incorporating the effects of revenue reduction for the whole economy. They celebrated the positive effects of a policy combining trade liberalisation and doubling of the irrigation water price, and simply added that '[t]he government budget still declines appreciably with tariff revenues, but this might be offset by alternative, nondistortionary sources of revenue' (p. 190). Needless to say, offsetting the budget deficit by any non-distortionary sources of revenue will have negative welfare impacts that offset, to a certain degree, the positive effects of trade liberalisation.

The number of trials of Monte Carlo simulations is set at 100. For demonstrative purposes this must be large enough. The planning period is set at 15 years.

6.3.3 Evaluation Indicators

Separation of the planning and the implementation processes and introducing Monte Carlo simulations for the latter allows the policy makers to evaluate policies from a wider perspective. It is expected that some policies could attain better mean values but they might be more risky in terms of a larger dispersion while some perform the other way around. The choice of safety margin clearly demonstrates this. There is no unique optimal policy but a range of alternative satisficing policies, and a choice of the 'best' policy necessarily depends on value judgements, for instance the degree of risk aversion, of the policy makers and the stakeholders in the policy-making process. This policy-making process matches an aphorism of Simon (1982): 'Optimizing in a simplified world is an important means for satisficing in the real world' (p. xx). Keeping such a policy-making process in mind, the following evaluation indicators are employed:

1. Social welfare
2. Probability of satisfying the sustainability constraints
3. Probability of satisfying the government budget constraint
4. Minimum consumption levels
5. Terminal stock level of total private capital
6. Terminal stock level of total public capital
7. Nationwide unemployment rates
8. Nationwide safe water access rates.

Indicators (1) – (3) measure the performance of policy from the viewpoint of the original government optimisation problem, whereas indicator (4) measures the severity of the least-favourable event. In addition to the original utility metric social welfare, money-metric social welfare is derived in order to grasp the magnitude of the welfare difference between policy scenarios. Money-metric social welfare is measured by equivalent variations (EV) defined as the amount of income which must be given up to make felicity levels under the base case and the alternative policy scenarios indifferent. More precisely, the EV in the year t is such a 'constant income stream' for the entire time horizon starting from the year t and expressed as

$$EV_t = \frac{\{(1-\tau_H)r_t^* - \nu\}(\hat{c}_t - \hat{c}_t^{base})}{1+(1-\tau_H)r_t^* - (1+\nu)\left\{\frac{1+(1-\tau_H)r_t^*}{1+\rho}\right\}^{1/\sigma}} \left(\frac{p_t}{\varphi_Q}\right)^{\varphi_Q} \prod_{i=R,I,U}\left(\frac{p_t^{ic}}{\varphi_i}\right)^{\varphi_i} \quad (6.3)$$

where $\hat{c}_t^{base}$ is the realised consumption of satisfaction under the base case scenario, and all the other variables correspond to each alternative policy scenario. The base case scenario corresponds to Business-as-Usual (BAU) policy under the Base-Base environment, which is explained in the next section.

Indicators (5) and (6) represent the terminal conditions of state variables of the original government optimisation problem (4.58). Indicators (7) and (8) are included as proxies of poverty alleviation in terms of a reduction in the socially disadvantaged population.

These indicators are obtained for each trial of the Monte Carlo simulation, and then the mean and the standard deviation across the trials are computed.

6.4 POLICY SCENARIOS

6.4.1 Policy Alternatives

The applied model contains two types of policy variables that are fully controlled by the government, that is: (1) rates of public charges; and (2) public investment allocation among three types of public capital. The policy alternatives are constructed as their combinations.

Pricing schedule for public charges

There are several CGE studies dealing with water pricing policy in Morocco.

Goldin and Roland-Holst (1995) investigated the effects of doubling the price of irrigation water. As de Melo commented in the discussion section, their model set-up, such as perfectly elastic water supply at a fixed cost, cannot capture the implications of a water shortage.

Löfgren et al. (1997) conducted policy simulations in which irrigation water pricing policy is located within rural development policy. They prepared two alternatives of the irrigation water tariff: one covered the operation and maintenance costs and the other covered the full costs of irrigation water supply. This study did not take into account the effects of water scarcity on the water supply or the water price.

The most interesting study in this regard is Decaluwé et al. (1999). They explicitly incorporated the effects of water scarcity into two types of water production functions, of which the first type represented the water produced by the existing dams and the second type represented a combination of retrieving both surface water and groundwater. The high degree of spatial heterogeneity of water availability in Morocco was captured by differentiating water production technology between the northern and the southern regions with a different segmentation of water markets. Then they conducted policy simulations with Boiteux-Ramsey pricing and marginal cost pricing along with tax reform policies.[2]

Unfortunately the Boiteux-Ramsey pricing is not applicable to this study due to the lack of a proper cost function. Still it is possible to derive marginal cost as a cost of a hypothetical additional unit of investment entailed by an infinitesimal additional demand.[3] Considering the importance of marginal cost pricing in the literature, this pricing rule was envisaged as an alternative pricing policy. A test trial of the simulation immediately revealed, however, that the marginal costs in this study fluctuate drastically, and the magnitude of prices could reach several hundreds times higher than the calibrated rates of charges. As a result, only one pricing policy, the optimal pricing policy such that the sustainable supplies and the optimal demands coincide, is employed.

Public investment allocation

The current public expenditure of the Moroccan government according to the World Bank (1995) is summarised in Table 6.1.

Table 6.1 Current annual public expenditure in the water sector

	1990–94		1995–2000	
	Share	Amount (mil. 1993DH)	Share	Amount (mil. 1993DH)
Water resource development (θ^R)	0.36	700	0.43	3000
Drinking water and sewerage(θ^G)	0.18	350	0.285	2000
Irrigation development(θ^I)	0.46	900	0.285	2000
Total	1.00	1950	1.00	7000

Based on the investment allocation pattern during the period between 1995 and 2000, the alternatives of investment policy are prepared as follows:

BAU (status-quo): $(\theta^R, \theta^G, \theta^I) = (0.43, 0.285, 0.285)$
Alt.1 (domestic water priority): $(\theta^R, \theta^G, \theta^I) = (0.285, 0.43, 0.285)$
Alt.2 (irrigation priority): $(\theta^R, \theta^G, \theta^I) = (0.285, 0.285, 0.43)$
Alt.3 (raw and domestic water priority): $(\theta^R, \theta^G, \theta^I) = (0.43, 0.43, 0.14)$
Alt.4 (domestic water and irrigation priority): $(\theta^R, \theta^G, \theta^I) = (0.14, 0.43, 0.43)$
Alt.5 (raw water and irrigation priority): $(\theta^R, \theta^G, \theta^I) = (0.43, 0.14, 0.43)$

6.4.2 Policy Environments

In addition to the above two types of policy variables, the applied model contains several exogenous variables and parameters that determine the policy environment. It is expected that the performance of a policy alternative depends on the policy environment. For example, worsened vulnerability in rain-fed agriculture due to climate change may give increased priority to irrigation development in comparison with raw water production or water supply development. Some policy alternatives may be more robust than others in terms of stable performance under different environments. Investigating such influences of policy environments on the performance of policy alternatives will be instrumental in understanding sustainable development policy. In particular, it seems worth investigating the policy implications of the following alternative policy environments.

International aid flows

In developing countries, insufficient public capital stock is one of the most challenging problems and it often triggers a vicious circle in which insufficient public capital stock results in low service quality which hinders sufficient investment in public capital due to an inadequate level of cost recovery. Apart from low service quality, it is often observed that full cost recovery pricing, which is beneficial in the long run, is not feasible due to negative welfare effects in the short run. For these cases, international aid flows, either as grants or as loans, can play a vital role in promoting sustainable development.

The volume of international aid flows is mostly determined by donor countries, and it can be regarded as a key instrument of sustainable development policies of the global community. It is interesting to see how the international aid flows affect an individual nation's sustainable development policies; in particular how they facilitate policy implementation.

The base environment (IAbase) assumes no international aid flow, and the alternative environment (IA1) assumes availability of external loans such that initial public capital stocks increase 20 per cent. Repayment conditions for loans are set as follows:

- Interest rate: 7 per cent per annum including grace period
- Grace period: 5 years with interest payment
- Maturity period: 15 years including grace period.

Risk aversion of a society represented by sustainability coefficients

Sustainability coefficients employed in the construction of sustainable production functions are chosen in an ad hoc manner, and they are subject to sensitivity analysis. Moreover, it is possible to interpret this sensitivity analysis as a policy experiment of society's preference on risk aversion that is necessarily embodied in the sustainability coefficients. In reality, no sustainable production function can eliminate risks of violating sustainability constraints or, in other words, losing ecosystem resilience due to a high degree of uncertainty. Although it is not necessarily possible to assign the probability of losing ecosystem resilience to particular values of sustainability coefficients, there generally exists a trade-off between reducing risks of violating sustainability constraints and reducing economic costs associated with large sustainability coefficients. Policy simulations with different values of sustainability coefficients provide policy implications of different degrees of risk aversion of a society.

The base environment (SCbase) employs sustainability coefficients of 1.3 for raw water, 1.8 for treated water and 1.5 for irrigation land, as explained in Chapter 5. These values are increased by 20 per cent for the alternative environment (SC1), that is, 1.56 for raw water, 2.16 for treated water and 1.8 for irrigation land.

Climate change

Most of Africa, including Morocco, has experienced secular climate change in terms of annual rainfall reduction and increased temperatures, and several studies warn that climate change in Africa could accelerate in the future (Hulme et al. 1995; Parish and Funnell 1999; Knippertz et al. 2003). Assessment of climate change impacts entails such a high degree of uncertainty that we could not conclude whether annual rainfall will increase or decrease (Hulme et al. 1995; Knippertz et al. 2003). Nevertheless, there seems to be a consensus that climate change would be manifested as more frequent extreme events such as droughts and floods (Hulme et al. 1995). A larger coefficient of variation of rain-fed productivity could represent such a climate change scenario. The possibility that climate change could affect the water production process is, however, not incorporated. The status quo value of the coefficient of variation (0.366) is selected as the base environment (CCbase), and a value 50 per cent higher (0.55) is chosen as an alternative environment (CC1).

Trade regime

Since the introduction of the Structural Adjustment Program in the early 1980s, trade liberalisation has been one of key political issues in Morocco. While Morocco is undertaking gradual trade liberalisation under WTO rules and the Association Agreement with the European Union and consequently most non-tariff barriers have been eliminated, there remain considerably high import tariffs which aim at protecting domestic production sectors, in particular agricultural sectors, as well as keeping this important revenue source for the government (Löfgren et al. 1999; Economist Intelligence Unit 2002). In spite of the reluctance of the government, further trade liberalisation is still discussed and it is interesting to investigate how it could influence sustainable development policies.

The status quo trade regime in 1994 is selected as the base environment (TRbase). As an alternative trade regime (TR1), a 20 per cent reduction of import tax rate resulting in no earmarked tax revenue for the water sector is chosen consulting with Löfgren et al. (1999), as they provided the most detailed account of Moroccan trade liberalisation policy among Moroccan CGE studies introduced so far.[4] In their model the government savings level is kept constant by adjusting the rate of the value added tax. This specification enables their model to capture the welfare effects of revenue reduction due to trade liberalisation. The employed assumptions in this study also aim to reflect these negative effects of trade liberalisation.

Urban minimum wage

A wage gap between urban and rural areas is the principal determinant of the urban unemployment rate in a Harris-Todaro type migration equilibrium model, which is employed in the applied model. Considering the importance of the urban unemployment problem from the social welfare viewpoint, it is interesting to see how a reduction of urban unskilled labour wages affects sustainable development policy via a reduction of urban unemployment.

The status quo minimum wage for urban unskilled labour in 1994 is selected as the base environment (MWbase), and a 10 per cent reduction of the minimum wage is chosen as an alternative environment (MW1), following Agénor and Aynaoui (2003) who analysed economic impacts of Moroccan labour market policy using a CGE model. They explicitly introduced not only urban–rural differentiation but also a formal–informal dichotomy of the urban production sector in order to capture the potential impacts of labour market reforms in a realistic manner. Their policy experiments consist of a 5 per cent minimum-wage reduction, which affects only unskilled workers in the urban informal sector, and a 5 per cent payroll tax rate reduction, which affects urban formal employers of unskilled workers. The main message of their study is that labour-market reforms such as minimum-wage cuts or payroll tax cuts alone cannot have long-lasting positive effects on the labour market but have to be combined with wider economic policy changes, such as a public investment policy aiming at economic growth. This is exactly what this study can do, although the specifications related to the labour market policy in the applied model are much cruder than those in their model.

6.4.3 Policy Scenarios to be Simulated

Considering the objectives of the policy simulations explained in 6.1, the performance of policy alternatives is investigated in the context of the following combinations of policy environments:

Base Set: IAbase-SCbase	CCbase-TRbase-MWbase	[Base-Base environment]
	CC1-TRbase-MWbase	[Base-CC1 environment]
	CCbase-TR1-MWbase	[Base-TR1 environment]
	CCbase-TRbase-MW1	[Base-MW1 environment]
IA1 Set: IA1-SCbase	CCbase-TRbase-MWbase	[IA1-Base environment]
	CC1-TRbase-MWbase	[IA1-CC1 environment]
	CCbase-TR1-MWbase	[IA1-TR1 environment]
	CCbase-TRbase-MW1	[IA1-MW1 environment]
SC1 Set: IAbase-SC1	CCbase-TRbase-MWbase	[SC1-Base environment]
	CC1-TRbase-MWbase	[SC1-CC1 environment]
	CCbase-TR1-MWbase	[SC1-TR1 environment]
	CCbase-TRbase-MW1	[SC1-MW1 environment]

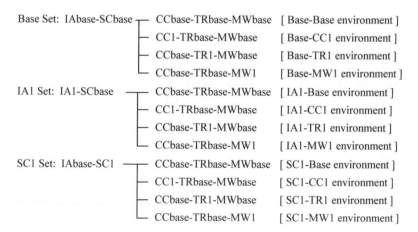

The following Sections 6.5.1, 6.5.2 and 6.5.3 report the policy simulation results under the policy environments corresponding to the Base set, the IA1 set and the SC1 set, respectively.

6.5 SIMULATION RESULTS

6.5.1 Sustainable Development Policies under the Base Set Environments

Optimal pricing schedules

Given the investment allocation policy as a policy alternative, sustainable development policies are presented as the optimal pricing schedules for three public charges.

Figure 6.3 shows the optimal pricing schedules of domestic water charges.

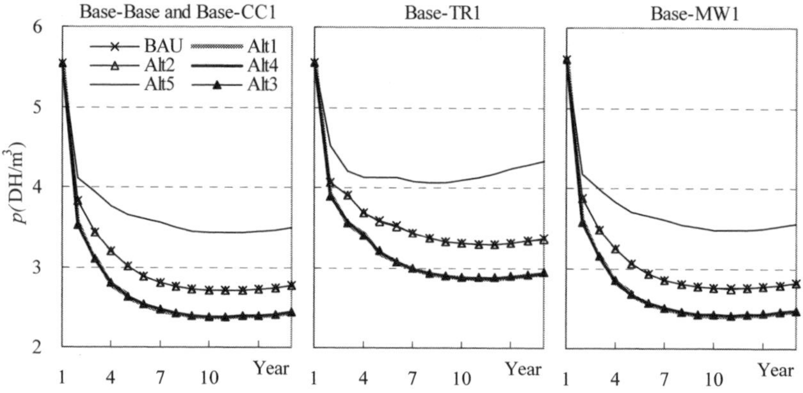

Figure 6.3 Optimal pricing schedules for domestic water charges

Note that there is no difference between policies in the Base-Base and the Base-CC1 environments because the difference in the coefficients of variation of production risk between the two environments plays a role only in the policy implementation process, not in the planning process. In addition, Alt.1, Alt.3 and Alt.4 have almost identical optimal domestic water pricing schedules, and so do BAU and Alt.2. Remember that Alt.1, Alt.3 and Alt.4 share the same θ^G (= 0.43) and BAU and Alt.2 share $\theta^G = 0.285$. This fact suggests that there is little difference between policy alternatives in total public capital accumulation in spite of the heterogeneous composition of G^R, G and G^I, and that domestic water demand is hardly affected by the levels of G^R and G^I.

Figures 6.4 and 6.5 show the optimal pricing schedules for irrigation water charges and irrigation land charges, respectively.

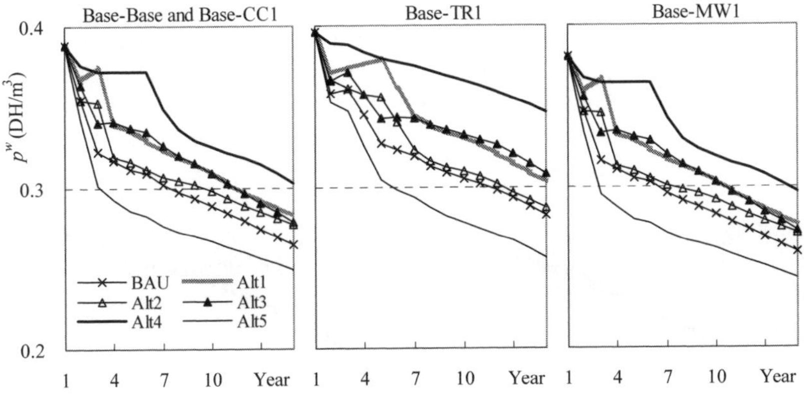

Figure 6.4 Optimal pricing schedules for irrigation water charges

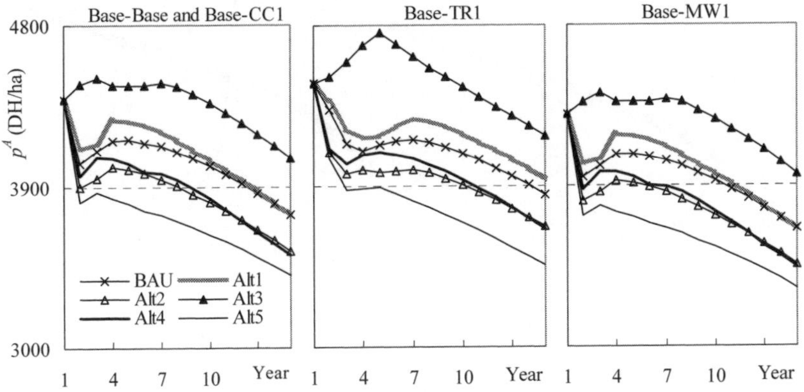

Figure 6.5 Optimal pricing schedules for irrigation land charges

These two figures show more complicated pricing schedules than those for domestic water charges. The non-smooth shape of these pricing schedules reflects the kinked shape of the sustainable production functions (see Figures 5.6–5.8). The fact that all the policy alternatives have unique pricing schedules indicates that all three types of public capital stock G^R, G and G^I affect the demand for irrigation water and irrigation land. It is observed that reducing the minimum wage (MW1 environment) has very little effect on optimal pricing schedules while tariff reduction (TR1 environment) affects them significantly.

Social welfare

Figures 6.6 and 6.7 show the simulated trajectories of mean per capita consumption of satisfaction and mean per user consumption of publicly supplied water. Note that in the calculation of the per user water consumption, it is not only the person of working age but also his or her dependent who is counted as 'one capita'. By contrast, the term 'per capita' always means per each person of working age including his or her dependents.

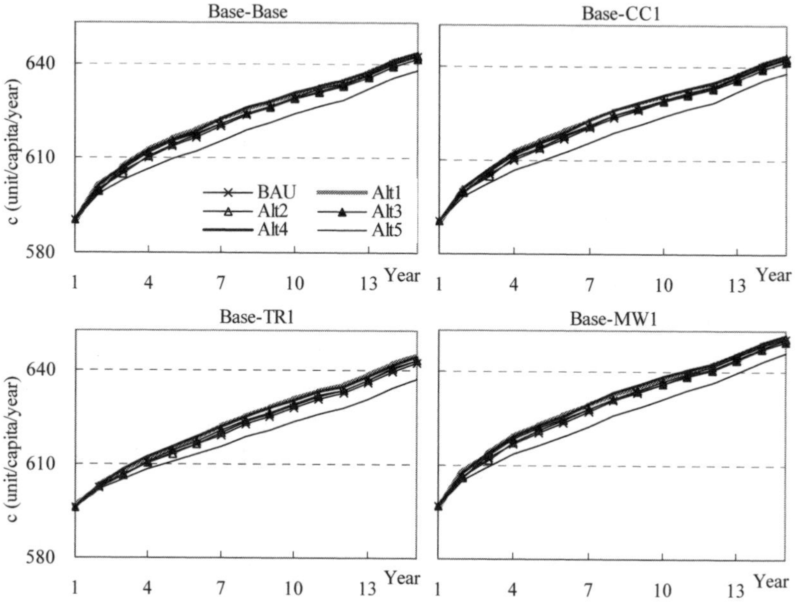

Figure 6.6 Mean per capita satisfaction consumption

It is observed that publicly supplied water consumption is severely suppressed in the first year, to less than 40 per cent of the level with status quo public charges (90 lcd). This suppression is considerably mitigated in the next year and further diminished throughout the planning period, but the status quo level of 90 lcd is not achieved even in the terminal year. This severe suppression of water consumption has only marginal impacts on the level of satisfaction consumption of which reduction from the level with status quo public charges (600 unit/capita/year) is less than 1.6 per cent in the first year, and in most cases the levels of satisfaction consumption exceed this status quo level in the second year.

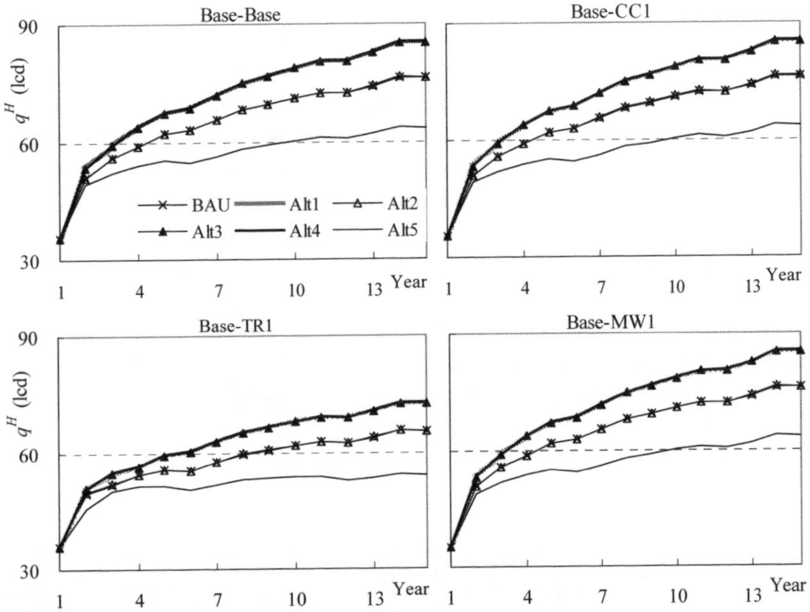

Figure 6.7 Mean per user publicly supplied water consumption

Table 6.2 shows the simulated money-metric social welfare in terms of the net present values of equivalent variations (EV) under the Base set environments.

Table 6.2 Net present value of equivalent variations (EV)

Policy			Policy environment			
			Base-Base	Base- CC1	Base- TR1	Base- MW1
BAU	Mean	(DH/capita)	–	-21.9	192.1	1961.4
	(c.v.)	(%)	–	(2414.0)	(10.7)	(2.1)
Alt.1	Mean	(DH/capita)	486.8	464.8	***781.1***	2449.4
	(c.v.)	(%)	(2.9)	(114.0)	(2.7)	(2.2)
Alt.2	Mean	(DH/capita)	130.9	109.0	330.0	2091.9
	(c.v.)	(%)	(3.9)	(486.9)	(6.2)	(2.1)
Alt.3	Mean	(DH/capita)	127.8	105.9	404.5	2092.2
	(c.v.)	(%)	(6.0)	(497.7)	(4.7)	(2.2)
Alt.4	Mean	(DH/capita)	***490.7***	***468.7***	740.4	***2452.7***
	(c.v.)	(%)	(2.8)	(113.2)	(2.8)	(2.2)
Alt.5	Mean	(DH/capita)	-988.5	-1010.3	-662.0	975.8
	(c.v.)	(%)	(3.1)	(52.2)	(6.5)	(2.0)

The abbreviation 'c.v.' in Table 6.2 stands for coefficients of variation and the bold italics indicate the best policy alternative in each environment; the same notation is applied to the following tables throughout this chapter.

Good performance of Alt.1 and Alt.4 and poor performance of Alt.5 collectively imply the importance of investment in the treated water production sector, while relatively poor performance of Alt.3 indicates that excessively low irrigation investment could reduce the welfare improvement effects of public investment in treated water production.

Another interesting finding is the effect of policy environments on sustainable development policies. Alt. 4 achieves the highest social welfare in the Base-Base, the Base-CC1, and the Base-MW1 environments, while Alt.1 does in the Base-TR1 environment.

The welfare implications of each policy alternative are more clearly illustrated by the trajectories of mean annual EV shown in Figure 6.8

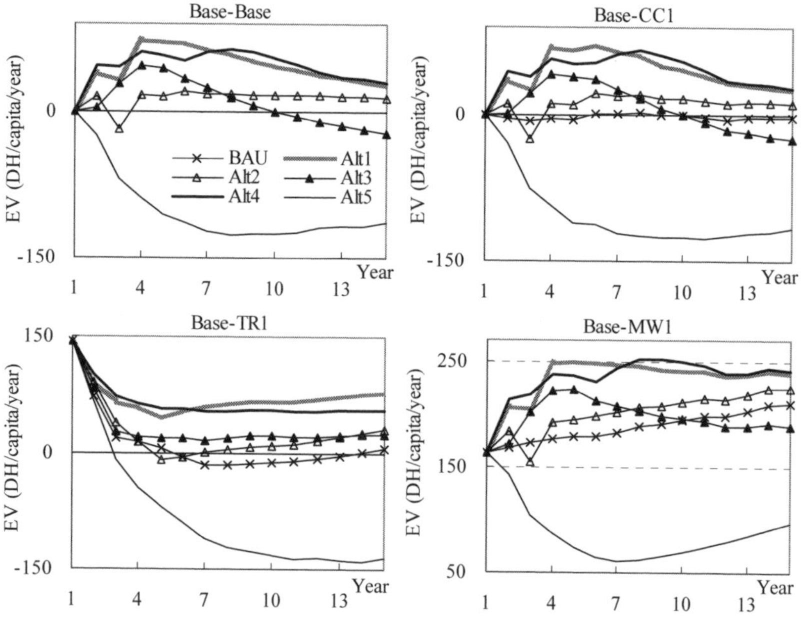

Figure 6.8 Mean annual equivalent variations (EV)

A common pattern for all environments is that Alt.4 achieves the highest EV at the beginning but after several years Alt.1 overtakes it. Whether or not Alt.4 overtakes Alt.1 once again depends on the policy environment. It can be inferred that higher social welfare could be achieved by altering the policy between Alt.1 and Alt.4 appropriately. Figure 6.8 provides useful information for designing such an optimal policy.

Figure 6.8 also shows that the trajectories in the Base-Base, the Base-CC1 and the Base-MW1 environments have essentially the same shape, while those in the Base-TR1 environment have a different shape. In particular trajectories under the Base-Base and the Base-CC1 environments have an almost identical shape. These facts correspond well to the shape of optimal pricing schedules.

The main implication of future climate change represented by the CC1 environment is not revealed in the mean values but in drastically increased coefficients of variation shown in Table 6.2. This implication is graphically illustrated in Figure 6.9, which depicts trajectories of annual EV of every fifth trials (5th, 10th, 15th, ⋯) among 100 trials associated with Alt.4 under the Base-Base and the Base-CC1 environments.

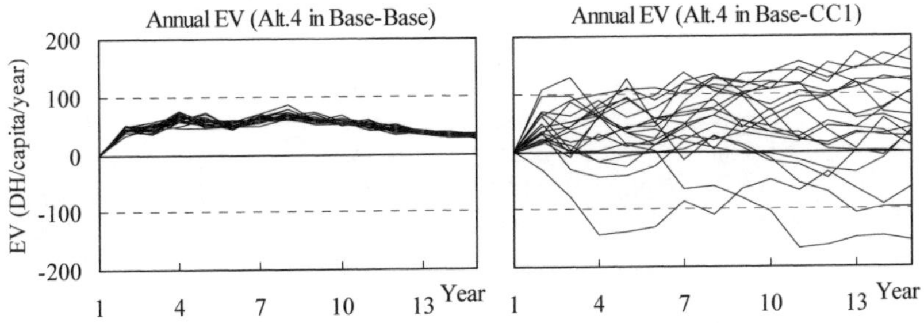

Figure 6.9 Effects of climate change on annual EV paths

Figure 6.9 shows that drastically amplified uncertainty makes comparison between policy alternatives almost impossible under the Base-CC1 environment. This amplified uncertainty is also reflected in the trajectories of minimum satisfaction consumption among 100 trials shown in Figure 6.10.

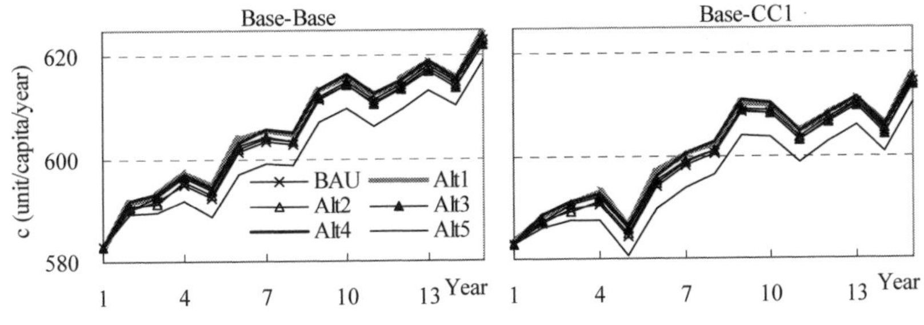

Figure 6.10 Effects of climate change on minimum satisfaction consumption

Figure 6.10 shows that the amplified uncertainty significantly pulls down the minimum values of satisfaction consumption among 100 trials but that it does not change the ranking of policy alternatives.

Observance of constraints

Tables 6.3 and 6.4 show how likely policy alternatives violate sustainability constraints and the government budget constraint, respectively.

Table 6.3 Probability of violating sustainability constraints

Policy			Policy environment			
			Base-Base	Base-CC1	Base-TR1	Base-MW1
BAU	Mean	(%)	13.3	13.3	13.3	13.3
	(c.v.)	(%)	(67.5)	(65.2)	(67.1)	(67.5)
Alt.1	Mean	(%)	13.3	13.3	13.3	13.3
	(c.v.)	(%)	(66.9)	(65.3)	(67.1)	(67.5)
Alt.2	Mean	(%)	13.3	13.3	13.3	13.3
	(c.v.)	(%)	(66.9)	(65.2)	(67.1)	(67.5)
Alt.3	Mean	(%)	13.3	13.3	13.3	13.3
	(c.v.)	(%)	(67.5)	(65.2)	(67.1)	(67.5)
Alt.4	Mean	(%)	13.3	13.3	13.3	13.3
	(c.v.)	(%)	(66.9)	(65.3)	(67.1)	(67.5)
Alt.5	Mean	(%)	13.3	13.5	13.5	13.5
	(c.v.)	(%)	(67.5)	(67.5)	(66.6)	(66.0)

Table 6.4 Probability of budget deficits

Policy			Policy environment			
			Base-Base	Base-CC1	Base-TR1	Base-MW1
BAU	Mean	(%)	4.4	7.7	8.7	4.4
	(c.v.)	(%)	(210.2)	(222.2)	(149.1)	(210.2)
Alt.1	Mean	(%)	4.4	7.7	8.6	4.4
	(c.v.)	(%)	(210.2)	(222.2)	(148.8)	(210.2)
Alt.2	Mean	(%)	4.4	7.7	8.7	4.4
	(c.v.)	(%)	(210.2)	(222.2)	(148.6)	(210.2)
Alt.3	Mean	(%)	4.4	7.7	8.7	4.4
	(c.v.)	(%)	(210.2)	(222.2)	(149.1)	(210.2)
Alt.4	Mean	(%)	4.4	7.7	8.6	4.4
	(c.v.)	(%)	(210.2)	(222.2)	(148.8)	(210.2)
Alt.5	Mean	(%)	4.4	7.7	8.9	4.5
	(c.v.)	(%)	(210.2)	(222.2)	(152.7)	(207.9)

The results show no significant difference between policy alternatives, although policy environments do have some effect on the government budget constraint. It is particularly interesting that high uncertainty under the Base-CC1 environment has no effect on observance of sustainability constraints. Note that both probabilities are associated with large coefficients of variation. If these constraints are strict, it is necessary to apply lower safety factors, which also pulls down the attainable levels of social welfare.

Terminal capital stock levels

The terminal values of both public and private capital stocks have important implications for social welfare after the planning period.

Tables 6.5 and 6.6 show the terminal values of per capita private capital stock consisting of household assets (m) and rain-fed capital (K^R) and the terminal values of total public capital stock, respectively.

Table 6.5 Terminal values of per capita private capital stock

Policy			Policy environment			
			Base-Base	Base-CC1	Base-TR1	Base-MW1
BAU	Mean	(unit/capita)	6799.8	6799.8	6810.7	6828.6
	(c.v.)	(%)	(3.0)	(4.4)	(3.0)	(3.0)
Alt.1	Mean	(unit/capita)	6805.5	6805.5	***6818.9***	6834.3
	(c.v.)	(%)	(3.0)	(4.4)	(3.0)	(2.9)
Alt.2	Mean	(unit/capita)	6802.0	6802.0	6813.1	6830.8
	(c.v.)	(%)	(3.0)	(4.4)	(3.0)	(3.0)
Alt.3	Mean	(unit/capita)	6799.3	6799.3	6812.5	6828.2
	(c.v.)	(%)	(3.0)	(4.4)	(3.0)	(3.0)
Alt.4	Mean	(unit/capita)	***6805.6***	***6805.6***	6817.9	***6834.4***
	(c.v.)	(%)	(3.0)	(4.4)	(3.0)	(2.9)
Alt.5	Mean	(unit/capita)	6786.2	6786.2	6798.5	6815.3
	(c.v.)	(%)	(3.0)	(4.4)	(3.0)	(3.0)

Table 6.6 Terminal values of total public capital stock (million units)

Policy	Policy environment		
	Base-Base and Base-CC1	Base-TR1	Base-MW1
BAU	12 697.4	7142.6	12 611.9
Alt.1	12 803.3	***7293.6***	12 718.5
Alt.2	12 752.8	7191.9	12 667.2
Alt.3	12 651.0	7170.7	12 567.0
Alt.4	***12 807.5***	7268.6	***12 722.5***
Alt.5	12 394.3	6896.9	12 310.4

Remember that public investment schedules are the committed policy variables and consequently the levels of public capital stocks are deterministic. The difference in capital accumulation between policy alternatives is much less than 1 per cent of the stock for private capital and less than 2 per cent for public capital, if we exclude Alt.5. This observation is consistent with what domestic water optimal pricing schedules imply (see Figure 6.3).

A policy alternative associated with the largest terminal values in each environment coincides with the best policy alternative in terms of net present value of EV. This fact precludes trade-offs between social welfare during the planning period and after the planning period, and makes it easy to identify the best policy alternative in each environment.

Note that the coincidence of order between the net present value of EV and the terminal values of capital stock is not entirely general. For example, under the Base environment Alt.3 ranks fourth in the net present value of EV but it ranks fifth in the terminal values of either private or public capital stock.

Unemployment and access to safe water

As explained in Chapter 1, meeting basic human needs is at the heart of sustainable development. In policy simulations of this study, basic human needs are represented by access to safe water and employment. Figure 6.11 shows the mean values of nationwide rates of access to safe water.

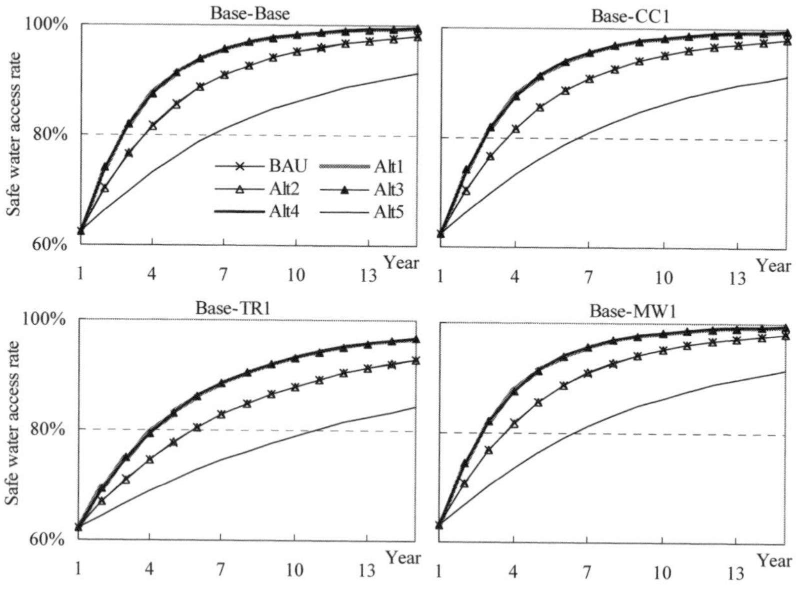

Figure 6.11 Mean values of nationwide safe water access rates

Similarly to the optimal pricing schedules of domestic water charges, the policy alternatives associated with the same investment allocation θ^G (for example, BAU and Alt.2) have almost identical paths of the nationwide rates of access to safe water . The achievement of sustainable development policies, in particular policy alternatives that prioritise domestic water supply, is remarkably successful in providing access to safe water.

Figure 6.12 shows the mean values of nationwide unemployment rates.

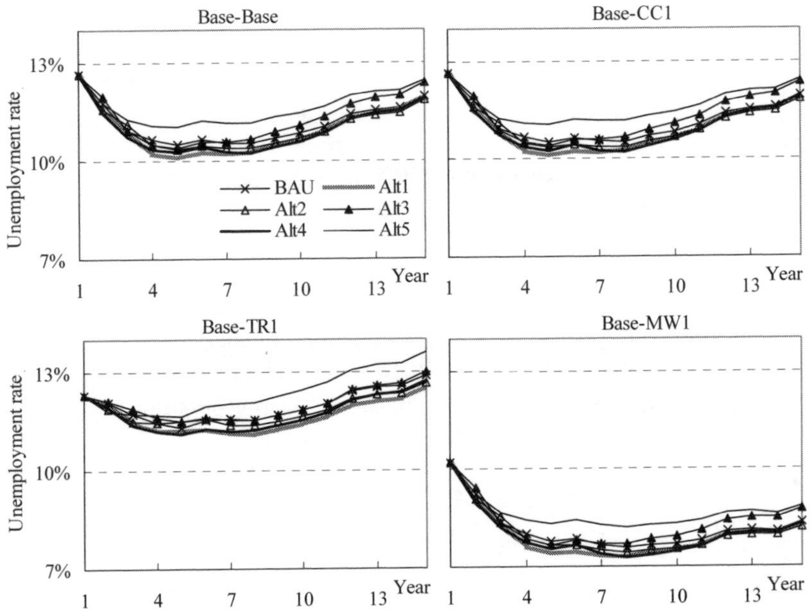

Figure 6.12 Mean values of nationwide unemployment rates

In contrast to the provision of access to safe water, the performance of sustainable development policies in reducing unemployment is disappointing. Nationwide unemployment rates rapidly decrease for the first few years, but then they start rising again. This poor performance is mainly due to population concentration into urban areas with positive population growth, because the probability of urban unskilled labourers getting jobs in the urban modern sector (θ^E) generally increases throughout the planning period, as shown in Figure 6.13. Recall the generalised Harris-Todaro model (Proposition 4.1). The fact that the shape of trajectories in Figure 6.13 is similar to that of the rate of access to safe water indicates that the rise in probability of getting an urban job is mainly due to the improvement in rural access to safe water.

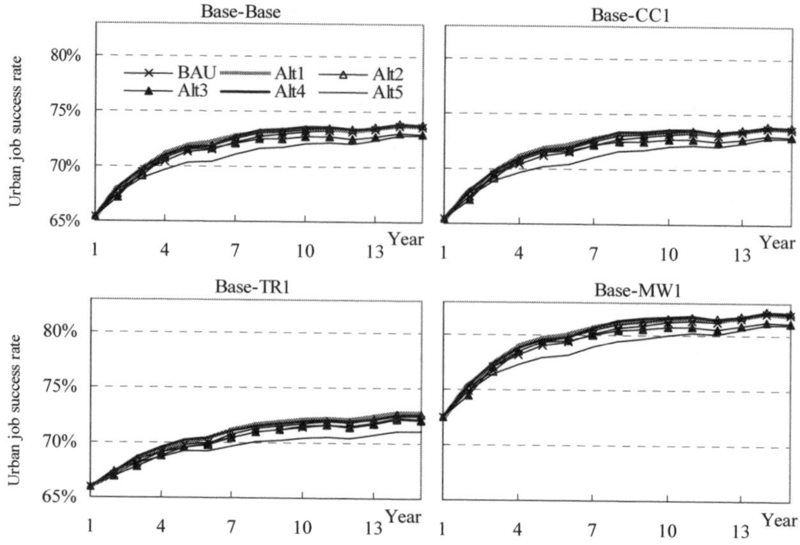

Figure 6.13 Mean probabilities to get urban unskilled jobs

In fact, no policy alternative is sufficiently effective in raising the irrigation labour wage in the long run, as shown in Figure 6.14.

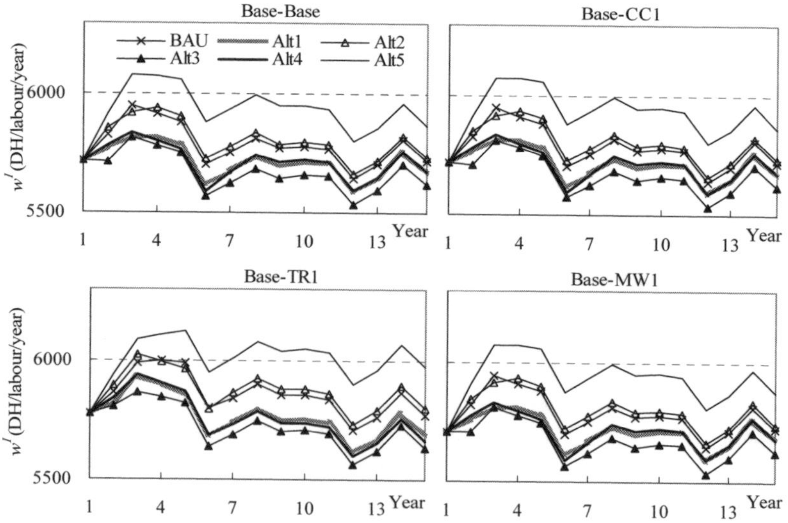

Figure 6.14 Mean values of irrigation labour wage rates

In order to reduce unemployment further, additional policies may be necessary. Relatively high irrigation labour wages associated with Alt.5 may suggest the possibility of raising the irrigation labour wage by investing more in the production of both raw water and irrigation land.

6.5.2 Policy Implications of International Aid Flows

The policy simulations under the IA1 set environments provide policy implications of international aid flows.

Optimal pricing schedules

Figures 6.15 to 6.17 show the optimal pricing schedules under the IA1 set environments.

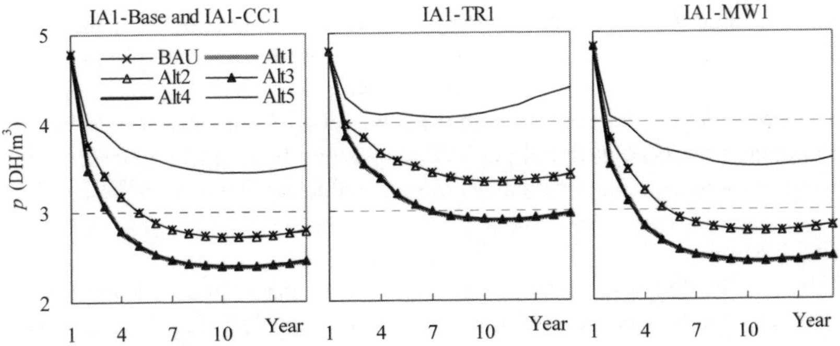

Figure 6.15 Optimal pricing schedules for domestic water charges in IA1 set environments

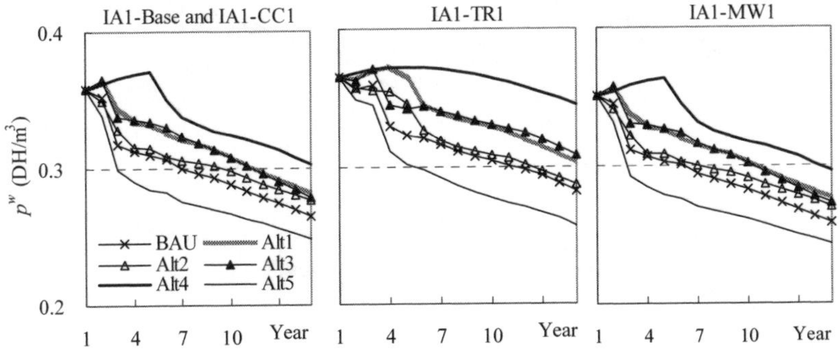

Figure 6.16 Optimal pricing schedules for irrigation water charges in IA1 set environments

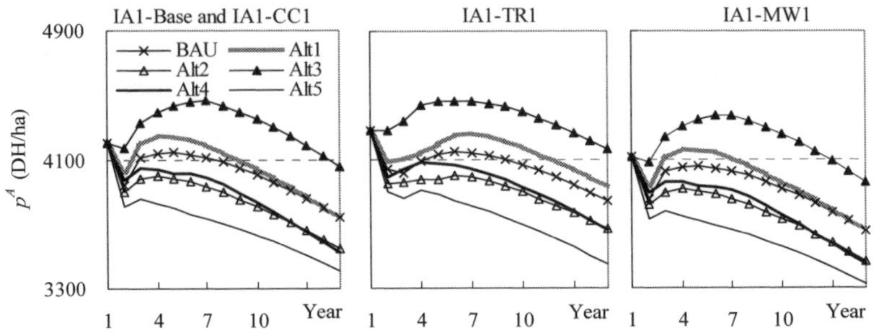

Figure 6.17 Optimal pricing schedules for irrigation land charges in IA1 set environments

The optimal domestic water pricing schedules of the policy alternatives with the same θ^G are almost identical, as observed in Figure 6.3. The increased initial public capital stock significantly reduces the optimal prices at the beginning, but after several years the optimal prices tend to converge on the counterpart pricing schedules under the Base set environments. It seems that a 20 per cent increase in initial public capital stock financed by external loans does not induce qualitative changes in sustainable development policies.

Social welfare

Figures 6.18 and 6.19 show the paths of mean per capita consumption of satisfaction and mean per user consumption of publicly supplied water in the IA1 set environments.

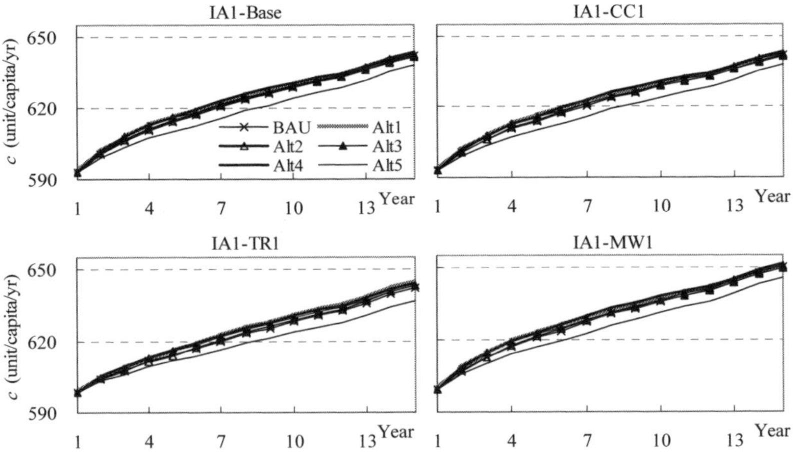

Figure 6.18 Mean satisfaction consumption in IA1 set environments

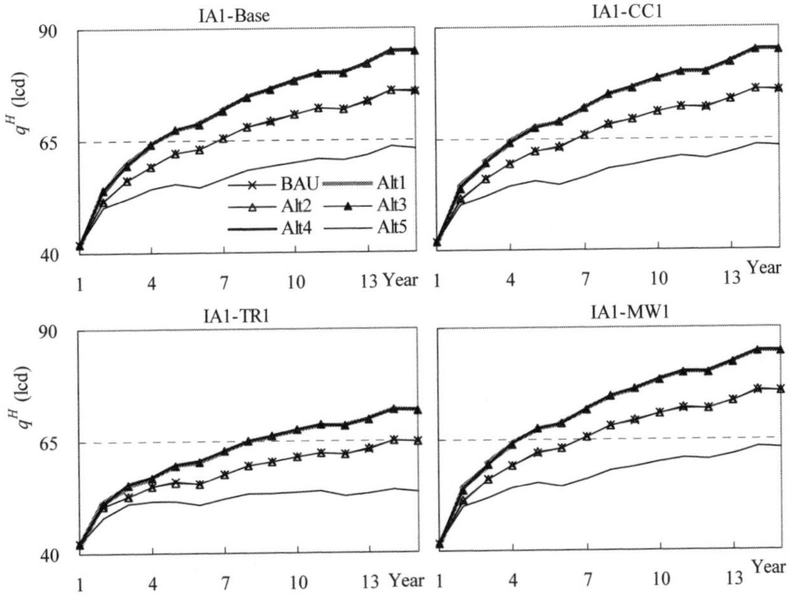

Figure 6.19 Mean per user publicly supplied water consumption in IA1 set environments

The suppression of publicly supplied water consumption in the first year is mitigated by the increased initial public capital stock. Although the first year consumption of 42 lcd is still less than half the status quo level, this mitigation of water consumption suppression improves the feasibility of sustainable development policy. The convergence property of optimal trajectories is observed again and there is almost no difference in the terminal values of satisfaction consumption after 15 years between the IAbase set and the IA1 set environments.

Table 6.7 shows the simulated net present values of equivalent variations (EV) under the IA1 set environments.

Comparison between the IAbase results (Table 6.2) and the IA1 results (Table 6.7) shows that Alt.3 enjoys the largest benefits in terms of the increased net present values of EV, and Alt.1 and Alt.4 follow it, all of which are associated with $\theta^G = 0.43$. This observation demonstrates the effectiveness of public investment in the treated water sector for improving social welfare.

To confirm this, an additional alternative environment (IA2) is prepared, in which the same amount of external loans as in IA1 environment is exclusively invested in G. Figure 6.20 shows the comparison of mean annual values of EV between the IA1 and the IA2 environments.

Table 6.7 Net present value of EV in IA1 set environments

Policy			Policy environment			
			IA1-Base	IA1-CC1	IA1-TR1	IA1-MW1
BAU	Mean	(DH/capita)	134.8	112.9	363.4	2094.8
	(c.v.)	(%)	(8.1)	(469.1)	(8.5)	(2.2)
Alt.1	Mean	(DH/capita)	***644.9***	***622.9***	***963.7***	***2605.6***
	(c.v.)	(%)	(3.1)	(85.1)	(3.3)	(2.3)
Alt.2	Mean	(DH/capita)	272.3	250.3	479.1	2231.5
	(c.v.)	(%)	(4.3)	(211.9)	(6.3)	(2.3)
Alt.3	Mean	(DH/capita)	321.8	299.9	686.4	2285.2
	(c.v.)	(%)	(5.2)	(175.9)	(4.3)	(2.3)
Alt.4	Mean	(DH/capita)	643.7	621.7	903.3	2604.6
	(c.v.)	(%)	(3.0)	(85.3)	(3.5)	(2.3)
Alt.5	Mean	(DH/capita)	-858.4	-880.2	-499.5	1104.7
	(c.v.)	(%)	(3.7)	(59.9)	(9.8)	(2.6)

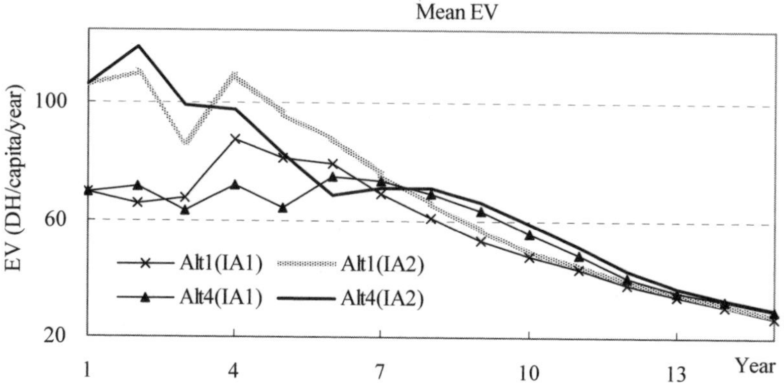

Figure 6.20 Welfare effects of exclusively investing external loans in treated water production capital

The figure illustrates the advantages of concentrating external loans on investment in treated water production capital *G*. In fact, the net present values of EV increase by more than 20 per cent and reach DH 794.8 per capita with Alt.1 and DH 797.8 per capita with Alt.4 under the IA2 environment.

The effects of international aid flows are more clearly observed in Figure 6.21.

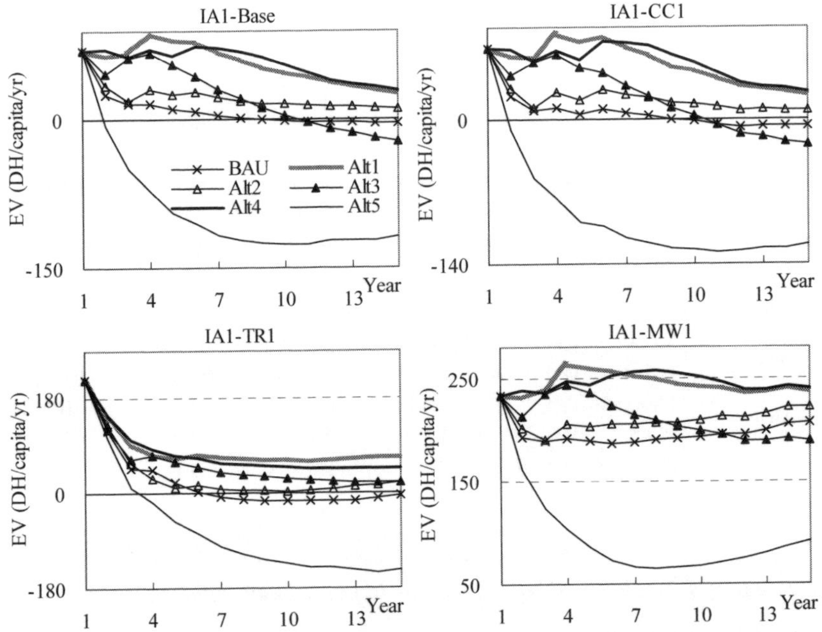

Figure 6.21 Mean annual EV in IA1 set environments

It is observed that the trajectories of mean annual EV generally shift upward in the IA1 set environments but tend to converge on those in the Base set environments towards the end of planning period. Furthermore, the relation between different policy alternatives, such as the overtaking point between Alt.1 and Alt.4, is not affected by the initial public capital increase. It suggests that a 20 per cent increase in initial public capital stock due to international aid flows does not structurally change the welfare effects of sustainable development policies.

Observance of constraints

Tables 6.8 and 6.9 show the probabilities of violating sustainability constraints and of running deficits in the government savings accounts in the IA1 set environments.

An increase in initial public capital stock barely affects these probabilities. It further suggests that safety factors are almost the sole determinants of these probabilities.

Table 6.8 Probability of violating sustainability constraints in IA1 set environments

Policy			Policy environment			
			IA1-Base	IA1-CC1	IA1-TR1	IA1-MW1
BAU	Mean	(%)	13.3	13.3	13.4	13.3
	(c.v.)	(%)	(67.5)	(65.2)	(66.6)	(67.5)
Alt.1	Mean	(%)	13.3	13.3	13.3	13.3
	(c.v.)	(%)	(66.9)	(65.3)	(67.5)	(67.5)
Alt.2	Mean	(%)	13.3	13.3	13.4	13.3
	(c.v.)	(%)	(66.9)	(65.2)	(66.6)	(67.5)
Alt.3	Mean	(%)	13.3	13.3	13.4	13.3
	(c.v.)	(%)	(67.5)	(65.2)	(66.6)	(67.5)
Alt.4	Mean	(%)	13.3	13.3	13.3	13.3
	(c.v.)	(%)	(66.9)	(65.3)	(67.5)	(67.5)
Alt.5	Mean	(%)	13.3	13.5	13.5	13.5
	(c.v.)	(%)	(67.5)	(65.7)	(66.3)	(66.0)

Table 6.9 Probability of budget deficits in IA1 set environments

Policy			Policy environment			
			IA1-Base	IA1-CC1	IA1-TR1	IA1-MW1
BAU	Mean	(%)	4.5	7.7	9.2	4.5
	(c.v.)	(%)	(204.7)	(221.7)	(151.6)	(204.7)
Alt.1	Mean	(%)	4.5	7.7	9.2	4.5
	(c.v.)	(%)	(204.7)	(222.2)	(151.6)	(204.7)
Alt.2	Mean	(%)	4.5	7.7	9.2	4.5
	(c.v.)	(%)	(204.7)	(221.7)	(151.6)	(204.7)
Alt.3	Mean	(%)	4.5	7.7	9.2	4.5
	(c.v.)	(%)	(204.7)	(222.2)	(151.6)	(204.7)
Alt.4	Mean	(%)	4.5	7.7	9.2	4.5
	(c.v.)	(%)	(204.7)	(222.2)	(151.6)	(204.7)
Alt.5	Mean	(%)	4.6	7.8	9.4	4.6
	(c.v.)	(%)	(202.6)	(221.6)	(150.5)	(202.6)

Terminal capital stock levels

Tables 6.10 and 6.11 show terminal values of per capita private capital stock consisting of household assets (m) and rain-fed capital (K^R) and those of total public capital stock, in the IA1 set environments.

Table 6.10 Terminal values of per capita private capital stock in IA1 set environments

Policy			Policy environment			
			IA1-Base	IA1-CC1	IA1-TR1	IA1-MW1
BAU	Mean	(unit/capita)	6801.2	6801.2	6812.5	6830.0
	(c.v.)	(%)	(2.9)	(4.4)	(3.0)	(2.9)
Alt.1	Mean	(unit/capita)	6807.2	6807.3	***6820.9***	6836.0
	(c.v.)	(%)	(2.9)	(4.4)	(3.0)	(2.9)
Alt.2	Mean	(unit/capita)	6803.5	6803.5	6814.7	6832.3
	(c.v.)	(%)	(2.9)	(4.4)	(3.0)	(2.9)
Alt.3	Mean	(unit/capita)	6801.6	6801.6	6816.1	6830.5
	(c.v.)	(%)	(2.9)	(4.4)	(3.0)	(2.9)
Alt.4	Mean	(unit/capita)	***6807.4***	***6807.4***	6819.6	***6836.1***
	(c.v.)	(%)	(2.9)	(4.4)	(3.0)	(2.9)
Alt.5	Mean	(unit/capita)	6787.6	6787.6	6800.2	6816.6
	(c.v.)	(%)	(2.9)	(4.4)	(3.0)	(2.9)

Table 6.11 Terminal values of total public capital stock in IA1 set environments (million units)

Policy	Policy environment		
	IA1-Base and IA1-CC1	IA1-TR1	IA1-MW1
BAU	12 494.7	6 937.2	12 408.8
Alt.1	12 607.9	***7 093.1***	12 522.6
Alt.2	12 550.9	6 982.4	12 464.8
Alt.3	12 466.7	6 997.5	12 382.3
Alt.4	***12 613.6***	7 062.8	***12 528.2***
Alt.5	12 189.1	6 690.5	12 104.7

In comparison with their IAbase counterparts (Tables 6.5 and 6.6), these results are of great interest in two respects. First, the reduction of terminal public capital stock due to loan repayment is small at around 1.5 to 3 per cent, in spite of the relatively tough repayment conditions in terms of a short maturity period and an interest payment obligation during the grace period. If a portion of international aid flows can be given as grants, it is fully possible that international aid flows, even if they mainly consisted of external loans, could increase terminal capital stock.

Second, the coincidence between the best policy alternative in terms of social welfare and the best one in terms of terminal capital stock in each environment is not observed, except for the TR1 environment. This case poses a tough choice for policy makers, who must choose between social welfare during the planning period and the source of future social welfare after the planning period.

Unemployment and access to safe water

Figures 6.22 and 6.23 show the mean values of nationwide rates of access to safe water and nationwide unemployment rates in the IA1 set environments. The trajectories in the IA1-CC1 environment are omitted because they are almost identical to those in the IA1-Base environment. The policy alternatives with the same θ^G, for example BAU and Alt.2, have almost identical paths of rates of access to safe water, as observed in Figure 6.11.

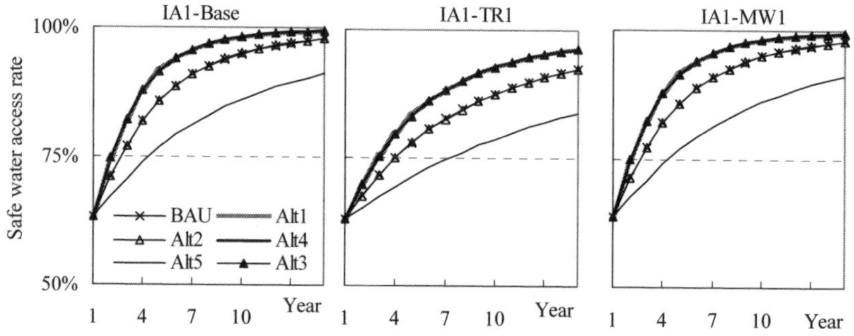

Figure 6.22 Mean values of nationwide rates of access to safe water in IA1 set environments

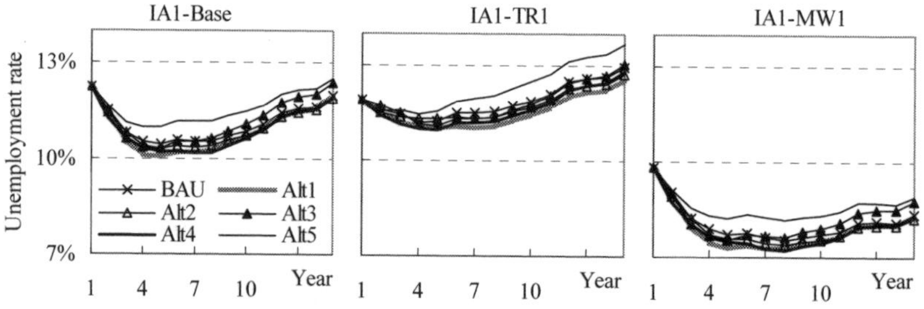

Figure 6.23 Mean values of nationwide unemployment rates in IA1 set environments

Although the benefits of increased initial public capital stock in meeting basic human needs are marginal, they are at least positive in terms of their mean value throughout the planning period. This fact guarantees the positive effects of international aid flows.

Figure 6.24 illustrates the effects of exclusively investing external loans in treated water production capital *G* for meeting basic human needs.

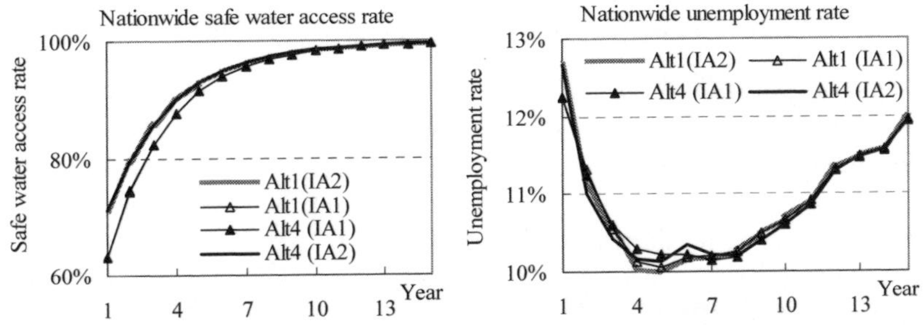

Figure 6.24 Effects of exclusively investing external loans in treated water production capital for basic human needs satisfaction

Note that the paths of the nationwide safe water access rates of Alt.1 and Alt.4 are almost identical in each environment. The only disadvantage of exclusively investing external loans in treated water production capital seems to be the 0.5 per cent higher nationwide unemployment rate in the first year, while there is almost no difference in period average nationwide unemployment rates in IA1 and IA2 environments. In the provision of safe water access there is a clear advantage in concentrating external loans on the investment into *G*.

6.5.3 Policy Implications of Sustainability Coefficients

This subsection reports the simulation results under the SC1 set environments in which sustainability coefficients are raised by 20 per cent. With modified sustainability coefficients each sustainable production function is recalibrated as follows:

Raw water production

$$
\begin{cases}
R_t = 11821.9 \times \left(1 - 167.75e^{-0.0085G_t^R}\right) & \text{for } G_t^R < 1500 \\
R_t = 13\,580.4 \times \left(1 - 21{,}143.18e^{-0.008G_t^R}\right) & \text{for } 1500 \le G_t^R < 2193 \\
R_t = 14\,312.4 \times \left(1 - 12.41e^{-0.0025G_t^R}\right) & \text{for } 2193 \le G_t^R < 3309 \\
R_t = 15\,080.9 \times \left(1 - 7.72e^{-0.0015G_t^R}\right) & \text{for } 3309 \le G_t^R < 4626 \\
R_t = 16\,795.9 \times \left(1 - 0.44e^{-0.0003G_t^R}\right) & \text{for } 4626 \le G_t^R < 7700 \\
R_t = 7884.7 \times \left(G_t^R\right)^{0.1} - 3225.51 & \text{for } G_t^R \ge 7700
\end{cases}
\quad (6.4)
$$

Treated water production

$$\begin{cases} Q_t = 525.9 \times \left(1 - 4.77e^{-0.012G_t}\right) & \text{for } G_t < 604 \\ Q_t = 614.6 \times \left(1 - 0.90e^{-0.003G_t}\right) & \text{for } 604 \le G_t < 1084 \\ Q_t = 79.9(G_t)^{0.3} - 56.92 & \text{for } G_t \ge 1084 \end{cases} \quad (6.5)$$

Irrigation land provision

$$\begin{cases} A_t = 728.9 \times \left(1 - 1.35e^{-0.003G_t^I}\right) & \text{for } G_t^I < 853 \\ A_t = 787.6 \times \left(1 - 66.96e^{-0.007G_t^I}\right) & \text{for } 853 \le G_t^I < 1097 \\ A_t = 892.2 \times \left(1 - 312.80e^{-0.007G_t^I}\right) & \text{for } 1097 \le G_t^I < 1715 \\ A_t = 738.0\left(G_t^I\right)^{0.1} - 663.58 & \text{for } G_t^I \ge 1715 \end{cases} \quad (6.6)$$

As a result, the proportions of the current sustainable production capacities to the current capacity with the present engineering practices become 55.7 per cent for raw water production, 50.9 per cent for treated water production, and 72.3 per cent for irrigation land provision. It is the raw water production that is most severely affected by the increase in the sustainability coefficients. Judging from this fact, it is anticipated that more public investment in raw water production may have favourable effects on social welfare.

Optimal pricing schedules

Figures 6.25 to 6.27 show the optimal pricing schedules in the SC1 set environments.

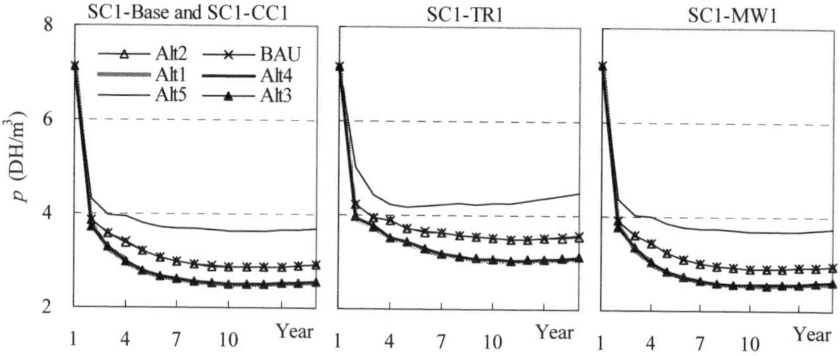

Figure 6.25 Optimal pricing schedules for domestic water charges in SC1 set environments

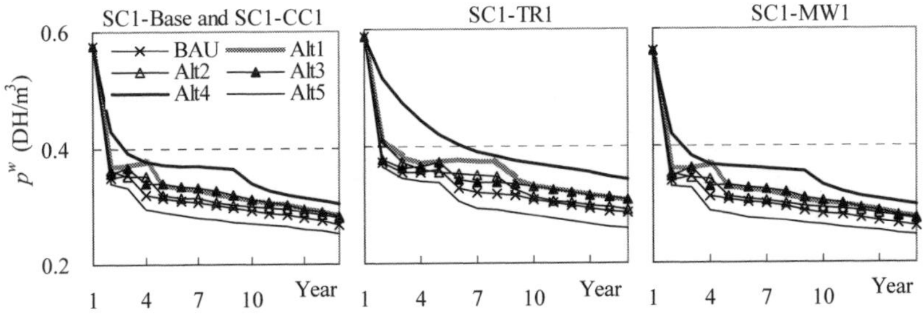

Figure 6.26 Optimal pricing schedules for irrigation water charges in SC1 set environments

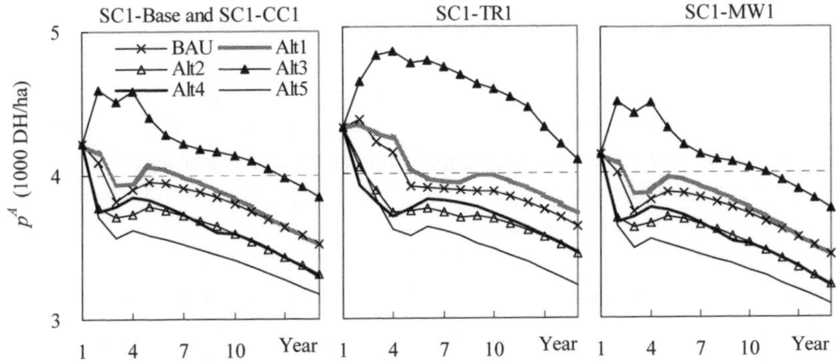

Figure 6.27 Optimal pricing schedules for irrigation land charges in SC1 set environments

As observed in Figure 6.3, the policy alternatives associated with the same θ^G such as BAU and Alt.2 have almost identical domestic water pricing schedules. A comparison between Figures 6.15−6.17 and their counterparts under the Base set environments reveals that the increased sustainability coefficients significantly raise the optimal prices in the first year but the differences tend to diminish towards the end of the planning period. It seems that a 20 per cent increase in sustainability coefficients does not induce a qualitative change in sustainable development policies.

Social welfare

Figures 6.28 and 6.29 show the paths of mean per capita satisfaction consumption and mean per user publicly supplied water consumption in the SC1 set environments.

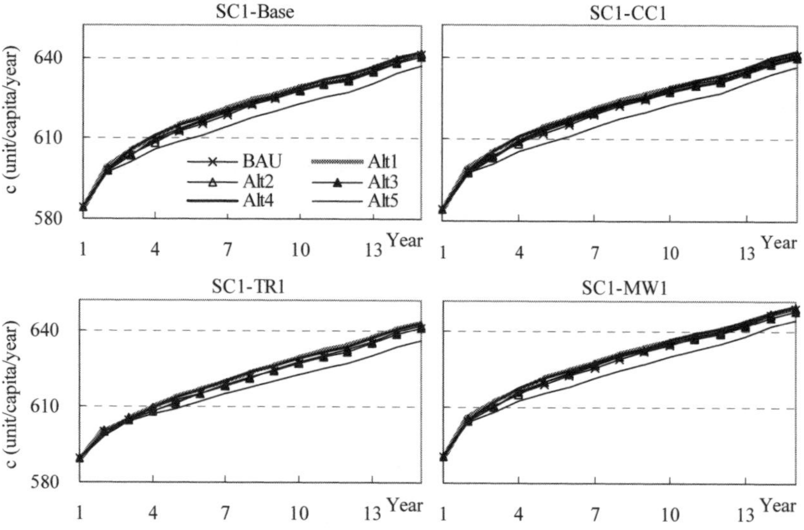

Figure 6.28 Mean per capita satisfaction consumption in SC1 set environments

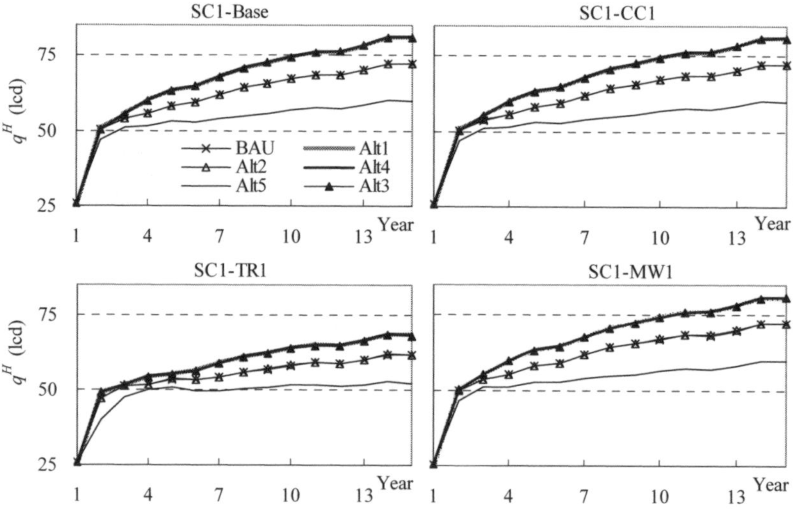

Figure 6.29 Mean per user publicly supplied water consumption in SC1 set environments

Although the suppression of domestic water consumption in the first year is much more severe in the SC1 environment than in the SCbase environment, the effect on satisfaction consumption is small, and there is almost no difference in the terminal values of satisfaction consumption after 15 years between the SCbase and the SC1 environments. This result corroborates our expectation of the convergence property of optimal trajectories observed in the experiments without supply side constraints.

Table 6.12 shows the simulated money-metric social welfare in terms of the net present values of EV under the SC1 set environments.

Table 6.12 Net present value of EV in SC1 set environments

Policy			Policy environment			
			SC1-Base	SC1-CC1	SC1-TR1	SC1-MW1
BAU	Mean	(DH/capita)	-498.2	-520.1	-385.3	1463.9
	(c.v.)	(%)	(4.5)	(101.7)	(5.9)	(2.1)
Alt.1	Mean	(DH/capita)	***-23.0***	***-44.9***	***138.1***	***1941.8***
	(c.v.)	(%)	(88.7)	(1178.4)	(10.4)	(2.3)
Alt.2	Mean	(DH/capita)	-356.4	-378.3	-259.6	1606.7
	(c.v.)	(%)	(5.8)	(140.1)	(7.8)	(2.2)
Alt.3	Mean	(DH/capita)	-433.7	-455.6	-400.6	1531.3
	(c.v.)	(%)	(5.0)	(115.5)	(5.6)	(2.2)
Alt.4	Mean	(DH/capita)	-82.9	-104.8	-24.7	1881.0
	(c.v.)	(%)	(24.7)	(504.6)	(64.8)	(2.3)
Alt.5	Mean	(DH/capita)	-1453.4	-1475.1	-1160.1	511.8
	(c.v.)	(%)	(3.0)	(35.8)	(4.0)	(1.9)

Comparison between the Base set results (Table 6.2) and the SC1 set results (Table 6.12) shows that in terms of net present value of EV the policy alternatives most severely affected by an increase in the sustainability coefficients are always Alt.3 and Alt.4, of which Alt.4 is the most affected one under the TRbase environment while Alt.3 is the most affected one under the TR1 environment. This means that the policy alternative most damaged by the SC1 set environments, in terms of social welfare, are not only the ones with a low investment allocation to raw water sector as expected but also those with a low investment allocation to irrigation land.

The more conspicuous difference between the Base set and the SC1 set environments is the drastic increase in coefficients of variation associated with Alt.1 and Alt.4 in the SC1 set environments. This does not mean, however, the dispersion of entire paths as observed in the CC1 environment. Instead, it is caused by the dispersion of annual EV only in the first year as shown in Figure 6.30.

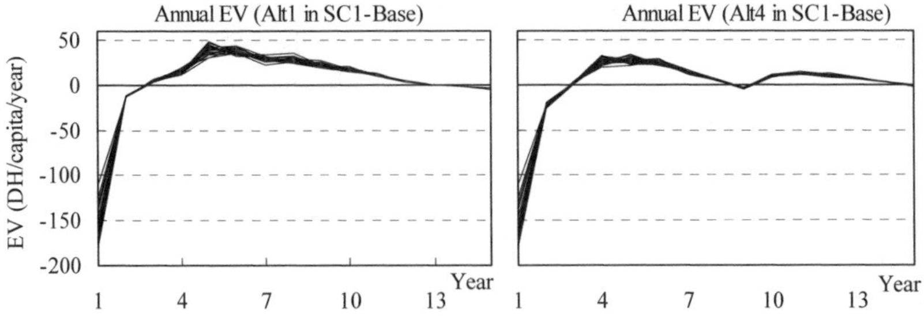

Figure 6.30 Effects of larger sustainability coefficients on annual EV paths

This observation is confirmed by the fact that elimination of the first-year values from the calculation of net present value of EV reduces the coefficients of variation from 88.7 per cent to 4.9 per cent for Alt.1 and from 24.7 per cent to 7.2 per cent for Alt.4 in SC1 environment.

Figure 6.31 shows the trajectories of mean annual EV in the SC1 set environments.

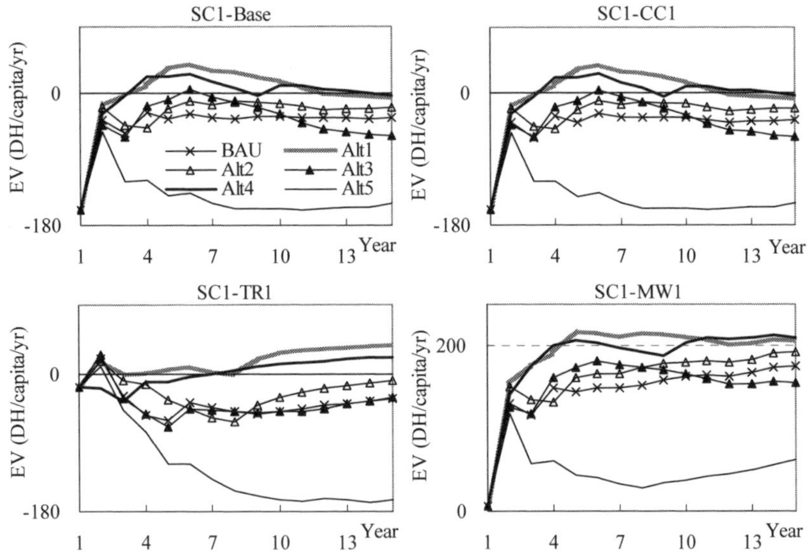

Figure 6.31 Mean annual EV in SC1 set environments

Except for the very low values recorded in the first year, the shape of trajectories associated with each policy alternative is very similar to the SCbase counterparts. It suggests that a 20 per cent increase in the sustainability coefficients does not structurally change the welfare effects of sustainable development policies. This observation is further supported by Figure 6.32.

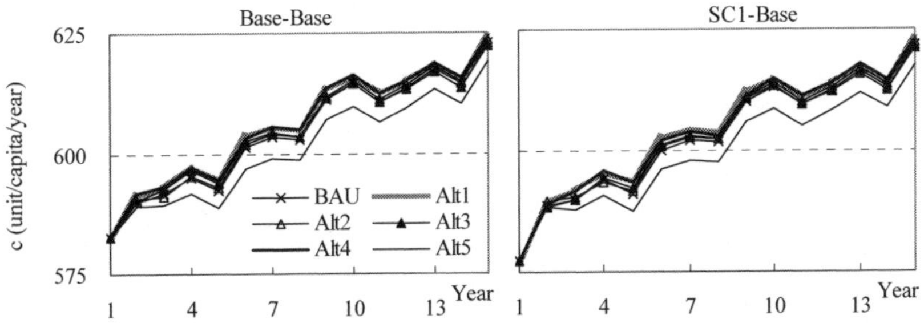

Figure 6.32 Effects of larger sustainability coefficients on minimum consumption

It can be observed that an increase in the sustainability coefficients only marginally affects the minimum values of satisfaction consumption in 100 trials, except for the first year.

Observance of constraints

Tables 6.13 and 6.14 show the probabilities of violating the sustainability constraints and of running deficits in the government savings accounts in the SC1 set environments, respectively.

Table 6.13 Probability of violating sustainability constraints in SC1 set environments

Policy			Policy environment			
			SC1-Base	SC1-CC1	SC1-TR1	SC1-MW1
BAU	Mean	(%)	13.3	13.4	13.7	13.4
	(c.v.)	(%)	(67.5)	(65.1)	(66.3)	(66.6)
Alt.1	Mean	(%)	13.3	13.3	13.4	13.3
	(c.v.)	(%)	(67.5)	(65.2)	(66.6)	(67.5)
Alt.2	Mean	(%)	13.3	13.3	13.5	13.3
	(c.v.)	(%)	(67.5)	(65.2)	(65.9)	(67.5)
Alt.3	Mean	(%)	13.3	13.4	13.8	13.4
	(c.v.)	(%)	(67.5)	(65.1)	(66.0)	(67.7)
Alt.4	Mean	(%)	13.3	13.3	13.5	13.3
	(c.v.)	(%)	(67.5)	(65.2)	(66.6)	(67.5)
Alt.5	Mean	(%)	13.3	13.5	13.6	13.6
	(c.v.)	(%)	(67.5)	(65.7)	(66.1)	(66.1)

Table 6.14 Probability of budget deficits in SC1 set environments

Policy			Policy environment			
			SC1-Base	SC1-CC1	SC1-TR1	SC1-MW1
BAU	Mean	(%)	4.5	7.6	8.9	4.5
	(c.v.)	(%)	(204.7)	(223.6)	(148.1)	(204.7)
Alt.1	Mean	(%)	4.5	7.6	8.7	4.5
	(c.v.)	(%)	(206.9)	(223.6)	(147.9)	(204.7)
Alt.2	Mean	(%)	4.5	7.6	8.8	4.5
	(c.v.)	(%)	(204.7)	(223.6)	(147.6)	(204.7)
Alt.3	Mean	(%)	4.5	7.6	8.9	4.5
	(c.v.)	(%)	(204.7)	(223.6)	(151.6)	(204.7)
Alt.4	Mean	(%)	4.5	7.6	8.9	4.5
	(c.v.)	(%)	(206.9)	(223.6)	(148.1)	(204.7)
Alt.5	Mean	(%)	4.5	7.6	8.9	4.5
	(c.v.)	(%)	(204.7)	(223.6)	(151.6)	(204.7)

An increase in the sustainability coefficients barely affects these probabilities. It implies that these probabilities are mostly determined by safety factors, not by sustainability coefficients.

Terminal capital stock levels

Table 6.15 shows terminal values of per capita private capital stock consisting of household assets (*m*) and rain-fed capital (K^R) in the SC1 set environments.

Table 6.15 Terminal values of per capita private capital stock in SC1 set environments

Policy			Policy environment			
			SC1-Base	SC1-CC1	SC1-TR1	SC1-MW1
BAU	Mean	(unit/capita)	6794.0	6794.0	6803.8	6822.9
	(c.v.)	(%)	(2.9)	(4.4)	(3.0)	(2.9)
Alt.1	Mean	(unit/capita)	***6799.7***	***6799.7***	***6811.1***	***6828.6***
	(c.v.)	(%)	(2.9)	(4.4)	(3.0)	(2.9)
Alt.2	Mean	(unit/capita)	6796.4	6796.4	6805.9	6825.3
	(c.v.)	(%)	(2.9)	(4.4)	(3.0)	(2.9)
Alt.3	Mean	(unit/capita)	6792.9	6792.9	6801.8	6821.9
	(c.v.)	(%)	(2.9)	(4.4)	(3.0)	(2.9)
Alt.4	Mean	(unit/capita)	6798.8	6798.9	6808.7	6827.7
	(c.v.)	(%)	(2.9)	(4.4)	(3.0)	(2.9)
Alt.5	Mean	(unit/capita)	6780.8	6780.8	6792.5	6809.9
	(c.v.)	(%)	(2.9)	(4.4)	(3.0)	(2.9)

Table 6.16 shows terminal values of total public capital stock in the SC1 set environments.

Table 6.16 Terminal values of total public capital stock in SC1 set environments (million units)

Policy	Policy environment		
	SC1-Base and SC1-CC1	SC1-TR1	SC1-MW1
BAU	12 579.7	7032.8	12 494.7
Alt.1	***12 685.9***	***7168.9***	***12 601.7***
Alt.2	12 637.1	7073.9	12 552.2
Alt.3	12 523.6	6985.0	12 440.1
Alt.4	12 668.2	7126.4	12 583.7
Alt.5	12 280.6	6798.2	12 197.2

There is no significant difference between the SCbase set and the SC1 set environments in terms of terminal capital stock. As in the Base set environments, a policy alternative associated with the largest terminal values in each environment achieves the highest net present value of EV.

Unemployment and access to safe water

Figures 6.33 and 6.34 show the mean values of nationwide rates of access to safe water and nationwide unemployment rates in the SC1 set environments. The trajectories in the SC1-CC1 environment are omitted because they are almost identical to those in the SC1-Base environment. As observed in Figure 6.11, the policy alternatives associated with the same θ^G have almost identical paths rates of access to safe water.

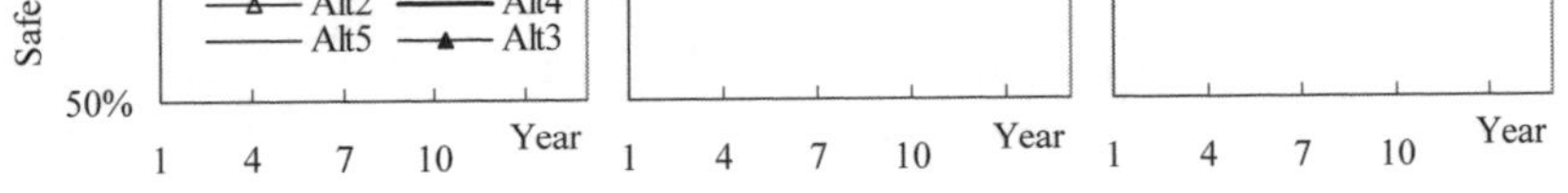

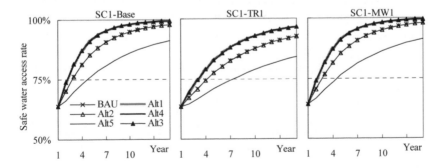

Figure 6.33 Mean values of nationwide rates of access to safe water in SC1 set environments

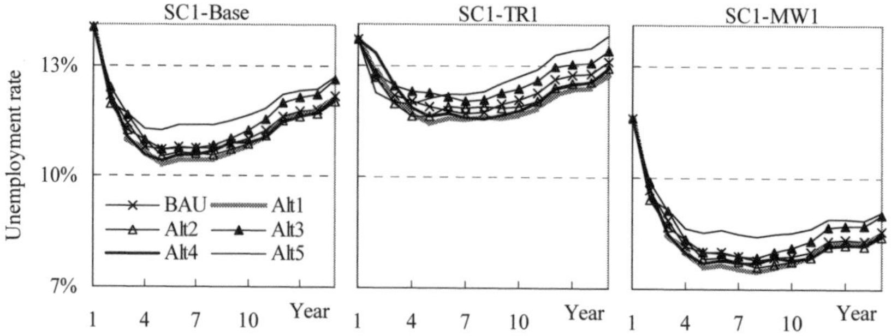

Figure 6.34 Mean values of nationwide unemployment rates in SC1 set environments

The influence of higher sustainability coefficients is not negligible in nationwide unemployment rates. In the first year the nationwide unemployment rates associated with each policy environment in the SC1 environment are 1.4 per cent higher than their counterparts in the SCbase environment. Except for the first year, the average differences in unemployment rates between the Base set and the SC1 set environments for each policy alternative for the planning period are 0.2–0.3 per cent in the TRbase environment, and this difference for Alt.3 in the TR1 environment reaches 0.54 per cent. Not only the reduction in EV but also this considerable increase in unemployment rates must be counted among the social costs of the higher sustainability coefficients.

The noticeable rise in unemployment rates coupled with almost unchanged rates of access to safe water in the SC1 set environments demonstrate downward effects of increased sustainability coefficients on irrigation labour wages. The irrigation labour wage in the SC1 set environments is shown in Figure 6.35.

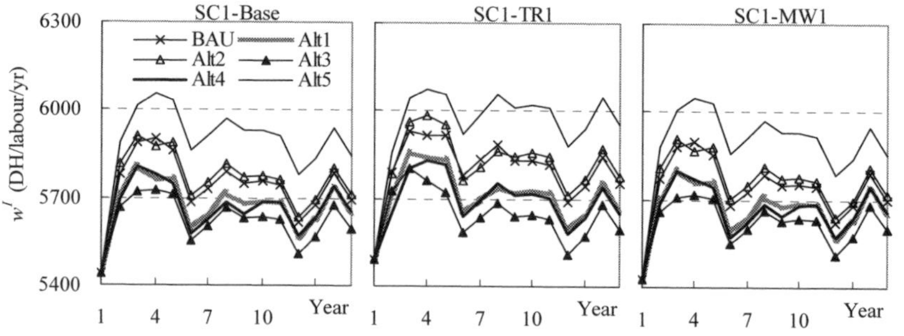

Figure 6.35 Mean values of the irrigation labour wage in SC1 set environments

A comparison between Figures 6.14 and 6.35 demonstrates this downward effect. In particular, it is clearly observed that the wage rate trajectory of Alt.3 in the SC1-TR1 environment goes down most conspicuously.

6.6 DISCUSSION

Before discussing the results it might be worthwhile to reconfirm what this book tries to demonstrate through policy simulations and what it does not.

This book tries to demonstrate the potential of the proposed methodology by providing concrete images of policy analysis based on that methodology. In addition, it aims to provide rough ideas of the policy implications of sustainable development policies.

This book does not, however, try to provide any guidance directly applicable to real policy making. Neither does it aim to seek the best sustainable development policies. For such purposes much more accurate sustainable production functions, amongst others, must be prepared based on highly interdisciplinary research efforts. The following discussion must read with this caveat.

6.6.1 Advantages of the Proposed Methodology

The policy simulations in this book analyse multiple aspects of sustainable development policies including: (1) social welfare during the planning period; (2) future ability to generate social welfare after the planning period; (3) observance of sustainability constraints; and (4) satisfaction of basic human needs. This rich analysis, which is rarely found in the existing literature, can not only facilitate the ability of policy makers to make decisions but can also improve the accountability of sustainable development policies. The simulation results contain interesting cases (IA1-Base, IA1-CC1 and IA1-MW1) in which the best policy alternatives from the aspect of the present social welfare and of the future ability to generate social welfare are different. Based on the proposed methodology it is not necessary to integrate these incompatible results into some unique indicator. Rather, policy makers can simulate the situation where the proposed policies were implemented and can choose more 'preferable' policies based on the simulation results.

The advantages of separating the planning and the implementation processes are also clearly demonstrated by the policy simulation results. It enables policy makers to see the implications of policies in terms of not only the expected values but also the minimum values or degree of dispersion of the simulated trajectories. The comparison between the CCbase set and the CC1 set environments most clearly demonstrates the merits of separating the planning and the implementation processes, in which the effects of increased variability of production risk factors presumably caused by climate change are manifested as both drastically dispersed annual EV trajectories and considerable reductions in minimum consumption values across 100 trials. These policy implications cannot be obtained without separating the policy planning simulation based on expectations from the Monte Carlo simulations of policy implementation process.

6.6.2 General Implications of Sustainable Development Policies

The general implications of the simulated outcomes of sustainable development policies can be described as follows:

- A slight suppression of satisfaction consumption in the first year followed by a steady growth at around 0.5 per cent annually throughout the planning period.
- A severe suppression of publicly supplied water consumption in the first year, which is more than a 60 per cent reduction from the simulated consumption level with status quo public charges. The consumption level rises considerably in the second year and continues to grow, but it remains at around 95 per cent of the status quo level in the terminal year even in the most preferable cases.
- Total private capital stock grows gradually at around 1 per cent a year, while total public capital stock grows rapidly at around 15 per cent a year on average.
- Access to safe water is quickly and drastically improved. In the terminal year nationwide rates of access to safe water often approach 100 per cent.
- Nationwide unemployment rates drop quickly in the first five to eight years by 2 to 3 per cent in the best case, but gradually increase afterwards.

Overall, sustainable development policies appear quite successful considering the fact that these outcomes are achieved under very severe sustainability constraints. On the other hand, a severe suppression of water consumption and a mediocre performance in fighting urban unemployment suggest that some additional policies might be necessary to realise sustainable development.

Throughout the policy simulations, the sustainable development trajectories show a tendency to converge towards the end of the planning period, and this tendency is shared by both the analytic and the applied models. It precludes the possibility for these models to generate poverty traps, which are of high empirical interest. There are several potential sources of this convergence property.

The most plausible one is a particular specification of the expectation formation process of households employed in this study. Because households always assume zero growth rates of exogenous prices (constant prices) regardless of their actual growth rates at any moment, this expectation formation process absorbs the fluctuations of exogenous variables.

Another strong candidate is the lack of human capital accumulation mechanisms, which are often regarded as a generator of poverty traps (Kremer and Chen 2002; De la Croix and Doepke 2003). For example, it might be plausible that there exists some threshold value of a society's wealth above which a better access to education increases the proportion of skilled workers to unskilled workers and leads to higher productivity, while below that value such a level of access to education cannot be realised and productivity drops as a result of fewer skilled workers. This kind of mechanism is not incorporated in the applied model.

6.6.3 Implications of Policy Alternatives

A comparison among the six policy alternatives reveals that either Alt.1 or Alt.4 always achieves the best outcomes in many respects, and Alt.5 is always the worst. The main implication is the importance of improving access to safe water for sustainable development. Although it is undeniably a product of the employed model specifications and assumptions, this policy implication seems to have empirical relevance.

Relatively poor performance of Alt.3, particularly in terms of nationwide unemployment rates, implies the necessity of maintaining an appropriate level of irrigation investment. Irrigation is often regarded as one of the main environmental threats. At the same time it is widely recognised that irrigation is indispensable not only for feeding the global population but also for establishing a sound rural economy in many developing countries. The simulation results support the latter view.

Another interesting finding is that the best policy alternatives switch depending upon the policy environments. The policy implication is that the government has to forecast the policy environment in order to determine the best strategy. In addition, it is observed that the policy alternatives associated with the highest mean annual EV alternate between Alt.1 and Alt.4 as time goes by. It provides useful information as to how to find better policy alternatives in which investment allocation is allowed to be time variant.

6.6.4 Implications of Policy Environments

The simulation results also yield several policy implications for each policy environment. The major implications are as follows:

- A 20 per cent increase in initial public capital stock financed by external loans (IA1 environment) greatly mitigates the negative welfare impacts of sustainable development policies in terms of the price escalation of public charges at the beginning of the planning period, while the negative effects of loan repayment on public capital stock are small. A comparison between the IAbase set and the IA1 set environments show that the reduction in terminal total public capital stock due to loan repayments is no more than 1.7 per cent.
- The adoption of safer sustainability coefficients (SC1 environment) has significant negative welfare impacts in the first year only. These negative impacts remain throughout the planning period but their magnitude is small.
- Severer climate change (CC1 environment) drastically disperses consumption paths, while their mean values are hardly affected. It makes the worst events more devastating and decision making more difficult.
- Trade liberalisation in terms of a 20 per cent tariff reduction (TR1 environment) has positive effects on social welfare in terms of EV due to a reduction in consumer prices. On the other hand, the consequent loss of tariff revenue earmarked for the water sector results in much lower levels of public investment, by more than 40 per cent, than in the Base set environments. The negative effects of the reduction in public investment are manifested in the form of poorer basic needs satisfaction performance in terms of both nationwide access to safe water and unemployment rates.
- A 10 per cent reduction in the urban unskilled labour wage (MW1 environment) improves the performance of sustainable development policy in every respect. This result highlights the importance of curbing urban unemployment for promoting sustainable development.

It should be noted that lack of distributional effects in the applied model results in the all-round triumph of minimum wage reduction (MW1) despite the fact that urban unskilled labourers are highly likely to be losers. The introduction of distributional issues into sustainable development policy analysis must be pursued in the future in order to have directly relevant implications for the actual policy making.

6.6.5 Feasibility of Sustainable Development Policies

The biggest threat to the feasibility of sustainable development policies in this study is severely suppressed water consumption, particularly in the first year. This drawback of the sustainable development policies can be mitigated by increasing the initial public capital stock to a certain degree, as demonstrated in the IA1 environment. In fact, if the government exclusively invests the same amount of external loans as in the IA1 environment into treated water production capital (IA2 environment), per user consumption of publicly supplied water in the first year becomes 52 lcd, which is nearly 50 per cent more than the value in the IAbase environment. Nevertheless, it is still much lower than the status quo consumption level of 90 lcd.

In order to improve the feasibility of sustainable development policies, it might be necessary not only to increase international aid flows but also to set transitional periods to apply to sustainable production functions. For instance, it might be practical to increase the values of sustainability coefficients gradually from unity to the target levels over, say, five years.

NOTES

1. For wider application of the Monte Carlo simulation, see Rubinstein (1981).
2. The Boiteux-Ramsey pricing rule is obtained as an interior solution to a consumer surplus maximisation problem under certain budgetary constraint (Boiteux 1956, p. 35). Although this rule is designed to achieve the second-best optimality, realisation of the second-best optimality along Boiteux-Ramsey pricing requires several restrictive assumptions regarding the elasticity of supply at marginal cost, convexity of demand in regard to the budgetary requirements, and so on (Dierker 1991).
3. This corresponds to the long-run marginal cost. In the applied model, the short-run marginal cost is zero because there are no variable costs.
4. Their simulations cover four policy alternatives combining tariff unification at two different levels (29 per cent and 10 per cent) and the elimination of non-tariff barriers.

7. Conclusion: Towards Policy-Relevant Sustainable Development Research

7.1 ACCOMPLISHMENT OF THIS STUDY

This book presents a coherent body of research work encompassing conceptual clarification, theoretical analysis and empirical analysis employing a case-study. The study detailed in this book was motivated by the call for policy-relevant sustainable development research. It rejects the mainstream definition of sustainable development based on the principle of non-declining social welfare for very long periods because of its irrelevance to the most imperative global policy goal embedded in the notion of sustainable development, that is, to meet 'the essential needs of the world's poor' (WCED 1987, p. 43). Instead, this book proposes the following operational principles of sustainable development:

- The primary objective of sustainable development is to meet basic human needs throughout the world, particularly in developing countries.
- Economic growth is required to meet basic human needs through higher material consumption and higher employment rates in developing countries, while appropriate policy interventions are also required to address distributional issues including infrastructure development such as the provision of access to safe water.
- The resilience of ecosystems underpinning life support systems must be maintained as the basis for future generations to meet their needs. For this purpose, sustainability constraints, mainly in terms of safe minimum standards, must be set and observed. The determination of sustainability constraints must follow the precautionary principle and scientific uncertainty cannot be an excuse not to implement them.

These operational principles form a cornerstone of this study. Unlike the prevailing interpretation of sustainable development in the existing literature, such as the famous three-pillars model of economy, environment and society, or weak–strong sustainability models, the established operational principles provide concrete policy goals that respond to real global concerns taking into account potential trade-offs between environmental protection and economic development.

7.1.1 Methodological Innovations

The proposed methodology is built on the foundation of microeconomic theory, in particular Ramsey-Cass-Koopmans (RCK) type neoclassical growth theory, but several basic constituents of the theory are replaced by the following innovative ideas:

- Instead of the standard interpretation of dynamic utility optimisation in which life-time utility of immortal agents is given as a discount sum of instantaneous utility, this study assumes that the maximand of RCK models is the utility level experienced at the moment of decision which is determined as a discounted sum of a stream of expected felicities, in which felicity is defined as enjoyment derived from the current conditions.
- Instead of the standard benevolent social planner setting, this study employs a two-stage optimisation setting in which optimisation processes of private agents and the government are separated in order to address the issue of controllability of the government policy.
- Instead of the standard perfect foresight assumption, it is assumed that households expect that the future trajectories of exogenous variables are constant at the current values but they are free to update these expectations based on the realised values at every moment.

These innovations offer several advantages in sustainable development research. The alternative interpretation of dynamic utility optimisation clarifies the difference between intertemporal and intergenerational aspects of dynamic utility optimisation. In the existing literature, an intertemporal utility function of the RCK model is often interpreted as an intergenerational welfare function, but such an interpretation invites insurmountable difficulties both in representing the welfare of the unborn future generation and in finding 'correct' discount factors. The alternative interpretation employed by this study is free from such difficulties as the subject of optimisation is defined as the utility of the present generation. The two-stage optimisation setting liberates households from the dictatorship of the benevolent social planner. Further, this setting resolves confusion over normative and positive aspects, which is often observed in the existing literature. The imperfect foresight assumption in household expectation formation clarifies the role of expectations in the optimisation process.

Model development of this study is in a stepwise manner and an analytic model and an applied model are developed sequentially.

The analytic model is a pioneering water-extended RCK model free from both a benevolent social planner setting and the perfect foresight assumption. The sustainability constraints are represented by sustainable water production functions that are defined as the relationship between public capital stock and capacity to produce clean water on condition that water production and consumption do not endanger the resilience of ecosystems underpinning life support systems. The analytic model serves as a model platform and provides key implications for constructing the applied model.

The applied model is a highly aggregate dynamic optimisation CGE model, which is developed based on the analytic model with the incorporation of four key stylised facts of water-stressed developing economies: (1) dominant water use share of irrigated agriculture; (2) high production risks of rain-fed agriculture; (3) high urban unemployment rates; and (4) poor access to safe water in the rural areas. The latter two stylised facts are modelled as a generalised Harris-Todaro rural–urban migration model in which indirect utilities derived from the expected income in the rural and the urban areas are equalised. The applied model is successfully calibrated and validated based on empirical data of Morocco between 1994 and 2002.

The following advantages of the proposed methodology prove its relevance to the established operational principles of sustainable development:

- Sustainable development policies can be evaluated in various aspects encompassing: social welfare during the planning period, terminal capital stock as a basis of future social welfare after the planning period, observance of sustainability constraints, rates of access to safe water and unemployment rates as measures of basic human needs satisfaction.
- Sustainability constraints are translated into sustainable production functions that are defined as the relationship between public capital stock and production capacity on condition that production and consumption of publicly supplied goods do not endanger resilience of ecosystems functioning as life support systems. Although the employed sustainable production functions are hypothetical, sustainability constraints are conceptually anchored in ecosystem resilience.
- The applied model addresses negative welfare impacts of lack of access to safe water, competition between domestic water use and irrigation water use, and effects of public investment in provision of access to safe water and irrigation on urban unemployment. These issues represent various pathways through which water affects sustainable development.
- The applied model can provide rich information useful for both policy making and accountability improvement. In addition, it can accommodate

various uncertainties in a straightforward manner, in which the uncertainties without probability distribution can also be dealt with.

7.1.2 Major Findings from Theoretical Analysis and Numerical Simulation of the Analytic Model

Theoretical analysis based on the analytic model has several policy implications. It reveals that two candidates of the optimal water pricing schedule exist: one is a water pricing schedule determined solely by water market clearance conditions (market-clearing pricing schedule) and the other corresponds to an interior solution when sustainable water supply capacity exceeds the optimal water demand (excess-supply pricing schedule). Although theoretical analysis cannot tell us which of them is the optimal water pricing schedule, it tells us that the optimal steady state must be associated with the market-clearing pricing schedule. The local stability analysis of the optimal steady state associated with the market-clearing pricing schedule shows that this steady state exhibits the saddle-path stability, which is commonly observed in the RCK model literature, and that the stability properties of the optimal steady state depend on whether or not the elasticity of sustainable water production with respect to public capital exceeds unity.

Numerical simulations of the analytic model provide more policy-relevant insights. These numerical simulations demonstrate that the market-clearing pricing schedule provides the optimum solution in practice. Another interesting finding from numerical simulations is that the optimal trajectories along the market-clearing pricing schedule are globally stable in a practical sense. This finding reveals the limited applicability of the linearised local stability analysis to highly non-linear systems. Many theoretical studies of RCK models have derived major conclusions from local stability analysis of the steady state, but this finding casts doubt on the practical relevance of such an analysis.

7.1.3 Major Findings from the Policy Simulations

The policy simulations generate highly interesting results. The major findings include:

- The importance of public investment in provision of access to safe water and the irrigation sector is unambiguously demonstrated.
- The best policy alternatives change in different policy environments.
- Severe consumption suppression of publicly supplied water is a major threat to the feasibility of sustainable development policy.
- The contribution of international aid flows (even without a grant element) to implement sustainable development is demonstrated.

Although it does not aim to provide any materials directly applicable to the real world, this study is expected both to fill the existing information gap in operationalising sustainable development to a certain extent and to stimulate research efforts, driven by the same motivation behind this study, with real-world applications.

The policy simulations provide rich information to assess the outcomes of sustainable development policies in various policy environments. It is observed that the best policy alternatives change according to policy environments. Further, the policy simulations identify severe consumption suppression of publicly supplied water as a potential threat to the feasibility of sustainable development, and also demonstrate the positive impacts of international aid flows on this feasibility.

7.2 FUTURE DIRECTIONS

7.2.1 Incorporation of Distributional Issues

Distributional issues are at the heart of sustainable development in terms of its implications for poverty and its importance for policy feasibility.

For the former, Drewnowski (1977) suggested the concept of relative poverty based upon which the poor are those who gain when income becomes more evenly distributed and the non-poor are those who lose. Furthermore, Lintott (1998) commented that 'once basic material needs are satisfied, it is an individual's relative, not absolute, consumption that counts for his or her welfare' (p. 242). This implies that intra-generational equity matters in sustainable development because the principal objective of sustainable development is poverty alleviation.

For the latter, it is well recognised that the Pareto optimality criterion is hardly applicable to real policy because policies always generate winners and losers. The political feasibility of sustainable development policies crucially depends on the proportion of losers and the magnitude of their loss. Evaluation of political feasibility based on the average of a society is thus neither reliable nor convincing.

The main reason why this study abandoned incorporating such an important issue into the applied model is the fact that the departure from a crucial assumption of the representative household would result in an undesirable model specification in which indexing all individuals or households based on their migration history is required. Consequently, incorporating distributional issues into the current analytical framework will drastically increase model complexity and make it difficult to keep analytical tractability. Nevertheless, this is a daunting but attractive challenge for future research and the pay-off for success would be immense.

7.2.2 Elaboration of Sustainable Production Functions

Construction of sustainable production functions in a reliable and operational manner may require truly interdisciplinary research projects in which ecologists contribute to understand impacts of production activity on ecosystem resilience, economists and sociologists play a crucial role in forming consensus on certain safe minimum standards to maintain this resilience, and scientists and engineers provide technological knowledge to achieve it. This is not necessarily a barrier to implement sustainable development but can be regarded as an excellent opportunity to conduct such an interdisciplinary project.

Successful construction of sustainable production functions not only improves the direct applicability of the proposed methodology to real policy analysis but also promotes genuinely interdisciplinary activities of which synergy effects could be substantial.

7.2.3 Integrated Treatment of Water and Energy

Water and energy are acknowledged as the most important issues for sustainable development. Furthermore, there are various direct and indirect linkages between water and energy, as described in Chapter 1. An example of linkages is energy input in water production. Suppose that the desalination of seawater is indispensable to increase water production capacity, and the necessary energy input exceeds the sustainable energy consumption level. Excluding energy from the analysis may provide fallacious prescriptions for sustainable development in such a case. It is thus highly desirable to address water and energy issues in an integrated manner.

An integrated treatment of water and energy issues is, however, expected to be costly in terms of analytical tractability. This is mainly why this study sets aside this integrated treatment. Nevertheless, the integration of water and energy is a potentially rewarding challenge for future policy-relevant sustainable development research.

7.3 CONCLUDING REMARKS

This book pioneers an unfamiliar path to responding to the urgent call for policy-relevant sustainable development research. Innovative features of this study imply both a large potential and the crudeness of the proposed methodology. As modelling analysis requires the difficult task of abstracting from a highly complex reality whilst keeping the important causal mechanisms underpinning the issues to be addressed, the policy relevance of quantitative applied models must be tested through empirical applications. The case-study of Morocco in this book illustrates the practical applicability of the proposed framework but it is sort of a pilot study and does not aim to provide any concrete policy recommendations to policy makers. Testing the policy relevance of the proposed framework through real-world applications is left for the follow-up studies to be conducted by the interested readers.

Readers may or may not agree with the proposed methodology, but I sincerely hope that readers unanimously agree with the necessity of innovating sustainable development research in order to address the real concerns of global society.

References

Académie du Royaume du Maroc (2000), *La politique de l'eau et la Sécurité Alimentaire du Maroc a l'Aube du XXI Siècle*, Rabat: Publications de l'Académie du Royaume du Maroc.

Agénor, Pierre-Richard and Karim El Aynaoui (2003), *Labor Market Policies and Unemployment in Morocco: A Quantitative Analysis*, Washington, DC: World Bank.

Aghion, Philippe and Peter Howitt (1998), *Endogenous Growth Theory*, Cambridge, MA: MIT Press.

Armington, Paul S. (1969), 'A theory of demand for products distinguished by place of production', *IMF Staff Papers*, **16**, 159–76.

Aronsson, Thomas, Karl-Gustaf Löfgren and Kenneth Backlund (2004), *Welfare Measurement in Imperfect Markets*, Cheltenham, UK and Northampton, MA, USA: Edward Elgar.

Arrow, Kenneth J., William R. Cline, Karl-Göran Mäler, Mohan Munasinghe, Ray Squitieri and Joseph Stiglitz (1996), 'Intertemporal equity, discounting, and economic efficiency', in James P. Bruce, Hoesung Lee and Erik F. Haites (eds), *Climate Change 1995: Economic and Social Dimensions of Climate Change*, Cambridge: Cambridge University Press, pp. 129–44.

Arrow, Kenneth J. and Mordecai Kurz (1970), *Public Investment, the Rate of Return, and Optimal Fiscal Policy*, Baltimore, MD: Resources for the Future.

Ayres, Robert U. and Allen V. Kneese (1969), 'Production, consumption and externalities', *American Economic Review*, **59** (3), 282–97.

Barbier, Edward B. (2004), 'Water and economic growth', *Economic Record*, **80**, 1–16.

Barro, Robert J. and Xabier Sala-i-Martin (1992), 'Public finance in models of economic growth', *Review of Economic Studies*, **59** (4), 645–61.

Barro, Robert J. and Xabier Sala-i-Martin (1995), *Economic Growth*, New York: McGraw Hill.

Becker, Egon, Thomas Jahn and Immanuel Stiess (1999), 'Exploring uncommon ground: sustainability and the social sciences', in Egon Becker and Thomas Jahn (eds), *Sustainability and the Social Sciences*, London: Zed Books, pp. 1–22.

Beladi, Hamid and Shigemi Yabuuchi (2001), 'Tariff-induced capital inflow and welfare in the presence of unemployment and informal sector', *Japan and the World Economy*, **13**, 51–60.

Bennis, Phyllis, Erik Leaver and the IPS Iraq Task Force (2005), *The Iraq Quagmire: The Mounting Costs of War and the Case for Bringing Home the Troops*, Washington, DC: Institute for Policy Studies.

Berentsen, Paul B.M., Gerard W.J. Giesen and Jan A. Renkema (1996), *Reality and Modelling: Operational Validation of an Environmental-Economic Model of a Dairy Farm*, Wageningen: Wageningen Agricultural University.

Bergson, Abram (1938), 'A reformulation of certain aspects of welfare economics', *Quarterly Journal of Economics*, **52**, 310–34.

Boiteux, Marcel (1956), 'Sur la gestion des Monopoles Publics astreints a l'equilibre budgetaire', *Econometrica*, **24** (1), 22–40.

Bouhia, Hynd (1998), 'Water in the Economy: Integrating Water Resources into National Economic Planning', Cambridge, MA: PhD Thesis, Harvard University.

Bouoiyour, Jamal (2003), 'The Determining Factors of Foreign Direct Investment in Morocco', 16–18 December, Marrakesh, Morocco: background paper for the ERF 10th Annual Conference.

Bourguignon, Francois and Pierre-André Chiappori (1992), 'Collective models of household behaviour: an introduction', *European Economic Review*, **36**, 355–64.

Brooke, Anthony, David Kendrick and Alexander Meeraus (1988), *GAMS: A User's Guide*, Redwood, CA: Scientific Press.

Cass, David (1965), 'Optimum growth in an aggregative model of capital accumulation', *Review of Economic Studies*, **32** (3), 233–40.

Central Intelligence Agency (2005), *The World Factbook*, Washington, DC: Central Intelligence Agency.

Choucri, Nazli (1999), 'The political logic of sustainability', in Egon Becker and Thomas Jahn (eds), *Sustainability and the Social Sciences*, London: Zed Books, pp. 143–61.

Ciriacy-Wantrup, Siegfried von (1967), 'Water policy and economic optimizing: some conceptual problems in water research', *American Economic Review*, **57** (2), 179–89.

Common, Michael S. (1995), *Sustainability and Policy; Limits to Economics*, Cambridge: Cambridge University Press.

De Janvry, Alain, Elisabeth Sadoulet, Marcel Fafchamps and Mohamed Raki (1992), 'Structural adjustment and the peasantry in Morocco: a computable household model', *European Review of Agricultural Economics*, **19**, 427–53.

De la Croix, David and Matthias Doepke (2003), 'Inequality and growth: why differential fertility matters', *American Economic Review*, **93** (4), 1091–1113.

Debreu, Gérard (1959), *Theory of Value: An Axiomatic Analysis of Economic Equilibrium*, New York: Wiley.

Decaluwé, Bernard, André Patry and Luc Savard (1999), *When Water is No Longer Heaven Sent: Comparative Pricing Analysis in an AGE Model*, Quebec: CREFA, University of Laval.

Devarajan, Shantayanan and Delfin S. Go (1998), 'The simplest dynamic general-equilibrium model of an open economy', *Journal of Policy Modeling*, **20** (6), 677–714.

Devarajan, Shantayanan, Margaret J. Miller and Eric V. Swanson (2002), *Goals for Development: History, Prospects, and Costs*, Washington, DC: World Bank.

Dierker, Egbert (1991), 'The optimality of Boiteux-Ramsey pricing', *Econometrica*, **59** (1), 99–121.

Dodds, Steve (1997), 'Towards a "science of sustainability": improving the way ecological economics understands human well-being', *Ecological Economics*, **23**, 95–111.

Drewnowski, Jan (1977), 'Poverty: its meaning and measurement', *Development and Change*, **8**, 183–208.

Economist Intelligence Unit (2002), *Country Profile Morocco 2002*, London: Economist Intelligence Unit.

Ekins, Paul (1992), 'Sustainability first', in Paul Ekins and Manfred Max-Neef (eds), *Real-Life Economics: Understanding Wealth Creation*, London: Routledge, pp. 412–22.

Fafchamps, Marcel, Christopher Udry and Katherine Czukas (1998), 'Drought and saving in West Africa: are livestock a buffer stock?' *Journal of Development Economics*, **55** (2), 273–305.

Gandolfo, Giancarlo (1997), *Economic Dynamics*, Berlin: Springer.

Gleick, Peter H. (1994), 'Water, war and peace in the Middle East', *Environment*, **36** (3), 6–42

Gleick, Peter H. (1998), 'Water and conflicts', in Peter H. Gleick (ed.), *World's Water 1998–1999*, Washington, DC: Island Press, pp. 105–35.

Goldin, Ian and David Roland-Holst (1995), 'Economic policies for sustainable resource use in Morocco', in Ian Goldin and L. Alan Winters (eds), *The Economics of Sustainable Development*, Cambridge: Cambridge University Press, pp. 175–96.

Gorman, William M. (1957), 'Convex indifference curves and diminishing marginal utility', *Journal of Political Economy*, **65** (1), 40–50.

Haddad, Lawrence and Ravi Kanbur (1992), 'Intrahousehold inequality and the theory of targeting', *European Economic Review*, **36**, 372–78.

Hamilton, Kirk and Michael Clemens (1999), 'Genuine savings rates in developing countries', *World Bank Economic Review*, **13**, 333–56.

Hanley, Nick, Jason F. Shogren and Ben White (1997), *Environmental Economics in Theory and Practice*, Oxford: Oxford University Press.

Harris, John R. and Michael P. Todaro (1970), 'Migration, unemployment and development: a two-sector analysis', *American Economic Review*, **60** (1), 126–42.

Harsanyi, John C. (1955), 'Cardinal welfare, individualistic ethics, and interpersonal comparisons of utility', *Journal of Political Economy*, **63** (4), 309–21.

Hoffman, Allan R. (2004), 'The connection: water and energy security', *Energy Security*, August 13, 2004. (http://www.iags.org/n0813043.htm)

Holling, Crawford S. (1973), 'Resilience and stability of ecological systems', *Annual Review of Ecology and Systematics*, **4**, 1–24.

Hulme, Mike, Declan Conway, P. Mick Kelly, Susan Subak and Thomas E. Downing (1995), *The Impacts of Climate Change on Africa*, Stockholm: Stockholm Environment Institute.

Jackson, Tim and Nic Marks (1999), 'Consumption, sustainable welfare and human needs – with reference to UK expenditure patterns between 1954 and 1994', *Ecological Economics*, **28**, 421–41.

Jacobs, Michael (1991), *The Green Economy: Environment, Sustainable Development and the Politics of the Future*, London: Pluto Press.

Jorgenson, Dale W. and Peter J. Wilcoxen (1993), 'Energy, the environment, and economic growth', in Allen V. Kneese and James L. Sweeney (eds), *Handbook of Natural Resource and Energy Economics, Volume III*, Amsterdam: Elsevier, pp. 1267–1349.

Kadi, Mohamed Ait (2002), 'Irrigation water pricing policy in Morocco's large scale irrigation projects', in Atef Hamdy, Cosimo Lacirignola and Nicola Lamaddalena (eds) *Water Valuation and Cost Recovery Mechanisms in the Developing Countries of the Mediterranean Region*, Bari: CIHEAM-IAMB, pp. 51–71

Karaky, Rabih and Channing Arndt (2002), 'Climate Variability and Agricultural Policy in Morocco', 5–7 June, Taipei, Taiwan: proceedings of the Fifth Annual Conference on Global Economic Analysis, 2B-13–2B-22.

King, Robert G. and Ross Levine (1994), 'Capital fundamentalism, economic development, and economic growth', *Carnegie-Rochester Conference Series on Public Policy*, **40**, 259–92.

Kneese, Allen V., Robert U. Ayres and Ralph C. d'Arge (1972), *Economics and the Environment: A Material Balance Approach*, Washington, DC: Resources for the Future.

Knippertz, Peter, Michael Christoph and Peter Speth (2003), 'Long-term precipitation variability in Morocco and the link to the large-scale circulation in recent and future climates', *Meteorology and Atmospheric Physics*, **83**, 67–88.

Kojima, Satoshi (2006), 'Reconsideration of dynamic utility optimisation and intergenerational equity in sustainable development studies', *International Journal of Ecological Economics and Statistics*, **6**, 26–36.

Koopmans, Tjalling C. (1965), 'On the concept of optimal economic growth', *Pontificae Academiae Scientiarum Scripta Varia*, **28**, 225–300.

Kremer, Michael and Daniel L. Chen (2002), 'Income distribution dynamics with endogenous fertility', *Journal of Economic Growth*, **7**, 227–58.

Lélé, Sharachchandra M. (1991), 'Sustainable development: a critical review', *World Development*, **19** (6), 607–21.

Lintott, John (1998), 'Beyond the economics of more: the place of consumption in ecological economics', *Ecological Economics*, **25**, 239–48.

Lipman, Barton L. (1991), 'How to decide how to decide how to ... : modeling limited rationality', *Econometrica*, **59** (4), 1105–25.

Lipsey, Richard G. and Kelvin Lancaster (1956), 'The general theory of second best', *Review of Economic Studies*, **24** (1), 11–32.

Löfgren, Hans, Rachid Doukkali, Hassan Serghini and Sherman Robinson (1997), *Rural Development in Morocco: Alternative Scenarios to the Year 2000*, Washington, DC: International Food Policy Research Institute.

Löfgren, Hans, Moataz El-Said and Sherman Robinson (1999), *Trade Liberalization and Complementary Domestic Policies: A Rural–Urban General Equilibrium Analysis of Morocco*, Washington, DC: International Food Policy Research Institute.

Mäler, Karl-Göran (1974), *Environmental Economics, A Theoretical Inquiry*, London: Johns Hopkins University Press.

Mangasarian, Olvi L. (1966), 'Sufficiency conditions for the optimal control of nonlinear systems', *SIAM Journal on Control*, **4**, 139–52.

Martens, André (1995), *La Matrice de Comptabilité Sociale du Maroc de 1985*, Rabat: Groupe de Recherche en Économic Internationale.

Mateus, Abel (1988), *A Multisector Framework for Analysis of Stabilization and Structural Adjustment Policies: The Case of Morocco*, Washington, DC: World Bank.

Max-Neef, Manfred (1992), 'Development and human needs', in Paul Ekins and Manfred Max-Neef (eds), *Real-life Economics: Understanding Wealth Creation*, London: Routledge, pp. 197–214.

McKinney, Daene C. and Ximing Cai (1997), *Multiobjective Water Resources Allocation Model for the Naryn-Syrdarya Cascade*, Almaty, Kazakhstan: Environmental Policies and Technology Project, US Agency for International Development.

Meade, James E. (1955), *Trade and Welfare*, London: Oxford University Press.

Miller, Ronald E. and Peter D. Blair (1985), *Input-Output Analysis: Foundations and Extensions*, Englewood Cliffs, NJ: Prentice-Hall.

Morris, Brian L., Adrian R.L. Lawrence, P.J.C. Chilton, Brian Adams, Roger C. Calow and Ben A. Klinck (2003), *Groundwater and its Susceptibility to Degradation: A Global Assessment of the Problem and Options for Management*, Nairobi: United Nations Environmental Programme.

Muth, John F. (1961), 'Rational expectations and the theory of price movements', *Econometrica*, **29** (3), 315–335.

Ng, Yew-Kwang (1975), 'Bentham or Bergson? Finite sensibility, utility functions and social welfare functions', *Review of Economic Studies*, **42** (4), 545–69.

Ostry, Jonathan D. and Carmen M. Reinhart (1992), 'Private saving and terms of trade shocks', *IMF Staff Papers*, **39** (3), 495–517.

Parish, Romola and Don C. Funnell (1999), 'Climate change in mountain regions: some possible consequences in the Moroccan High Atlas', *Global Environmental Change*, **9**, 45–58.

Pearce, David W. and Giles Atkinson (1993), 'Capital theory and the measurement of sustainable development: an indicator of weak sustainability', *Ecological Economics*, **8**, 103–8.

Perrings, Charles (1989), 'An optimal path to extinction? Poverty and resource degradation in the open agrarian economy', *Journal of Development Economics*, **30**, 1–24.

Perrings, Charles and Silvana Dalmazzone (1997), *Resilience and Stability in Ecological Economic Systems*, York: Department of Environmental Economics and Environmental Management, University of York.

Perrings, Charles, Karl-Göran Mäler, Carl Folke, Crawford S. Holling and Bengt-Owe Jansson (1995), 'Introduction: framing the problem of biodiversity loss', in Charles Perrings, Karl-Göran Mäler, Carl Folke, Crawford S. Holling and Bengt-Owe Jansson (eds), *Biodiversity Loss*, Cambridge: Cambridge University Press, pp. 1–17.

Postel, Sandra (1992), *Last Oasis: Facing Water Scarcity*, New York: W.W. Norton.

Postel, Sandra (1999), *Pillar of Sand: Can the Irrigation Miracle Last?* New York: W.W. Norton.

Ramsey, Frank P. (1928), 'A mathematical theory of saving', *Economic Journal*, **38**, 543–59.

Robinson, Sherman (1989), 'Multisectoral models', in Hollis Chenery and T.N. Srinivasan (eds), *Handbook of Development Economics, Volume 2*, Amsterdam: Elsevier, pp. 885–947.

Roland-Holst, David (1996), *SAMs for Morocco, 1990 and 1994* (in electronic form).

Rosegrant, Mark W., Ximing Cai and Sarah A. Cline (2002a), *World Water and Food to 2025: Dealing with Scarcity*, Washington, DC: International Food Policy Research Institute.

Rosegrant, Mark W., Ximing Cai, Sarah A. Cline and Naoko Nakagawa (2002b), *The Role of Rainfed Agriculture in the Future of Global Food Production*, Washington, DC: International Food Policy Research Institute.

Rosenfeld, Daniel (2000), 'Suppression of rain and snow by urban and industrial air pollution', *Science*, **287**, 1793–96.

Roumasett, James (1976), *Rice and Risk: Decision Making among Low-Income Farmers*, Amsterdam: North-Holland.

Royaume du Maroc (1982–85, 1990–2003), *Annuaire Statistique du Maroc*, Rabat: Direction de la Statistique.

Rubinstein, Reuven Y. (1981), *Simulation and Monte Carlo Method*, New York, NY: Wiley.

Rutherford, Thomas (1993), *MILES: a Mixed Inequality and Nonlinear Equation Solver*, Boulder, CO: Department of Economics, University of Colorado.

Sadoulet, Elisabeth and Alain de Janvry (1995), *Quantitative Development Policy Analysis*, Baltimore, MD: Johns Hopkins University Press.

Samuelson, Paul A. (1965), 'A caternary turnpike theorem involving consumption and the golden rule', *American Economic Review*, **55** (3), 486–96.

Shiva, Vandana (2002), *Water Wars: Privatization, Pollution, and Profit*, Cambridge, MA: South End Press.

Simon, Herbert A. (1955), 'A behavioral model of rational choice', *Quarterly Journal of Economics*, **69** (1), 99–118.

Simon, Herbert A. (1982), *Models of Bounded Rationality*, Cambridge, MA: MIT Press.

Stiglitz, Joseph (1974), 'Growth with exhaustible natural resources: the competitive economy', *Review of Economic Studies*, **41** (Symposium on the Economics of Exhaustible Resources), 139–52.

Stone, Richard (1961), *Input-Output and National Accounts*, Paris: OECD.

Strotz, Robert H. (1956), 'Myopia and inconsistency in dynamic utility maximisation', *Review of Economic Studies*, **23**, 165–80.

Tarascio, Vincent J. (1969), 'Paretian welfare theory: some neglected aspects', *Journal of Political Economy*, **77** (1), 1–20.

Tinbergen, Jan (1952), *On the Theory of Economic Policy*, Amsterdam: North-Holland.

Todaro, Michael P. (1969), 'A model of labor migration and urban unemployment in less developed countries', *American Economic Review*, **59** (1), 138–48.

Toman, Michael A., John C.V. Pezzy and Jeffrey Krautkraemer (1995), 'Neoclassical economic growth theory and "sustainability"', in Daniel W. Bromley (ed.), *Handbook of Environmental Economics*, Oxford: Blackwell, pp. 139–65.

Turnovsky, Stephen J. (1995), *Methods of Macroeconomic Dynamics*, Cambridge, MA: MIT Press.

Turnovsky, Stephen J. (1997), *International Macroeconomic Dynamics*, Cambridge, MA: MIT Press.

UNDP (2000, 2003), *Human Development Report*, Oxford: Oxford University Press.

United Nations (2003), *Water for People, Water for Life: The United Nations World Water Development Report*, Paris: UNESCO Publishing.

United Nations (2005), *The Millennium Development Goals Report 2005*, New York: United Nations.

WCED (1987), *Our Common Future*, Oxford: Oxford University Press.

Weitzman, Martin L. (1970), 'Optimal growth with scale economies in the creation of overhead capital', *Review of Economic Studies*, **37** (4), 555–70.

WHO (2005), *The World Health Report 2005: Make Every Mother and Child Count*, Geneva: World Health Organization.

WHO and UNICEF (2000), *Global Water Supply and Sanitation Assessment 2000 Report*, Geneva: United Nations.

WHO/UNICEF (1996, 2001), *WHO/UNICEF Joint Monitoring Programme for Water Supply and Sanitation*, Geneva: WHO.

World Bank (1995), *Kingdom of Morocco: Water Sector Review*, Washington, DC: World Bank.

World Bank (1998), *World Development Indicators 1998*, CD-ROM, Washington, DC: World Bank.

World Bank (2004), *Reforming Infrastructure: Privatization, Regulation, and Competition*, Washington, DC: World Bank.

Young, Robert A. and Robert H. Haveman (1985), 'Economics of water resources: a survey', in Allen V. Kneese and James L. Sweeney (eds), *Handbook of Natural Resource and Energy Economics, Volume II*, Amsterdam: Elsvier, pp. 465–529.

Zagdouni, Larbi and Driss Benatya (1990), 'Mechanization and agricultural employment in arid and semiarid zones of Morocco: the case of Upper Chaouia', in Dennis Tully (ed.), *Labor, Employment and Agricultural Development in West Asia and North Africa*, London: Kluwer, pp. 103–41.

Index